OCT 2 3 2015

RAILS

To: ESS

For: Small water damage

From: SCD

Notes:
Title: Catalan language : 101 Catalan verbs
Set In Transit: 08/04/2021 14:31

Printed in the USA

Catalan Language:

101 Catalan Verbs

By Lluc Tosell

Contents

Introduction to Catalan Verbs

Catalan verbs are one of the most complex things of the Catalan language. They are very rich in terms of grammar and morphology and they have dozens of different forms depending on the person, the gender, the tenses, etc.

In the following image it can be seen how the conjugation of a verb is divided.

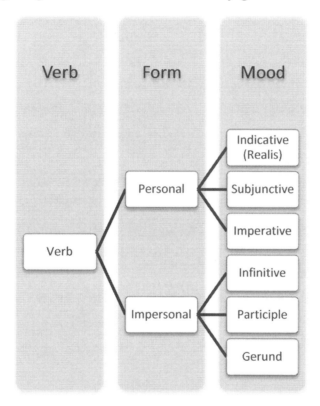

The Catalan verb has three grammatical persons, two numbers, three genders, two forms, six moods, sixteen verb tenses and three conjugations.

There are also auxiliary, regular and irregular verbs, most of them are regular but there are few exceptions, we'll talk about it later in this article.

Numbers, Grammatical Persons and Genders

The numbers are singular and plural and the genders are masculine and feminine. The masculine and feminine are the same for the first and second person.

	First person		Second Person		Third Person	
Number	**Masculine**	**Feminine**	**Masculine**	**Feminine**	**Masculine**	**Feminine**
Singular	Jo	Jo	Tu	Tu	Ell	Ella
Plural	Nosaltres	Nosaltres	Vosaltres	Vosaltres	Ells	Elles

In Catalan not always the person is used in a sentence. Since the conjugations are so rich and different depending on the subject they are often avoided.

For example:

The sentence *I sing a song* would be translated *Jo canto una cançó* but the subject is avoided, because canto already implies that the subject is JO. The right sentence is *Canto una cançó*, unless the person doing the action has to be emphasized.

Forms

There are two forms, Personal and Impersonal.

The personal form is conjugated according to the subject, so a subject is needed in front of the verb (it can be present or avoided but it has to be there in some way). This form will be developed later in the paper.

The impersonal form doesn't have a conjugation and doesn't have a subject.

It has three moods: Infinitive, Participle and Gerund.

Voices

The voice shows the relation between the subject and the action, depending on the role the subject plays in the sentence. In Catalan, as in English, the voice is presented by the auxiliary verb.

Active: I have *eaten* the apple – He *menjat* la poma

Passive: The apple has been *eaten* by me – La poma ha estat *menjada* per mi

Moods

The mood expresses the attitude of the speaker to the action. The following moods exist in Catalan:

- INDICATIVE (or REALIS) – Is used to indicate that something is a fact or a statement, either in the present, past or future.

- SUBJUNCTIVE – Is used to talk about statements that could happen but didn't happen yet. It usually appears in subordinated sentences.
- IMPERATIVE – It only has one verb tense and it is used to give orders.
- INFINITIVE – It's the "name" of the verb, and it can't be a part of a sentence unless it is in a form of a periphrasis (for example M'agrada CANTAR, as "I like to SING"). The infinitive is very important to know to what conjugation belongs the verb.
- PARTICIPLE – It is usually used for composed tenses (He ANAT as "I have GONE")
- GERUNDI – It works as the –ing ending in English.

Conjugations

The verbs in Catalan have three conjugations, which are determined by the last two letters:

The verbs from first conjugation end in AR – CantAR, BallAR, JugAR

The verbs from the second conjugation end in ER or RE – ViuRE, SabER, CauRE

The verbs from the third conjugation end in IR – MentIR, ServIR, SentIR

In the third conjugation there are two kinds of verbs, **Inchoative** and **Pure.** The pure are conjugated as the other two conjugations, but the inchoatives add the letters -eix at the middle of the conjugated verb.

For example verbs *Servir* (to serve) and *Dormir* (To sleep) are both from the third conjugation, *Servir* is an inchoative verb and *Dormir* is pure. In the following table the conjugation of the present indicative is provided:

	Servir	Dormir
Jo	Serveixo	Dormo
Tu	Serveixes	Dorms
Ell/Ella	Serveix	Dorm
Nosaltres	Servim	Dormim
Vosaltres	Serviu	Dormiu
Ells/Elles	Serveixen	Dormen

Auxiliary Verbs

An auxiliary verb is a verb that is written always besides another one to form specific verbal tenses, the passive voice, a periphrasis or other similar structures. In these structures the important verb is not the auxiliary but the other.

There are three auxiliary verbs in Catalan: SER (to be), HAVER (to have) and ANAR (to go).

Verbal tenses

Catalan verbs have sixteen verbal tenses in the personal forms and then there are three more for the impersonal (not conjugated).

PRESENT – INDICATIVE

Used to describe an action that is happening at the same time it is said, it is also used to express routines, habits and facts (the sky is blue, for example).

PRESENT - INDICATIVE				
PERSON	1st Conjugation	2nd Conjugation	3rd Conjugation (Pure)	3rd Conjugation (Inchoative)
Jo	-O	-O	-O	-EIXO
Tu	-ES	-S	-S	-EIXES
Ell/ella	-A	-	-	-EIX
Nosaltres	-EM	-EM	-IM	-IM
Vosaltres	-EU	-EU	-IU	-IU
Ells/Elles	-EN	-EN	-EN	-EIXEN

There are four verbs used as a base to build all the others, these will be used as an example during the following of this article.

The verbs will be separated in syllables and the strong one will be highlighted in bold letters.

	1st Conjugation	2nd Conjugation	3rd Conjugation (Pure)	3rd Conjugation (Inchoative)
	Can-**tar** (To sing)	Per-**dre** (To lose)	Dor-**mir** (To sleep)	Ser-**vir** (To serve)
Jo	**Can**-to	**Per**-do	**Dor**-mo	Ser-**vei**-xo
Tu	**Can**-tes	**Perds**	**Dorms**	Ser-**vei**-xes
Ell/Ella	**Can**-ta	**Perd**	**Dorm**	Ser-**veix**
Nosaltres	Can-**tem**	Per-**dem**	Dor-**mim**	Ser-**vim**
Vosaltres	Can-**teu**	Per-**deu**	Dor-**miu**	Ser-**viu**
Ells/Elles	**Can**-ten	**Per**-den	**Dor**-men	Ser-**vei**-xen

In the following table a translation to English can be seen

	To sing	**To lose**	**To sleep**	**To serve**
I/You/We/Them	Sing	Lose	Sleep	Serve
He/She/It	Sings	Loses	Sleeps	Serves

PERFET – INDICATIVE

It is used for a near past, actions finished today. It is similar to the Present perfect, but have in mind that this past goes further back than the present perfect. It can be used for something ended in the morning or in sentences like "How was your weekend?"

PAST INDEFINITE - INDICATIVE				
PERSON	1st Conjugation	2nd Conjugation	3rd Conjugation (Pure)	3rd Conjugation (Inchoative)
Jo	HE + participle	HE + participle	HE + participle	HE + participle
Tu	HAS + part.	HAS + part.	HAS + part.	HAS + part.
Ell/ella	HA + part.	HA + part.	HA + part.	HA + part.
Nosaltres	HEM + part.	HEM + part.	HEM + part.	HEM + part.
Vosaltres	HEU + part.	HEU + part.	HEU + part.	HEU + part.
Ells/Elles	HAN + part.	HAN + part.	HAN + part.	HAN + part.

	1st Conjugation	2nd Conjugation	3rd Conjugation (Pure)	3rd Conjugation (Inchoative)
	Can-**tar** (To sing)	Per-**dre** (To lose)	Dor-**mir** (To sleep)	Ser-**vir** (To serve)
Jo	**He** Can-**tat**	**He** Per-**dut**	**He** Dor-**mit**	**He** Ser-**vit**
Tu	**Has** Can-tat	**Has** Per-**dut**	**Has** Dor-mit	**Has** Ser-**vit**
Ell/Ella	**Ha** Can-tat	**Ha** Per-**dut**	**Ha** Dor-mit	**Ha** Ser-**vit**
Nosaltres	**Hem** Can-tat	**Hem** Per-dut	**Hem** Dor-mit	**Hem** Ser-vit
Vosaltres	**Heu** Can-tat	**Heu** Per-dut	**Heu** Dor-mit	**Heu** Ser-vit
Ells/Elles	**Han** Can-tat	**Han** Per-dut	**Han** Dor-mit	**Han** Ser-vit

	To sing	To lose	To sleep	To serve
I/You/We/Them	Have sung	Have lost	Have slept	Have served
He/She/It	Has sung	Has lost	Has slept	Has served

IMPERFET – INDICATIVE

There isn't a word to translate this tense, as this tense doesn't exist in English and it will be translated differently depending on the use being possible translations the Past continuous, Past simple, and the form "used to" or "would".

1. When it can be replaced by "estar + gerund" (To be + gerund) it's usually translated for past continuous.
   - Mentre jugava (= Mentre estava jugant), algú li va robar l'abric
     While he was playing, someone stole his coat

2. When the verb can't be replaced by a continuous construction is translated with past simple
   - Estava cansat
     I was tired

3. When it can be replaced by "Solia + infinitive" the literal translation of USED TO is used.
   - Abans cantava (= solia cantar) en una coral
     I used to sing in a choir

4. When it is used to explain a repeated action in the past it is translated as WOULD + infinitive.
   - Quan era petit solia trobar-me amb els amics els diumenges i nedàvem fins a l'hora de dinar.
     When I was young I used to meet my friends on Sundays and we would swim until lunchtime

IMPERFET - INDICATIVE				
PERSON	1st Conjugation	2nd Conjugation	3rd Conjugation (Pure)	3rd Conjugation (Inchoative)
Jo	-AVA	-IA	-IA	-IA
Tu	-AVES	-IES	-IES	-IES
Ell/ella	-AVA	-IA	-IA	-IA
Nosaltres	-ÀVEM	-ÍEM	-ÍEM	-ÍEM
Vosaltres	-ÀVEU	-ÍEU	-ÍEU	-ÍEU
Ells/Elles	-AVEN	-IEN	-IEN	-IEN

	1st Conjugation	2nd Conjugation	3rd Conjugation (Pure)	3rd Conjugation (Inchoative)
	Can-**tar** (To sing)	Per-**dre** (To lose)	Dor-**mir** (To sleep)	Ser-**vir** (To serve)
Jo	Can-**ta**-va	Per-**di**-a	Dor-**mi**-a	Ser-**vi**-a
Tu	Can-**ta**-ves	Per-**di**-es	Dor-**mi**-es	Ser-**vi**-es
Ell/Ella	Can-**ta**-va	Per-**di**-a	Dor-**mi**-a	Ser-**vi**-a
Nosaltres	Can-**tà**-vem	Per-**dí**-em	Dor-**mí**-em	Ser-**ví**-em
Vosaltres	Can-**tà**-veu	Per-**dí**-eu	Dor-**mí**-eu	Ser-**ví**-eu
Ells/Elles	Can-**ta**-ven	Per-**di**-en	Dor-**mi**-en	Ser-**vi**-en

PAST PLUSQUAMPERFET – INDICATIVE

It is used for a past action, already finished. It is translated with the past perfect.

PAST PLUSQUAMPERFET - INDICATIVE				
PERSON	1st Conjugation	2nd Conjugation	3rd Conjugation (Pure)	3rd Conjugation (Inchoative)
Jo	HAVIA + participle	HAVIA + participle	HAVIA + participle	HAVIA + participle
Tu	HAVIES + part.	HAVIES + part.	HAVIES + part.	HAVIES + part.
Ell/ella	HAVIA + part.	HAVIA + part.	HAVIA + part.	HAVIA + part.
Nosaltres	HAVÍEM + part.	HAVÍEM + part.	HAVÍEM + part.	HAVÍEM + part.
Vosaltres	HAVÍEU + part.	HAVÍEU + part.	HAVÍEU + part.	HAVÍEU + part.
Ells/Elles	HAVIEN + part.	HAVIEN + part.	HAVIEN + part.	HAVIEN + part.

	1st Conjugation	2nd Conjugation	3rd Conjugation (Pure)	3rd Conjugation (Inchoative)
	Can-**tar** (To sing)	Per-**dre** (To lose)	Dor-**mir** (To sleep)	Ser-**vir** (To serve)
Jo	Ha-**vi**-a Can-**tat**	Ha-**vi**-a Per-**dut**	Ha-**vi**-a Dor-**mit**	Ha-**vi**-a Ser-**vit**
Tu	Ha-**vi**-es Can-**tat**	Ha-**vi**-es Per-**dut**	Ha-**vi**-es Dor-**mit**	Ha-**vi**-es Ser-**vit**
Ell/Ella	Ha-**vi**-a Can-**tat**	Ha-**vi**-a Per-**dut**	Ha-**vi**-a Dor-**mit**	Ha-**vi**-a Ser-**vit**
Nosaltres	Ha-**ví**-em Can-**tat**	Ha-**ví**-em Per-**dut**	Ha-**ví**-em Dor-**mit**	Ha-**ví**-em Ser-**vit**
Vosaltres	Ha-**ví**-eu Can-**tat**	Ha-**ví**-eu Per-**dut**	Ha-**ví**-eu Dor-**mit**	Ha-**ví**-eu Ser-**vit**
Ells/Elles	Ha-**vi**-en Can-**tat**	Ha-**vi**-en Per-**dut**	Ha-**vi**-en Dor-**mit**	Ha-**vi**-en Ser-**vit**

	To sing	To lose	To sleep	To serve
I/You/We/Them	Had sung	Had lost	Had slept	Had served
He/She/It	Had sung	Had lost	Had slept	Had served

PAST SIMPLE – INDICATIVE

It is used for a past action, already finished. Nowadays it's only used in literature and cultivated language, often in the third person. It doesn't have a translation in English.

PAST SIMPLE - INDICATIVE				
PERSON	1st Conjugation	2nd Conjugation	3rd Conjugation (Pure)	3rd Conjugation (Inchoative)
Jo	-Í	-Í	-Í	-Í
Tu	-ARES	-ERES	-IRES	-IRES
Ell/ella	-À	-É	-Í	-Í
Nosaltres	-ÀREM	-ÉREM	-ÍREM	-ÍREM
Vosaltres	-ÀREU	-ÉREU	-ÍREU	-ÍREU
Ells/Elles	-AREN	-EREN	-IREN	-IREN

	1st Conjugation	2nd Conjugation	3rd Conjugation (Pure)	3rd Conjugation (Inchoative)
	Can-**tar** (To sing)	Per-**dre** (To lose)	Dor-**mir** (To sleep)	Ser-**vir** (To serve)
Jo	Can-**tí**	Per-**dí**	Dor-**mí**	Ser-**ví**
Tu	Can-**ta**-res	Per-**de**-res	Dor-**mi**-res	Ser-**vi**-res
Ell/Ella	Can-**tà**	Per-**dé**	Dor-**mí**	Ser-**ví**
Nosaltres	Can-**tà**-rem	Per-**dé**-rem	Dor-**mí**-rem	Ser-**ví**-rem
Vosaltres	Can-**tà**-reu	Per-**dé**-reu	Dor-**mí**-reu	Ser-**ví**-reu
Ells/Elles	Can-**ta**-ren	Per-**de**-ren	Dor-**mi**-ren	Ser-**vi**-ren

PAST ANTERIOR PERIFRASTIC – INDICATIVE

It is used for a past action, already finished when a second action starts. Nowadays it's only used in literature and cultivated language. It doesn't have a translation in English.

PAST ANTERIOR PERIFRASTIC - INDICATIVE				
PERSON	1st Conjugation	2nd Conjugation	3rd Conjugation (Pure)	3rd Conjugation (Inchoative)
Jo	VAIG + haver + partic.	VAIG + haver + partic.	VAIG + haver + partic.	VAIG + haver + partic.
Tu	VAS + haver + partic.	VAS + haver + partic.	VAS + haver + partic.	VAS + haver + partic.
Ell/ella	VA + haver + partic.	VA + haver + partic.	VA + haver + partic.	VA + haver + partic.
Nosaltres	VAM + haver + partic.	VAM + haver + partic.	VAM + haver + partic.	VAM + haver + partic.
Vosaltres	VAU + haver + partic.	VAU + haver + partic.	VAU + haver + partic.	VAU + haver + partic.
Ells/Elles	VAN + haver + partic.	VAN + haver + partic.	VAN + haver + partic.	VAN + haver + partic.

	1st Conjugation	2nd Conjugation	3rd Conjugation (Pure)	3rd Conjugation (Inchoative)
	Can-**tar** (To sing)	Per-**dre** (To lose)	Dor-**mir** (To sleep)	Ser-**vir** (To serve)
Jo	**Vaig** ha-**ver** Can-**tat**	**Vaig** ha-**ver** Per-**dut**	**Vaig** ha-**ver** Dor-**mit**	**Vaig** ha-**ver** Ser-**vit**
Tu	**Vas** ha-**ver** Can-**tat**	**Vas** ha-**ver** Per-**dut**	**Vas** ha-**ver** Dor-**mit**	**Vas** ha-**ver** Ser-**vit**
Ell/Ella	**Va** ha-**ver** Can-**tat**	**Va** ha-**ver** Per-**dut**	**Va** ha-**ver** Dor-**mit**	**Va** ha-**ver** Ser-**vit**
Nosaltres	**Vam** ha-**ver**	**Vam** ha-**ver**	**Vam** ha-**ver**	**Vam** ha-**ver**

	Can-**tat**	Per-**dut**	Dor-**mit**	Ser-**vit**
Vosaltres	**Vau** ha-**ver** Can-**tat**	**Vau** ha-**ver** Per-**dut**	**Vau** ha-**ver** Dor-**mit**	**Vau** ha-**ver** Ser-**vit**
Ells/Elles	**Van** ha-**ver** Can-**tat**	**Van** ha-**ver** Per-**dut**	**Van** ha-**ver** Dor-**mit**	**Van** ha-**ver** Ser-**vit**

PAST PERIFRASTIC – INDICATIVE

It is the equivalent of the English Past Simple.

PAST PERIFRASTIC - INDICATIVE				
PERSON	1st Conjugation	2nd Conjugation	3rd Conjugation (Pure)	3rd Conjugation (Inchoative)
Jo	VAIG + Infinitive	VAIG + Infinitive	VAIG + Infinitive	VAIG + Infinitive
Tu	VAS + Inf.	VAS + Inf.	VAS + Inf.	VAS + Inf.
Ell/ella	VA + Inf.	VA + Inf.	VA + Inf.	VA + Inf.
Nosaltres	VAM + Inf.	VAM + Inf.	VAM + Inf.	VAM + Inf.
Vosaltres	VAU + Inf.	VAU + Inf.	VAU + Inf.	VAU + Inf.
Ells/Elles	VAN + Inf.	VAN + Inf.	VAN + Inf.	VAN + Inf.

	1st Conjugation	2nd Conjugation	3rd Conjugation (Pure)	3rd Conjugation (Inchoative)
	Can-**tar** (To sing)	Per-**dre** (To lose)	Dor-**mir** (To sleep)	Ser-**vir** (To serve)
Jo	**Vaig** Can-**tar**	**Vaig** Per-**dre**	**Vaig** Dor-**mir**	**Vaig** Ser-**vir**
Tu	**Vas** Can-**tar**	**Vas** Per-**dre**	**Vas** Dor-**mir**	**Vas** Ser-**vir**

Ell/Ella	**Va** Can-**tar**	**Va** Per-**dre**	**Va** Dor-**mir**	**Va** Ser-**vir**
Nosaltres	**Vam** Can-**tar**	**Vam** Per-**dre**	**Vam** Dor-**mir**	**Vam** Ser-**vir**
Vosaltres	**Vau** Can-**tar**	**Vau** Per-**dre**	**Vau** Dor-**mir**	**Vau** Ser-**vir**
Ells/Elles	**Van** Can-**tar**	**Van** Per-**dre**	**Van** Dor-**mir**	**Van** Ser-**vir**

	To sing	**To lose**	**To sleep**	**To serve**
I/You/We/Them	Sang	Lost	Slept	Served
He/She/It	Sang	Lost	Slept	Served

FUTURE SIMPLE – INDICATIVE

The future tenses are much easier than the past. The Future Simple is the equivalent of the Future in English.

FUTURE SIMPLE - INDICATIVE				
PERSON	1st Conjugation	2nd Conjugation	3rd Conjugation (Pure)	3rd Conjugation (Inchoative)
Jo	-ARÉ	-RÉ	-IRÉ	-IRÉ
Tu	-ARÀS	-RÀS	-IRÀS	-IRÀS
Ell/ella	-ARÀ	-RÀ	-IRÀ	-IRÀ
Nosaltres	-AREM	-REM	-IREM	-IREM
Vosaltres	-AREU	-REU	-IREU	-IREU
Ells/Elles	-ARAN	-RAN	-IRAN	-IRAN

	1st Conjugation	2nd Conjugation	3rd Conjugation (Pure)	3rd Conjugation (Inchoative)
	Can-**tar** (To sing)	Per-**dre** (To lose)	Dor-**mir** (To sleep)	Ser-**vir** (To serve)
Jo	Can-ta-**ré**	Per-**dré**	Dor-mi-**ré**	Ser-vi-**ré**
Tu	Can-ta-**ràs**	Per-**dràs**	Dor-mi-**ràs**	Ser-vi-**ràs**
Ell/Ella	Can-ta-**rà**	Per-**drà**	Dor-mi-**rà**	Ser-vi-**rà**
Nosaltres	Can-ta-**rem**	Per-**drem**	Dor-mi-**rem**	Ser-vi-**rem**
Vosaltres	Can-ta-**reu**	Per-**dreu**	Dor-mi-**reu**	Ser-vi-**reu**
Ells/Elles	Can-ta-**ran**	Per-**dran**	Dor-mi-**ran**	Ser-vi-**ran**

	To sing	**To lose**	**To sleep**	**To serve**
I/You/We/Them	Will sing	Will lose	Will sleep	Will serve
He/She/It	Will sing	Will lose	Will sleep	Will serve

FUTURE COMPOUND – INDICATIVE

The other future tense is the Future Compound, the equivalent in English Future Perfect.

FUTURE COMPOUND - INDICATIVE				
PERSON	1st Conjugation	2nd Conjugation	3rd Conjugation (Pure)	3rd Conjugation (Inchoative)
Jo	HAURÉ + Participle	HAURÉ + Participle	HAURÉ + Participle	HAURÉ + Participle
Tu	HAURÀS + Partic.	HAURÀS + Partic.	HAURÀS + Partic.	HAURÀS + Partic.
Ell/ella	HAURÀ + partic.	HAURÀ + partic.	HAURÀ + partic.	HAURÀ + partic.
Nosaltres	HAUREM + partic.	HAUREM + partic.	HAUREM + partic.	HAUREM + partic.

14

	HAUREU + partic.	HAUREU + partic.	HAUREU + partic.	HAUREU + partic.
Vosaltres	HAUREU + partic.	HAUREU + partic.	HAUREU + partic.	HAUREU + partic.
Ells/Elles	HAURAN + partic.	HAURAN + partic.	HAURAN + partic.	HAURAN + partic.

	1st Conjugation	2nd Conjugation	3rd Conjugation (Pure)	3rd Conjugation (Inchoative)
	Can-**tar** (To sing)	Per-**dre** (To lose)	Dor-**mir** (To sleep)	Ser-**vir** (To serve)
Jo	Hau-**ré** Can-**tat**	Hau-**ré** Per-**dut**	Hau-**ré** Dor-**mit**	Hau-**ré** Ser-**vit**
Tu	Hau-**ràs** Can-**tat**	Hau-**ràs** Per-**dut**	Hau-**ràs** Dor-**mit**	Hau-**ràs** Ser-**vit**
Ell/Ella	Hau-**rà** Can-**tat**	Hau-**rà** Per-**dut**	Hau-**rà** Dor-**mit**	Hau-**rà** Ser-**vit**
Nosaltres	Hau-**rem** Can-**tat**	Hau-**rem** Per-**dut**	Hau-**rem** Dor-**mit**	Hau-**rem** Ser-**vit**
Vosaltres	Hau-**reu** Can-**tat**	Hau-**reu** Per-**dut**	Hau-**reu** Dor-**mit**	Hau-**reu** Ser-**vit**
Ells/Elles	Hau-**ran** Can-**tat**	Hau-**ran** Per-**dut**	Hau-**ran** Dor-**mit**	Hau-**ran** Ser-**vit**

	To sing	To lose	To sleep	To serve
I/You/We/Them	Will have sung	Will have lost	Will have slept	Will have served
He/She/It	Will have sung	Will have lost	Will have slept	Will have served

CONDITIONAL SIMPLE – INDICATIVE

The conditional Simple works exactly as the Would + verb works in English.

CONDITIONAL SIMPLE - INDICATIVE				
PERSON	1st Conjugation	2nd Conjugation	3rd Conjugation (Pure)	3rd Conjugation (Inchoative)
Jo	-ARIA	-RIA	-IRIA	-IRIA
Tu	-ARIES	-RIES	-IRIES	-IRIES
Ell/ella	-ARIA	-RIA	-IRIA	-IRIA
Nosaltres	-ARÍEM	-RÍEM	-IRÍEM	-IRÍEM
Vosaltres	-ARÍEU	-RÍEU	-IRÍEU	-IRÍEU
Ells/Elles	-ARIEN	-RIEN	-IRIEN	-IRIEN

	1st Conjugation	2nd Conjugation	3rd Conjugation (Pure)	3rd Conjugation (Inchoative)
	Can-**tar** (To sing)	Per-**dre** (To lose)	Dor-**mir** (To sleep)	Ser-**vir** (To serve)
Jo	Can-ta-**ri**-a	Per-**dri**-a	Dor-mi-**ri**-a	Ser-vi-**ri**-a
Tu	Can-ta-**ri**-es	Per-**dri**-es	Dor-mi-**ri**-es	Ser-vi-**ri**-es
Ell/Ella	Can-ta-**ri**-a	Per-**dri**-a	Dor-mi-**ri**-a	Ser-vi-**ri**-a
Nosaltres	Can-ta-**rí**-em	Per-**drí**-em	Dor-mi-**rí**-em	Ser-vi-**rí**-em
Vosaltres	Can-ta-**rí**-eu	Per-**drí**-eu	Dor-mi-**rí**-eu	Ser-vi-**rí**-eu
Ells/Elles	Can-ta-**ri**-en	Per-**dri**-en	Dor-mi-**ri**-en	Ser-vi-**ri**-en

	To sing	To lose	To sleep	To serve
I/You/We/Them	Would sing	Would lose	Would sleep	Would serve
He/She/It	Would sing	Would lose	Would sleep	Would serve

CONDITIONAL COMPOUND – INDICATIVE

The conditional Compound works exactly as the Would Have + participle works in English

CONDITIONAL COMPOUND - INDICATIVE				
PERSON	1st Conjugation	2nd Conjugation	3rd Conjugation (Pure)	3rd Conjugation (Inchoative)
Jo	HAURIA + participle.	HAURIA + participle.	HAURIA + participle.	HAURIA + participle.
Tu	HAURIES + partic.	HAURIES + partic.	HAURIES + partic.	HAURIES + partic.
Ell/ella	HAURIA + partic.	HAURIA + partic.	HAURIA + partic.	HAURIA + partic.
Nosaltres	HAURÍEM + partic.	HAURÍEM + partic.	HAURÍEM + partic.	HAURÍEM + partic.
Vosaltres	HAURÍEU + partic.	HAURÍEU + partic.	HAURÍEU + partic.	HAURÍEU + partic.
Ells/Elles	HAURIEN + partic.	HAURIEN + partic.	HAURIEN + partic.	HAURIEN + partic.

	1st Conjugation	2nd Conjugation	3rd Conjugation (Pure)	3rd Conjugation (Inchoative)
	Can-**tar** (To sing)	Per-**dre** (To lose)	Dor-**mir** (To sleep)	Ser-**vir** (To serve)
Jo	Hau-**ri**-a Can-**tat**	Hau-**ri**-a Per-**dut**	Hau-**ri**-a Dor-**mit**	Hau-**ri**-a Ser-**vit**
Tu	Hau-**ri**-es Can-**tat**	Hau-**ri**-es Per-**dut**	Hau-**ri**-es Dor-**mit**	Hau-**ri**-es Ser-**vit**
Ell/Ella	Hau-**ri**-a Can-**tat**	Hau-**ri**-a Per-**dut**	Hau-**ri**-a Dor-**mit**	Hau-**ri**-a Ser-**vit**
Nosaltres	Hau-**rí**-em Can-**tat**	Hau-**rí**-em Per-**dut**	Hau-**rí**-em Dor-**mit**	Hau-**rí**-em Ser-**vit**

Vosaltres	Hau-**rí**-eu Can-tat	Hau-**rí**-eu Per-dut	Hau-**rí**-eu Dor-mit	Hau-**rí**-eu Ser-vit
Ells/Elles	Hau-**ri**-en Can-tat	Hau-**ri**-en Per-dut	Hau-**ri**-en Dor-mit	Hau-**ri**-en Ser-vit

	To sing	**To lose**	**To sleep**	**To serve**
I/You/We/Them	Would have sung	Would have lost	Would have slept	Would have served
He/She/It	Would have sung	Would have lost	Would have slept	Would have served

PRESENT – SUBJUNCTIVE

It is used for something that has a hypothetical value, it's not sure, desirable... and it always appears in subordinate sentences. It is translated with the present simple:

- We'll go there when we <u>have</u> the money
- I'm interested in everything that <u>has to do</u> with movies
- He denies that he ever <u>makes</u> mistakes

It is also used as imperative in the negative form. (For example: No Cantis – Don't sing)

PRESENT - SUBJUNCTIVE				
PERSON	1st Conjugation	2nd Conjugation	3rd Conjugation (Pure)	3rd Conjugation (Inchoative)
Jo	-I	-I	-I	-EIXI
Tu	-IS	-IS	-IS	-EIXIS
Ell/ella	-I	-I	-I	-EIXI
Nosaltres	-EM	-EM	-IM	-IM
Vosaltres	-EU	-EU	-IU	-IU
Ells/Elles	-IN	-IN	-IN	-EIXIN

	1st Conjugation	2nd Conjugation	3rd Conjugation (Pure)	3rd Conjugation (Inchoative)
	Can-**tar** (To sing)	Per-**dre** (To lose)	Dor-**mir** (To sleep)	Ser-**vir** (To serve)
Jo	**Can**-ti	**Per**-di	**Dor**-mi	Ser-**vei**-xi
Tu	**Can**-tis	**Per**-dis	**Dor**-mis	Ser-**vei**-xis
Ell/Ella	**Can**-ti	Per-di	**Dor**-mi	Ser-**vei**-xi
Nosaltres	Can-**tem**	Per-**dem**	Dor-**mim**	Ser-**vim**
Vosaltres	Can-**teu**	Per-**deu**	Dor-**miu**	Ser-**viu**
Ells/Elles	**Can**-tin	**Per**-din	**Dor**-min	Ser-**vei**-xin

	To sing	**To lose**	**To sleep**	**To serve**
I/You/We/Them	Sing	Lose	Sleep	Serve
He/She/It	Sings	Loses	Sleeps	Serves

PERFET – SUBJUNCTIVE

It is used for conditional sentences and it is translated with the present perfect:

- You can leave when you <u>have finished</u> your homework
- I hope you <u>have enjoyed</u> the movie!

PERFET - SUBJUNCTIVE				
PERSON	1st Conjugation	2nd Conjugation	3rd Conjugation (Pure)	3rd Conjugation (Inchoative)
Jo	HAGI + participle.	HAGI + participle.	HAGI + participle.	HAGI + participle.
Tu	HAGIS + partic.	HAGIS + partic.	HAGIS + partic.	HAGIS + partic.
Ell/ella	HAGI + partic.	HAGI + partic.	HAGI + partic.	HAGI + partic.
Nosaltres	HÀGIM + partic.	HÀGIM + partic.	HÀGIM + partic.	HÀGIM + partic.
Vosaltres	HÀGIU + partic.	HÀGIU + partic.	HÀGIU + partic.	HÀGIU + partic.
Ells/Elles	HAGIN + partic.	HAGIN + partic.	HAGIN + partic.	HAGIN + partic.

	1st Conjugation	2nd Conjugation	3rd Conjugation (Pure)	3rd Conjugation (Inchoative)
	Can-**tar** (To sing)	Per-**dre** (To lose)	Dor-**mir** (To sleep)	Ser-**vir** (To serve)
Jo	**Ha**-gi Can-**tat**	**Ha**-gi Per-**dut**	**Ha**-gi Dor-**mit**	**Ha**-gi Ser-**vit**
Tu	**Ha**-gis Can-**tat**	**Ha**-gis Per-**dut**	**Ha**-gis Dor-**mit**	**Ha**-gis Ser-**vit**
Ell/Ella	**Ha**-gi Can-**tat**	**Ha**-gi Per-**dut**	**Ha**-gi Dor-**mit**	**Ha**-gi Ser-**vit**
Nosaltres	**Hà**-gim Can-**tat**	**Hà**-gim Per-**dut**	**Hà**-gim Dor-**mit**	**Hà**-gim Ser-**vit**
Vosaltres	**Hà**-giu Can-**tat**	**Hà**-giu Per-**dut**	**Hà**-giu Dor-**mit**	**Hà**-giu Ser-**vit**
Ells/Elles	**Ha**-gin Can-**tat**	**Ha**-gin Per-**dut**	**Ha**-gin Dor-**mit**	**Ha**-gin Ser-**vit**

	To sing	To lose	To sleep	To serve
I/You/We/Them	Have sung	Have lost	Have slept	Have served
He/She/It	Has sung	Has lost	Has slept	Has served

IMPERFET PAST – SUBJUNCTIVE

It is used for hypothetical actions, imaginary or a desire. It is translated with the past simple:

- If I <u>knew</u> I'd tell you
- If it <u>rained</u> I would open the umbrella

PERFET - SUBJUNCTIVE				
PERSON	1st Conjugation	2nd Conjugation	3rd Conjugation (Pure)	3rd Conjugation (Inchoative)
Jo	-ÉS	-ÉS	-ÍS	-ÍS
Tu	-ESSIS	-ESSIS	-ISSIS	-ISSIS
Ell/ella	-ÉS	-ÉS	-ÍS	-ÍS
Nosaltres	-ÉSSIM	-ÉSSIM	-ÍSSIM	-ÍSSIM
Vosaltres	-ÉSSIU	-ÉSSIU	-ÍSSIU	-ÍSSIU
Ells/Elles	-ESSIN	-ESSIN	-ISSIN	-ISSIN

	1st Conjugation	2nd Conjugation	3rd Conjugation (Pure)	3rd Conjugation (Inchoative)
	Can-**tar** (To sing)	Per-**dre** (To lose)	Dor-**mir** (To sleep)	Ser-**vir** (To serve)
Jo	Can-**tés**	Per-**dés**	Dor-**mís**	Ser-**vís**
Tu	Can-**tes**-sis	Per-**des**-sis	Dor-**mis**-sis	Ser-**vis**-sis
Ell/Ella	Can-**tés**	Per-**dés**	Dor-**mís**	Ser-**vís**
Nosaltres	Can-**tés**-sim	Per-**dés**-sim	Dor-**mís**-sim	Ser-**vís**-sim

Vosaltres	Can-**tés**-siu	Per-**dés**-siu	Dor-**mís**-siu	Ser-**vís**-siu
Ells/Elles	Can-**tes**-sin	Per-**des**-sin	Dor-**mis**-sin	Ser-**vis**-sin

	To sing	**To lose**	**To sleep**	**To serve**
I/You/We/Them	Sang	Lost	Slept	Served
He/She/It	Sang	Lost	Slept	Served

PLUSQUAMPERFET PAST – SUBJUNCTIVE

It is used to express a condition in a sentence. It's almost always translated with the past perfect.

- I you <u>had scored</u> a goal we wouldn't have lost
- It puzzled me that they <u>had been</u> in Rome
- I really doubted that they <u>had passed</u> the exam

PERFET - SUBJUNCTIVE				
PERSON	1st Conjugation	2nd Conjugation	3rd Conjugation (Pure)	3rd Conjugation (Inchoative)
Jo	HAGUÉS + participle.	HAGUÉS + participle.	HAGUÉS + participle.	HAGUÉS + participle.
Tu	HAGUESSIS + partic.	HAGUESSIS + partic.	HAGUESSIS + partic.	HAGUESSIS + partic.
Ell/ella	HAGUÉS + partic.	HAGUÉS + partic.	HAGUÉS + partic.	HAGUÉS + partic.
Nosaltres	HAGUÉSSIM + partic.	HAGUÉSSIM + partic.	HAGUÉSSIM + partic.	HAGUÉSSIM + partic.
Vosaltres	HAGUÉSSIU + partic.	HAGUÉSSIU + partic.	HAGUÉSSIU + partic.	HAGUÉSSIU + partic.
Ells/Elles	HAGUESSIN + partic.	HAGUESSIN + partic.	HAGUESSIN + partic.	HAGUESSIN + partic.

	1st Conjugation	2nd Conjugation	3rd Conjugation (Pure)	3rd Conjugation (Inchoative)
	Can-**tar** (To sing)	Per-**dre** (To lose)	Dor-**mir** (To sleep)	Ser-**vir** (To serve)
Jo	Ha-**gués** Can-**tat**	Ha-**gués** Per-**dut**	Ha-**gués** Dor-**mit**	Ha-**gués** Ser-**vit**
Tu	Ha-**gues**-sis Can-**tat**	Ha-**gues**-sis Per-**dut**	Ha-**gues**-sis Dor-**mit**	Ha-**gues**-sis Ser-**vit**
Ell/Ella	Ha-**gués** Can-**tat**	Ha-**gués** Per-**dut**	Ha-**gués** Dor-**mit**	Ha-**gués** Ser-**vit**
Nosaltres	Ha-**gués**-sim Can-**tat**	Ha-**gués**-sim Per-**dut**	Ha-**gués**-sim Dor-**mit**	Ha-**gués**-sim Ser-**vit**
Vosaltres	Ha-**gués**-siu Can-**tat**	Ha-**gués**-siu Per-**dut**	Ha-**gués**-siu Dor-**mit**	Ha-**gués**-siu Ser-**vit**
Ells/Elles	Ha-**gues**-sin Can-**tat**	Ha-**gues**-sin Per-**dut**	Ha-**gues**-sin Dor-**mit**	Ha-**gues**-sin Ser-**vit**

	To sing	To lose	To sleep	To serve
I/You/We/Them	Had sung	Had lost	Had slept	Had served
He/She/It	Had sung	Had lost	Had slept	Had served

IMPERATIVE

It is used to express an order. The subject is not used in the imperative mood.

IMPERATIVE				
PERSON	1st Conjugation	2nd Conjugation	3rd Conjugation (Pure)	3rd Conjugation (Inchoative)
(Jo)				
(Tu)	-A	-	-	-EIX
(Ell/ella)	-I	-I	-I	-EIXI

(Nosaltres)	-EM	-EM	-IM	-IM
(Vosaltres)	-EU	-EU	-IU	-IU
(Ells/Elles)	-IN	-IN	-IN	-EIXIN

	1st Conjugation	2nd Conjugation	3rd Conjugation (Pure)	3rd Conjugation (Inchoative)
	Can-**tar** (To sing)	Per-**dre** (To lose)	Dor-**mir** (To sleep)	Ser-**vir** (To serve)
Tu	**Can**-ta	**Perd**	**Dorm**	Ser-**veix**
Ell/Ella	**Can**-ti	**Per**-di	**Dor**-mi	Ser-**vei**-xi
Nosaltres	Can-**tem**	Per-**dem**	Dor-**mim**	Ser-**vim**
Vosaltres	Can-**teu**	Per-**deu**	Dor-**miu**	Ser-**viu**
Ells/Elles	**Can**-tin	**Per**-din	**Dor**-min	Ser-**vei**-xin

	To sing	To lose	To sleep	To serve
I/You/We/Them	Sing	Lose	Sleep	Serve
He/She/It	Sing	Lose	Sleep	Serve

INFINITIVE

It's the name of the verb. It is used for:

- Knowing the conjugation the verb belongs to
- Building periphrasis

There are two forms, simple and compound.

The SIMPLE is build with the root + the ending (AR, ER, RE or IR)

- CANT-AR
- PERD-RE
- DORM-IR
- SERV-IR

The COMPOUND is build with the infinitive of the verb To Have + participle.

- HAVER CANTAT
- HAVER PERDUT
- HAVER DORMIT
- HAVER SERVIT

PARTICIPLE

It is used to build periphrasis and, sometimes, as an adjective (The lost book, for example)

It is formed with the root + AT (1st), UT (2nd) and IT (3rd)

- CANT-AT
- PERD-UT
- DORM-IT
- SERV-IT

GERUND

It works as the gerund in English, with the ING ending.

There are also two forms, Simple and Compound

The SIMPLE is build with the root + ANT (1st), ENT (2nd) and INT (3rd)

- CANT-ANT (Singing)
- PERD-ENT (Losing)
- DORM-INT (Sleeping)
- SERV-INT (Serving)

The COMPOUND is build with the gerund of the verb have (HAVENT) + participle

- HAVENT CANTAT (Having sung)
- HAVENT PERDUT (Having lost)
- HAVENT DORMIT (Having slept)
- HAVENT SERVIT (Having served)

IRREGULAR VERBS

Most of the Catalan verbs are regular, although some of them, as in any other language, are not. Here is the list of the most common irregular verbs:

Catalan	English	Catalan	English
Absoldre	To Absolve	Anar	To Go
Aprendre	To Learn	Atendre	To Attend
Beure	To Drink	Complaure	To Please
Córrer	To Run	Créixer	To Grow
Cabre	To Fit	Canviar	To Change
Caure	To Fall	Concloure	To Conclude
Collir	To Harvest	Començar	To Start
Conèixer	To Know	Cruixir	To Rustle
Dir	To Say	Donar	To Give
Dur	To Carry	Eixir	To Leave
Enaiguar	To Flood	Escriure	To Write
Esglaiar	To Scare	Fer	To Do
Fondre	To Melt	Fugir	To Run Away
Haver	To Have	Heure	To Achieve
Jeure	To Lay Down	Jugar	To Play
Lluir	To Show off	Nàixer o Néixer	To Born
Obrir	To Open	Obtenir	To Obtain
Passejar	To Stroll	Percudir	To tarnish
Pertànyer	To Belong	Poder	Can
Rebre	To Receive	Riure	To laugh
Vendre	To Sell		

TO ACCEPT – ACCEPTAR

PERSONAL							
INDICATIVE				**SUBJUNCTIVE**			
SIMPLE		**COMPOUND**		**SIMPLE**		**COMPOUND**	
Present		*Past Indefinite*		*Present*		*Past Perfet*	
Jo	Ac-**cep**-to	Jo	**He** ac-cep-**tat**	Jo	Ac-**cep**-ti	Jo	**Ha**-gi ac-cep-**tat**
Tu	Ac-**cep**-tes	Tu	**Has** ac-cep-**tat**	Tu	Ac-**cep**-tis	Tu	**Ha**-gis ac-cep-**tat**
Ell	Ac-**cep**-ta	Ell	**Ha** ac-cep-**tat**	Ell	Ac-**cep**-ti	Ell	**Ha**-gi ac-cep-**tat**
No.	Ac-cep-**tem**	Nos.	**Hem** ac-cep-**tat**	Nos.	Ac-cep-**tem**	Nos.	**Hà**-gim ac-cep-**tat**
Vos.	Ac-cep-**teu**	Vos.	**Heu** ac-cep-**tat**	Vos.	Ac-cep-**teu**	Vos.	**Hà**-giu ac-cep-**tat**
Ells	Ac-**cep**-ten	Ells	**Han** ac-cep-**tat**	Ells	Ac-cep-**tin**	Ells	**Ha**-gin ac-cep-**tat**
Imperfet		*Past Plusquamperfet*		*Imperfet past*		*Plusquamperfet past*	
Jo	Ac-cep-**ta**-va	Jo	Ha-**vi**-a ac-cep-**tat**	Jo	Ac-cep-**tés**	Jo	Ha-**gués** ac-cep-**tat**
Tu	Ac-cep-**ta**-ves	Tu	Ha-**vi**-es ac-cep-**tat**	Tu	Ac-cep-**tes**-sis	Tu	Ha-**gues**-sis ac-cep-**tat**
Ell	Ac-cep-**ta**-va	Ell	Ha-**vi**-a ac-cep-**tat**	Ell	Ac-cep-**tés**	Ell	Ha-**gués** ac-cep-**tat**
No.	Ac-cep-**tà**-vem	Nos.	Ha-**ví**-em ac-cep-**tat**	Nos.	Ac-cep-**tés**-sim	Nos.	Ha-**gués**-sim ac-cep-**tat**
Vos.	Ac-cep-**tà**-veu	Vos.	Ha-**ví**-eu ac-cep-**tat**	Vos.	Ac-cep-**tés**-siu	Vos.	Ha-**gués**-siu ac-cep-**tat**
Ells	Ac-cep-**ta**-ven	Ells	Ha-**vi**-en ac-cep-**tat**	Ells	Ac-cep-**tes**-sin	Ells	Ha-**gues**-sin ac-cep-**tat**

Past Simple		*Past Perifrastic*	*Past Anterior perifrastic*
Jo	Ac-cep-**tí**	**Vaig** ac-cep-**tar**	**Vaig** ha-**ver** ac-cep-**tat**
Tu	Ac-cep-**ta**-res	**Vas** ac-cep-**tar**	**Vas** ha-**ver** ac-cep-**tat**
Ell	Ac-cep-**tà**	**Va** ac-cep-**tar**	**Va** ha-**ver** ac-cep-**tat**
Nos.	Ac-cep-**tà**-rem	**Vam** ac-cep-**tar**	**Vam** ha-**ver** ac-cep-**tat**
Vos.	Ac-cep-**tà**-reu	**Vau** ac-cep-**tar**	**Vau** ha-**ver** ac-cep-**tat**
Ells	Ac-cep-**tà**-ren	**Van** ac-cep-**tar**	**Van** ha-**ver** ac-cep-**tat**

Future Simple		*Future Compound*	
Jo	Ac-cep-ta-**ré**	Jo	Hau-**ré** ac-cep-**tat**
Tu	Ac-cep-ta-**ràs**	Tu	Hau-**ràs** ac-cep-**tat**
Ell	Ac-cep-ta-**rà**	Ell	Hau-**rà** ac-cep-**tat**
Nos.	Ac-cep-ta-**rem**	Nos.	Hau-**rem** ac-cep-**tat**
Vos.	Ac-cep-tar-**eu**	Vos.	Hau-**reu** ac-cep-**tat**
Ells	Ac-cep-ta-**ran**	Ells	Hau-**ran** ac-cep-**tat**

Conditional Simple		*Conditional Compound*		**IMPERATIVE**		
Jo	Ac-cep-ta-**ri**-a	Jo	Hau-**ri**-a ac-cep-**tat**			
Tu	Ac-cep-ta-**ri**-es	Tu	Hau-**ri**-es ac-cep-**tat**	Ac-**cep**-ta	(Tu)	
Ell	Ac-cep-ta-**ri**-a	Ell	Hau-**ri**-a ac-cep-**tat**	Ac-**cep**-ti	(Ell)	
Nos.	Ac-cep-ta-**rí**-em	Nos.	Hau-**rí**-em ac-cep-**tat**	Ac-cep-**tem**	(Nos.)	
Vos.	Ac-cep-ta-**rí**-eu	Vos.	Hau-**rí**-eu ac-cep-**tat**	Ac-cep-**teu**	(Vos.)	
Ells	Ac-cep-ta-**ri**-en	Ells	Hau-**ri**-en ac-cep-**tat**	Ac-cep-**tin**	(Ells)	

IMPERSONAL		
	SIMPLE	**COMPOUND**
Infinitive	Ac-cep-**tar**	Ha-**ver** ac-cep-**tat**
Participle	Ac-cep-**tat**	-
Gerund	Ac-cep-**tant**	Ha-**vent** ac-cep-**tat**

TO ADMIT - ADMETRE

PERSONAL				
INDICATIVE			**SUBJUNCTIVE**	
SIMPLE	**COMPOUND**		**SIMPLE**	**COMPOUND**

INDICATIVE / SUBJUNCTIVE

Present		Past Indefinite		Present		Past Perfet	
Jo	Ad-**me**-to	Jo	**He** ad-**mès**	Jo	Ad-**me**-ti	Jo	**Ha**-gi ad-**mès**
Tu	Ad-**mets**	Tu	**Has** ad-**mès**	Tu	Ad-**me**-tis	Tu	**Ha**-gis ad-**mès**
Ell	Ad-**met**	Ell	**Ha** ad-**mès**	Ell	Ad-**me**-ti	Ell	**Ha**-gi ad-**mès**
No.	Ad-me-**tem**	Nos.	**Hem** ad-**mès**	Nos.	Ad-me-**tem**	Nos.	**Hà**-gim ad-**mès**
Vos.	Ad-me-**teu**	Vos.	**Heu** ad-**mès**	Vos.	Ad-me-**teu**	Vos.	**Hà**-giu ad-**mès**
Ells	Ad-**me**-ten	Ells	**Han** ad-**mès**	Ells	Ad-**me**-tin	Ells	**Ha**-gin ad-**mès**

Imperfet		Past Plusquamperfet		Imperfet past		Plusquamperfet past	
Jo	Ad-me-**ti**-a	Jo	Ha-**vi**-a ad-**mès**	Jo	Ad-me-**tés**	Jo	Ha-**gués** ad-**mès**
Tu	Ad-me-**ti**-es	Tu	Ha-**vi**-es ad-**mès**	Tu	Ad-me-**tes**-sis	Tu	Ha-**gues**-sis ad-**mès**
Ell	Ad-me-**ti**-a	Ell	Ha-**vi**-a ad-**mès**	Ell	Ad-me-**tés**	Ell	Ha-**gués** ad-**mès**
No.	Ad-me-**tí**-em	Nos.	Ha-**ví**-em ad-**mès**	Nos.	Ad-me-**tés**-sim	Nos.	Ha-**gués**-sim ad-**mès**
Vos.	Ad-me-**tí**-eu	Vos.	Ha-**ví**-eu ad-**mès**	Vos.	Ad-me-**tés**-siu	Vos.	Ha-**gués**-siu ad-**mès**
Ells	Ad-me-**ti**-en	Ells	Ha-**vi**-en ad-**mès**	Ells	Ad-me-**tes**-sin	Ells	Ha-**gues**-sin ad-**mès**

Past Simple		Past Perifrastic		Past Anterior perifrastic
Jo	Ad-me-**tí**	Jo	**Vaig** ad-**me**-tre	**Vaig** ha-**ver** ad-**mès**
Tu	Ad-me-**te**-res	Tu	**Vas** ad-**me**-tre	**Vas** ha-**ver** ad-**mès**
Ell	Ad-me-**té**	Ell	**Va** ad-**me**-tre	**Va** ha-**ver** ad-**mès**
Nos.	Ad-me-**té**-rem	Nos.	**Vam** ad-**me**-tre	**Vam** ha-**ver** ad-**mès**
Vos.	Ad-me-**té**-reu	Vos.	**Vau** ad-**me**-tre	**Vau** ha-**ver** ad-**mès**
Ells	Ad-me-**te**-ren	Ells	**Van** ad-**me**-tre	**Van** ha-**ver** ad-**mès**

Future Simple		Future Compound	
Jo	Ad-me-**tré**	Jo	Hau-**ré** ad-**mès**
Tu	Ad-me-**tràs**	Tu	Hau-**ràs** ad-**mès**
Ell	Ad-me-**trà**	Ell	Hau-**rà** ad-**mès**
Nos.	Ad-me-**trem**	Nos.	Hau-**rem** ad-**mès**
Vos.	Ad-me-**treu**	Vos.	Hau-**reu** ad-**mès**
Ells	Ad-me-**tran**	Ells	Hau-**ran** ad-**mès**

Conditional Simple		Conditional Compound		IMPERATIVE	
Jo	Ad-me-**tri**-a	Jo	Hau-**ri**-a ad-**mès**		
Tu	Ad-me-**tri**-es	Tu	Hau-**ri**-es ad-**mès**	Ad-**met**	(Tu)
Ell	Ad-me-**tri**-a	Ell	Hau-**ri**-a ad-**mès**	Ad-**me**-ti	(Ell)
Nos.	Ad-me-**trí**-em	Nos.	Hau-**rí**-em ad-**mès**	Ad-me-**tem**	(Nos.)
Vos.	Ad-me-**trí**-eu	Vos.	Hau-**rí**-eu ad-**mès**	Ad-me-**teu**	(Vos.)
Ells	Ad-me-**tri**-en	Ells	Hau-**ri**-en ad-**mès**	Ad-**me**-tin	(Ells)

IMPERSONAL		
	SIMPLE	**COMPOUND**
Infinitive	Ad-**me**-tre	Ha-**ver** ad-**mès**
Participle	Ad-**mès**	-
Gerund	Ad-me-**tent**	Ha-**vent** ad-**mès**

TO ANSWER - RESPONDRE

PERSONAL				
INDICATIVE		**SUBJUNCTIVE**		

SIMPLE		**COMPOUND**		**SIMPLE**		**COMPOUND**	
Present		*Past Indefinite*		*Present*		*Past Perfet*	
Jo	Res-**ponc**	Jo	**He** res-**post**	Jo	Res-**pon**-gui	Jo	**Ha**-gi res-**post**
Tu	Res-**pons**	Tu	**Has** res-**post**	Tu	Res-**pon**-guis	Tu	**Ha**-gis res-**post**
Ell	Res-**pon**	Ell	**Ha** res-**post**	Ell	Res-**pon**-gui	Ell	**Ha**-gi res-**post**
No.	Res-po-**nem**	Nos.	**Hem** res-**post**	Nos.	Res-pon-**guem**	Nos.	**Hà**-gim res-**post**
Vos.	Res-po-**neu**	Vos.	**Heu** res-**post**	Vos.	Res-pon-**gueu**	Vos.	**Hà**-giu res-**post**
Ells	Res-po-nen	Ells	**Han** res-**post**	Ells	Res-**pon**-guin	Ells	**Ha**-gin res-**post**
Imperfet		*Past Plusquamperfet*		*Imperfet past*		*Plusquamperfet past*	
Jo	Res-po-**ni**-a	Jo	**Ha**-**vi**-a res-**post**	Jo	Res-pon-**gués**	Jo	**Ha**-**gués** res-**post**
Tu	Res-po-**ni**-es	Tu	**Ha**-**vi**-es res-**post**	Tu	Res-pon-**gues**-sis	Tu	**Ha**-**gues**-sis res-**post**
Ell	Res-po-**ni**-a	Ell	**Ha**-**vi**-a res-**post**	Ell	Res-pon-**gués**	Ell	**Ha**-**gués** res-**post**
No.	Res-po-**ní**-em	Nos.	**Ha**-**ví**-em res-**post**	Nos	Res-pon-**gués**-sim	Nos.	**Ha**-**gués**-sim res-**post**
Vos.	Res-po-**ní**-eu	Vos.	**Ha**-**ví**-eu res-**post**	Vos.	Res-pon-**gués**-siu	Vos.	**Ha**-**gués**-siu res-**post**
Ells	Res-po-**ni**-en	Ells	**Ha**-**vi**-en res-**post**	Ells	Res-pon-**gues**-sin	Ells	**Ha**-**gues**-sin res-**post**

Past Simple		*Past Perifrastic*		*Past Anterior perifrastic*
Jo	Res-pon-**guí**	Jo	**Vaig** res-**pon**-dre	**Vaig** ha-**ver** res-**post**
Tu	Res-pon-**gue**-res	Tu	**Vas** res-**pon**-dre	**Vas** ha-**ver** res-**post**
Ell	Res-pon-**gué**	Ell	**Va** res-**pon**-dre	**Va** ha-**ver** res-**post**
Nos	Res-pon-**gué**-rem	Nos.	**Vam** res-**pon**-dre	**Vam** ha-**ver** res-**post**
Vos.	Res-pon-**gué**-reu	Vos.	**Vau** res-**pon**-dre	**Vau** ha-**ver** res-**post**
Ells	Res-pon-**gue**-ren	Ells	**Van** res-**pon**-dre	**Van** ha-**ver** res-**post**

Future Simple		*Future Compound*	
Jo	Res-pon-**dré**	Jo	Hau-**ré** res-**post**
Tu	Res-pon-**dràs**	Tu	Hau-**ràs** res-**post**
Ell	Res-pon-**drà**	Ell	Hau-**rà** res-**post**
Nos.	Res-pon-**drem**	Nos.	Hau-**rem** res-**post**
Vos.	Res-pon-**dreu**	Vos.	Hau-**reu** res-**post**
Ells	Res-pon-**dran**	Ells	Hau-**ran** res-**post**

Conditional Simple		*Conditional Compound*		IMPERATIVE	
Jo	Res-pon-**dri**-a	Jo	Hau-**ri**-a res-**post**		
Tu	Res-pon-**dri**-es	Tu	Hau-**ri**-es res-**post**	Res-**pon**	*(Tu)*
Ell	Res-pon-**dri**-a	Ell	Hau-**ri**-a res-**post**	Res-**pon**-gui	*(Ell)*
Nos.	Res-pon-**drí**-em	Nos.	Hau-**rí**-em res-**post**	Res-pon-**guem**	*(Nos.)*
Vos.	Res-pon-**drí**-eu	Vos.	Hau-**rí**-eu res-**post**	Res-po-**neu**	*(Vos.)*
Ells	Res-pon-**dri**-en	Ells	Hau-**ri**-en res-**post**	Res-**pon**-guin	*(Ells)*

IMPERSONAL		
	SIMPLE	**COMPOUND**
Infinitive	Res-**pon**-dre	Ha-**ver** res-**post**
Participle	Res-**post**	-
Gerund	Res-po-**nent**	Ha-**vent** res-**post**

TO APPEAR – APARÈIXER

PERSONAL				
INDICATIVE			**SUBJUNCTIVE**	
SIMPLE	**COMPOUND**		**SIMPLE**	**COMPOUND**

Present		*Past Indefinite*		*Present*		*Past Perfet*		
Jo	A-pa-**rec** / a-pa-**rei**-xo	Jo	**He** a-pa-re-**gut**	Jo	a-pa-**re**-gui	Jo	**Ha**-gi a-pa-re-**gut**	
Tu	A-pa-**rei**-xes	Tu	**Has** a-pa-re-**gut**	Tu	a-pa-**re**-guis	Tu	**Ha**-gis a-pa-re-**gut**	
Ell	A-pa-**reix**	Ell	**Ha** a-pa-re-**gut**	Ell	a-pa-**re**-gui	Ell	**Ha**-gi a-pa-re-**gut**	
No.	A-pa-rei-**xem**	Nos.	**Hem** a-pa-re-**gut**	Nos	a-pa-re-**guem**	Nos	**Hà**-gim a-pa-re-**gut**	
Vos.	A-pa-rei-**xeu**	Vos.	**Heu** a-pa-re-**gut**	Vos.	a-pa-re-**gueu**	Vos.	**Hà**-giu a-pa-re-**gut**	
Ells	A-pa-**rei**-xen	Ells	**Han** a-pa-re-**gut**	Ells	a-pa-**re**-guin	Ells	**Ha**-gin a-pa-re-**gut**	
Imperfet		*Past Plusquamperfet*		*Imperfet past*		*Plusquamperfet past*		
Jo	A-pa-rei-**xi**-a	Jo	Ha-**vi**-a a-pa-re-**gut**	Jo	a-pa-re-**gués**	Jo	Ha-**gués** a-pa-re-**gut**	
Tu	A-pa-rei-**xi**-es	Tu	Ha-**vi**-es a-pa-re-**gut**	Tu	a-pa-re-**gues**-sis	Tu	Ha-**gues**-sis a-pa-re-**gut**	
Ell	A-pa-rei-**xi**-a	Ell	Ha-**ví**-a a-pa-re-**gut**	Ell	a-pa-re-**gués**	Ell	Ha-**gués** a-pa-re-**gut**	
No.	A-pa-rei-**xí**-em	Nos.	Ha-**ví**-em a-pa-re-**gut**	Nos	a-pa-re-**gués**-sim	Nos	Ha-**gués**-sim a-pa-re-**gut**	
Vos.	A-pa-rei-**xí**-eu	Vos.	Ha-**ví**-eu a-pa-re-**gut**	Vos.	a-pa-re-**gués**-siu	Vos.	Ha-**gués**-siu a-pa-re-**gut**	
Ells	A-pa-rei-**xi**-en	Ells	Ha-**vi**-en a-pa-re-**gut**	Ells	a-pa-re-**gues**-sin	Ells	Ha-**gues**-sin a-pa-re-**gut**	

Past Simple		*Past Perifrastic*		*Past Anterior perifrastic*		
Jo	A-pa-re-**guí**	Jo	**Vaig** a-pa-**rèi**-xer	**Vaig** ha-**ver** a-pa-re-**gut**		
Tu	A-pa-re-**gue**-res	Tu	**Vas** a-pa-**rèi**-xer	**Vas** ha-**ver** a-pa-re-**gut**		
Ell	A-pa-re-**gué**	Ell	**Va** a-pa-**rèi**-xer	**Va** ha-**ver** a-pa-re-**gut**		
Nos	A-pa-re-**gué**-rem	Nos.	**Vam** a-pa-**rèi**-xer	**Vam** ha-**ver** a-pa-re-**gut**		
Vos.	A-pa-re-**gué**-reu	Vos.	**Vau** a-pa-**rèi**-xer	**Vau** ha-**ver** a-pa-re-**gut**		
Ells	A-pa-re-**gue**-ren	Ells	**Van** a-pa-**rèi**-xer	**Van** ha-**ver** a-pa-re-**gut**		

Future Simple		*Future Compound*		
Jo	a-pa-rei-xe-**ré**	Jo	Hau-**ré** a-pa-re-**gut**	
Tu	a-pa-rei-xe-**ràs**	Tu	Hau-**ràs** a-pa-re-**gut**	
Ell	a-pa-rei-xe-**rà**	Ell	Hau-**rà** a-pa-re-**gut**	
Nos.	a-pa-rei-xe-**rem**	Nos.	Hau-**rem** a-pa-re-**gut**	
Vos.	a-pa-rei-xe-**reu**	Vos.	Hau-**reu** a-pa-re-**gut**	
Ells	a-pa-rei-xe-**ran**	Ells	Hau-**ran** a-pa-re-**gut**	

Conditional Simple		*Conditional Compound*		**IMPERATIVE**	
Jo	a-pa-rei-xe-**ri**-a	Jo	Hau-**ri**-a a-pa-re-**gut**		
Tu	a-pa-rei-xe-**ri**-es	Tu	Hau-**ri**-es a-pa-re-**gut**	a-pa-**reix**	(Tu)
Ell	a-pa-rei-xe-**ri**-a	Ell	Hau-**ri**-a a-pa-re-**gut**	a-pa-**re**-gui	(Ell)
Nos	a-pa-rei-xe-**rí**-em	Nos.	Hau-**rí**-em a-pa-re-**gut**	a-pa-re-**guem**	(Nos.)
Vos.	a-pa-rei-xe-**rí**-eu	Vos.	Hau-**rí**-eu a-pa-re-**gut**	a-pa-rei-**xeu**	(Vos.)
Ells	a-pa-rei-xe-**ri**-en	Ells	Hau-**ri**-en a-pa-re-**gut**	a-pa-**re**-guin	(Ells)

IMPERSONAL		
	SIMPLE	**COMPOUND**
Infinitive	A-pa-**rèi**-xer	Ha-**ver** a-pa-re-**gut**
Participle	A-pa-re-**gut**	-
Gerund	A-pa-rei-**xent**	Ha-**vent** a-pa-re-**gut**

30

TO ASK - PREGUNTAR

PERSONAL			
INDICATIVE		**SUBJUNCTIVE**	
SIMPLE	**COMPOUND**	**SIMPLE**	**COMPOUND**

Present		*Past Indefinite*		*Present*		*Past Perfet*	
Jo	Pre-**gun**-to	Jo	**He** pre-gun-**tat**	Jo	Pre-**gun**-ti	Jo	**Ha**-gi pre-gun-**tat**
Tu	Pre-**gun**-tes	Tu	**Has** pre-gun-**tat**	Tu	Pre-**gun**-tis	Tu	**Ha**-gis pre-gun-**tat**
Ell	Pre-**gun**-ta	Ell	**Ha** pre-gun-**tat**	Ell	Pre-**gun**-ti	Ell	**Ha**-gi pre-gun-**tat**
No.	Pre-gun-**tem**	Nos.	**Hem** pre-gun-**tat**	Nos	Pre-gun-**tem**	Nos.	**Hà**-gim pre-gun-**tat**
Vos.	Pre-gun-**teu**	Vos.	**Heu** pre-gun-**tat**	Vos.	Pre-gun-**teu**	Vos.	**Hà**-giu pre-gun-**tat**
Ells	Pre-**gun**-ten	Ells	**Han** pre-gun-**tat**	Ells	Pre-**gun**-tin	Ells	**Ha**-gin pre-gun-**tat**

Imperfet		*Past Plusquamperfet*		*Imperfet past*		*Plusquamperfet past*	
Jo	Pre-gun-**ta**-va	Jo	Ha-**vi**-a pre-gun-**tat**	Jo	Pre-gun-**tés**	Jo	Ha-**gués** pre-gun-**tat**
Tu	Pre-gun-**ta**-ves	Tu	Ha-**vi**-es pre-gun-**tat**	Tu	Pre-gun-**tes**-sis	Tu	Ha-**gues**-sis pre-gun-**tat**
Ell	Pre-gun-**ta**-va	Ell	Ha-**vi**-a pre-gun-**tat**	Ell	Pre-gun-**tés**	Ell	Ha-**gués** pre-gun-**tat**
No.	Pre-gun-**tà**-vem	Nos.	Ha-**ví**-em pre-gun-**tat**	Nos	Pre-gun-**tés**-sim	Nos	Ha-**gués**-sim pre-gun-**tat**
Vos.	Pre-gun-**tà**-veu	Vos.	Ha-**ví**-eu pre-gun-**tat**	Vos.	Pre-gun-**tés**-siu	Vos.	Ha-**gués**-siu pre-gun-**tat**
Ells	Pre-gun-**ta**-ven	Ells	Ha-**vi**-en pre-gun-**tat**	Ells	Pre-gun-**tes**-sin	Ells	Ha-**gues**-sin pre-gun-**tat**

Past Simple		*Past Perifrastic*		*Past Anterior perifrastic*			
Jo	Pre-gun-**tí**	Jo	**Vaig** pre-gun-**tar**	**Vaig** ha-**ver** pre-gun-**tat**			
Tu	Pre-gun-**ta**-res	Tu	**Vas** pre-gun-**tar**	**Vas** ha-**ver** pre-gun-**tat**			
Ell	Pre-gun-**tà**	Ell	**Va** pre-gun-**tar**	**Va** ha-**ver** pre-gun-**tat**			
Nos	Pre-gun-**tà**-rem	Nos.	**Vam** pre-gun-**tar**	**Vam** ha-**ver** pre-gun-**tat**			
Vos.	Pre-gun-**tà**-reu	Vos.	**Vau** pre-gun-**tar**	**Vau** ha-**ver** pre-gun-**tat**			
Ells	Pre-gun-**ta**-ren	Ells	**Van** pre-gun-**tar**	**Van** ha-**ver** pre-gun-**tat**			

Future Simple		*Future Compound*			
Jo	Pre-gun-ta-**ré**	Jo	Hau-**ré** pre-gun-**tat**		
Tu	Pre-gun-ta-**ràs**	Tu	Hau-**ràs** pre-gun-**tat**		
Ell	Pre-gun-ta-**rà**	Ell	Hau-**rà** pre-gun-**tat**		
Nos.	Pre-gun-ta-**rem**	Nos.	Hau-**rem** pre-gun-**tat**		
Vos.	Pre-gun-ta-**reu**	Vos.	Hau-**reu** pre-gun-**tat**		
Ells	Pre-gun-ta-**ran**	Ells	Hau-**ran** pre-gun-**tat**		

Conditional Simple		*Conditional Compound*		**IMPERATIVE**	
Jo	Pre-gun-ta-**ri**-a	Jo	Hau-**ri**-a pre-gun-**tat**		
Tu	Pre-gun-ta-**ri**-es	Tu	Hau-**ri**-es pre-gun-**tat**	Pre-**gun**-ta	(Tu)
Ell	Pre-gun-ta-**ri**-a	Ell	Hau-**ri**-a pre-gun-**tat**	Pre-**gun**-ti	(Ell)
Nos	Pre-gun-ta-**rí**-em	Nos.	Hau-**rí**-em pre-gun-**tat**	Pre-gun-**tem**	(Nos.)
Vos.	Pre-gun-ta-**rí**-eu	Vos.	Hau-**rí**-eu pre-gun-**tat**	Pre-gun-**teu**	(Vos.)
Ells	Pre-gun-ta-**ri**-en	Ells	Hau-**ri**-en pre-gun-**tat**	Pre-**gun**-tin	(Ells)

IMPERSONAL		
	SIMPLE	**COMPOUND**
Infinitive	Pre-gun-**tar**	Ha-**ver** pre gun-**tat**
Participle	Pre-gun-**tat**	-
Gerund	Pre-gun-**tant**	Ha-**vent** pre-gun-**tat**

TO BE (someone or something) – SER / ÉSSER

PERSONAL							

INDICATIVE				SUBJUNCTIVE			
SIMPLE		**COMPOUND**		**SIMPLE**		**COMPOUND**	
Present		*Past Indefinite*		*Present*		*Past Perfet*	
Jo	**Sóc**	Jo	**He** es-**tat**	Jo	**Si**-gui	Jo	**Ha**-gi es-**tat**
Tu	**Ets**	Tu	**Has** es-**tat**	Tu	**Si**-guis	Tu	**Ha**-gis es-**tat**
Ell	**És**	Ell	**Ha** es-**tat**	Ell	**Si**-gui	Ell	**Ha**-gi es-**tat**
No.	**Som**	Nos.	**Hem** es-**tat**	Nos.	**Si**-**guem**	Nos.	**Hà**-gim es-**tat**
Vos.	**Sou**	Vos.	**Heu** es-**tat**	Vos.	**Si**-**gueu**	Vos.	**Hà**-giu es-**tat**
Ells	**Són**	Ells	**Han** es-**tat**	Ells	**Si**-guin	Ells	**Ha**-gin es-**tat**
Imperfet		*Past Plusquamperfet*		*Imperfet past*		*Plusquamperfet past*	
Jo	**E**-ra	Jo	Ha-**vi**-a es-**tat**	Jo	**Fos**	Jo	Ha-**gués** es-**tat**
Tu	**E**-res	Tu	Ha-**vi**-es es-**tat**	Tu	**Fos**-sis	Tu	Ha-**gues**-sis es-**tat**
Ell	**E**-ra	Ell	Ha-**vi**-a es-**tat**	Ell	**Fos**	Ell	Ha-**gués** es-**tat**
No.	**É**-rem	Nos.	Ha-**ví**-em es-**tat**	Nos	**Fós**-sim	Nos.	Ha-**gués**-sim es-**tat**
Vos.	**É**-reu	Vos.	Ha-**ví**-eu es-**tat**	Vos.	**Fós**-siu	Vos.	Ha-**gués**-siu es-**tat**
Ells	**E**-ren	Ells	Ha-**vi**-en es-**tat**	Ells	**Fos**-sin	Ells	Ha-**gués**-sin es-**tat**

Past Simple		*Past Perifrastic*		*Past Anterior perifrastic*			
Jo	**Fui**	Jo	**Vaig ser**	**Vaig** ha-**ver** es-**tat**			
Tu	**Fo**-res	Tu	**Vas ser**	**Vas** ha-**ver** es-**tat**			
Ell	**Fou**	Ell	**Va ser**	**Va** ha-**ver** es-**tat**			
Nos	**Fó**-rem	Nos.	**Vam ser**	**Vam** ha-**ver** es-**tat**			
Vos.	**Fó**-reu	Vos.	**Vau ser**	**Vau** ha-**ver** es-**tat**			
Ells	**Fo**-ren	Ells	**Van ser**	**Van** ha-**ver** es-**tat**			

Future Simple		*Future Compound*					
Jo	Se-**ré**	Jo	Hau-**ré** es-**tat**				
Tu	Se-**ràs**	Tu	Hau-**ràs** es-**tat**				
Ell	Se-**rà**	Ell	Hau-**rà** es-**tat**				
Nos.	Se-**rem**	Nos.	Hau-**rem** es-**tat**				
Vos.	Se-**reu**	Vos.	Hau-**reu** es-**tat**				
Ells	Se-**ran**	Ells	Hau-**ran** es-**tat**				

Conditional Simple		*Conditional Compound*		IMPERATIVE			
Jo	**Fó**-ra / se-**ri**-a	Jo	Hau-**ri**-a es-**tat**				
Tu	**Fo**-res / se-**ri**-es	Tu	Hau-**ri**-es es-**tat**	**Si**-gues		(Tu)	
Ell	**Fó**-ra / se-**ri**-a	Ell	Hau-**ri**-a es-**tat**	**Si**-gui		(Ell)	
Nos	**Fó**-rem / se-**rí**-em	Nos.	Hau-**rí**-em es-**tat**	**Si**-**guem**		(Nos.)	
Vos.	**Fó**-reu / se-**rí**-eu	Vos.	Hau-**rí**-eu es-**tat**	**Si**-**gueu**		(Vos.)	
Ells	**Fo**-ren / se-**ri**-en	Ells	Hau-**ri**-en es-**tat**	**Si**-guin		(Ells)	

IMPERSONAL		
	SIMPLE	**COMPOUND**
Infinitive	**És**-ser / **Ser** *	Ha-**ver** es-**tat**
Participle	Es-**tat** / **Set** / Si-**gut** **	-
Gerund	**Sent**	Ha-**vent** es-**tat**

*Both mean the same and are interchangeable, although SER is more common, ÉSSER is for literature
**All three words mean the same and are interchangeable; the only difference is that ESTAT is slightly more polite

TO BE (somewhere) - ESTAR

PERSONAL							
INDICATIVE				**SUBJUNCTIVE**			
SIMPLE		**COMPOUND**		**SIMPLE**		**COMPOUND**	
Present		*Past Indefinite*		*Present*		*Past Perfet*	
Jo	Es-**tic**	Jo	**He** es-**tat**	Jo	Es-**ti**-gui	Jo	**Ha**-gi es-**tat**
Tu	Es-**tàs**	Tu	**Has** es-**tat**	Tu	Es-**ti**-guis	Tu	**Ha**-gis es-**tat**
Ell	Es-**tà**	Ell	**Ha** es-**tat**	Ell	Es-**ti**-gui	Ell	**Ha**-gi es-**tat**
No.	Es-**tem**	Nos.	**Hem** es-**tat**	Nos.	Es-**ti**-**guem**	Nos.	**Hà**-gim es-**tat**
Vos.	Es-**teu**	Vos.	**Heu** es-**tat**	Vos.	Es-**ti**-**gueu**	Vos.	**Hà**-giu es-**tat**
Ells	Es-**tan**	Ells	**Han** es-**tat**	Ells	Es-**ti**-guin	Ells	**Ha**-gin es-**tat**
Imperfet		*Past Plusquamperfet*		*Imperfet past*		*Plusquamperfet past*	
Jo	Es-**ta**-va	Jo	Ha-**vi**-a es-**tat**	Jo	Es-ti-**gués**	Jo	Ha-**gués** es-**tat**
Tu	Es-**ta**-ves	Tu	Ha-**vi**-es es-**tat**	Tu	Es-ti-**gues**-sis	Tu	Ha-**gues**-sis es-**tat**
Ell	Es-**ta**-va	Ell	Ha-**vi**-a es-**tat**	Ell	Es-ti-**gués**	Ell	Ha-**gués** es-**tat**
No.	Es-**tà**-vem	Nos.	Ha-**ví**-em es-**tat**	Nos	Es-ti-**gués**-sim	Nos.	Ha-**gués**-sim es-**tat**
Vos.	Es-**tà**-veu	Vos.	Ha-**ví**-eu es-**tat**	Vos.	Es-ti-**gués**-siu	Vos.	Ha-**gués**-siu es-**tat**
Ells	Es-**ta**-ven	Ells	Ha-**vi**-en es-**tat**	Ells	Es-ti-**gues**-sin	Ells	Ha-**gues**-sin es-**tat**

Past Simple		*Past Perifrastic*		*Past Anterior perifrastic*
Jo	Es-ti-**guí**	Jo	**Vaig** es-**tar**	**Vaig** ha-**ver** es-**tat**
Tu	Es-ti-**gue**-res	Tu	**Vas** es-**tar**	**Vas** ha-**ver** es-**tat**
Ell	Es-ti-**gué**	Ell	**Va** es-**tar**	**Va** ha-**ver** es-**tat**
Nos	Es-ti-**gué**-rem	Nos.	**Vam** es-**tar**	**Vam** ha-**ver** es-**tat**
Vos.	Es-ti-**gué**-reu	Vos.	**Vau** es-**tar**	**Vau** ha-**ver** es-**tat**
Ells	Es-ti-**gue**-ren	Ells	**Van** es-**tar**	**Van** ha-**ver** es-**tat**

Future Simple		*Future Compound*	
Jo	Es-ta-**ré**	Jo	Hau-**ré** es-**tat**
Tu	Es-ta-**ràs**	Tu	Hau-**ràs** es-**tat**
Ell	Es-ta-**rà**	Ell	Hau-**rà** es-**tat**
Nos.	Es-ta-**rem**	Nos.	Hau-**rem** es-**tat**
Vos.	Es-ta-**reu**	Vos.	Hau-**reu** es-**tat**
Ells	Es-ta-**ran**	Ells	Hau-**ran** es-**tat**

Conditional Simple		*Conditional Compound*		**IMPERATIVE**	
Jo	Es-ta-**ri**-a	Jo	Hau-**ri**-a es-**tat**		
Tu	Es-ta-**ri**-es	Tu	Hau-**ri**-es es-**tat**	Es-**ti**-gues	(Tu)
Ell	Es-ta-**ri**-a	Ell	Hau-**ri**-a es-**tat**	Es-**ti**-gui	(Ell)
Nos	Es-ta-**rí**-em	Nos.	Hau-**rí**-em es-**tat**	Es-**ti**-guem	(Nos.)
Vos.	Es-ta-**rí**-eu	Vos.	Hau-**rí**-eu es-**tat**	Es-**ti**-gueu	(Vos.)
Ells	Es-ta-**ri**-en	Ells	Hau-**ri**-en es-**tat**	Es-**ti**-guin	(Ells)

IMPERSONAL		
	SIMPLE	**COMPOUND**
Infinitive	Es-**tar**	Ha-**ver** es-**tat**
Participle	Es-**tat**	-
Gerund	Es-**tant**	Ha-**vent** es-**tat**

TO BECOME – CONVERTIR-SE*

PERSONAL							
INDICATIVE				**SUBJUNCTIVE**			
SIMPLE		**COMPOUND**		**SIMPLE**		**COMPOUND**	
Present		*Past Indefinite*		*Present*		*Past Perfet*	
Jo	**Em** con-ver-**tei**-xo	Jo	**M'he** con-ver-**tit**	Jo	**Em** con-ver-**tei**-xi	Jo	**M'ha**-gi con-ver-**tit**
Tu	**Et** con-ver-**tei**-xes	Tu	**T'has** con-ver-**tit**	Tu	**Et** con-ver-**tei**-xis	Tu	**T'ha**-gis con-ver-**tit**
Ell	**Es** con-ver-**teix**	Ell	**S'ha** con-ver-**tit**	Ell	**Es** con-ver-**tei**-xi	Ell	**S'ha**-gi con-ver-**tit**
No.	**Ens** con-ver-**tim**	Nos.	**Ens hem** con-ver-**tit**	Nos.	**Ens** con-ver-**tim**	Nos.	**Ens hà**-gim con-ver-**tit**
Vos.	**Us** con-ver-**tiu**	Vos.	**Us heu** con-ver-**tit**	Vos.	**Us** con-ver-**tiu**	Vos.	**Us hà**-giu con-ver-**tit**
Ells	**Es** con-ver-**tei**-xen	Ells	**S'han** con-ver-**tit**	Ells	**Es** con-ver-**tei**-xin	Ells	**S'ha**-gin con-ver-**tit**
Imperfet		*Past Plusquamperfet*		*Imperfet past*		*Plusquamperfet past*	
Jo	**Em** con-ver-**ti**-a	Jo	M'ha-**vi**-a con-ver-**tit**	Jo	**Em** con-ver-**tís**	Jo	M'ha-**gués** con-ver-**tit**
Tu	**Et** con-ver-**ti**-es	Tu	T'ha-**vi**-es con-ver-**tit**	Tu	**Et** con-ver-**tis**-sis	Tu	T'ha-**gues**-sis con-ver-**tit**
Ell	**Es** con-ver-**ti**-a	Ell	S'ha-**vi**-a con-ver-**tit**	Ell	**Es** con-ver-**tís**	Ell	S'ha-**gués** con-ver-**tit**
No.	**Ens** con-ver-**tí**-em	Nos.	**Ens** ha-**ví**-em con-ver-**tit**	Nos	**Ens** con-ver-**tís**-sim	Nos.	Ens ha-**gués**-sim con-ver-**tit**
Vos.	**Us** con-ver-**tí**-eu	Vos.	**Us** ha-**ví**-eu con-ver-**tit**	Vos.	**Us** con-ver-**tís**-siu	Vos.	Us ha-**gués**-siu con-ver-**tit**
Ells	**Es** con-ver-**ti**-en	Ells	S'ha-**vi**-en con-ver-**tit**	Ells	**Es** con-ver-**tis**-sin	Ells	S'ha-**gues**-sin con-ver-**tit**

Past Simple		*Past Perifrastic**, ****		*Past Anterior periphrastic***			
Jo	**Em** con-ver-**tí**	Jo	**Vaig** con.ver.**tir**-me	**Vaig** ha.**ver**-me con.ver.**tit**			
Tu	**Et** con-ver-**ti**-res	Tu	**Vas** con.ver.**tir**-te	**Vas** ha.**ver**-te con.ver.**tit**			
Ell	**Es** con-ver-**tí**	Ell	**Va** con.ver.**tir**-se	**Va** ha.**ver**-se con.ver.**tit**			
Nos	**Ens** con-ver-**tí**-rem	Nos	**Vam** con.ver.**tir**-nos	**Vam** ha.**ver**-nos con.ver.**tit**			
Vos.	**Us** con-ver-**tí**-reu	Vos.	**Vau** con.ver.**tir**-vos	**Vau** ha.**ver**-vos con.ver.**tit**			
Ells	**Es** con-ver-**ti**-ren	Ells	**Van** con.ver.**tir**-se	**Van** ha.**ver**-se con.ver.**tit**			
Future Simple		*Future Compound*					
Jo	**Em** con-ver-ti-**ré**	Jo	**M'hau**-**ré** con-ver-**tit**				
Tu	**Et** con-ver-ti-**ràs**	Tu	**T'hau**-**ràs** con-ver-**tit**				
Ell	**Es** con-ver-ti-**rà**	Ell	**S'hau**-**rà** con-ver-**tit**				
Nos.	**Ens** con-ver-ti-**rem**	Nos.	**Ens hau**-**rem** con-ver-**tit**				
Vos.	**Us** con-ver-ti-**reu**	Vos.	**Us hau**-**reu** con-ver-**tit**				
Ells	**Es** con-ver-ti-**ran**	Ells	**S'hau**-**ran** con-ver-**tit**				
Conditional Simple		*Conditional Compound*		**IMPERATIVE***			
Jo	**Em** con-ver-ti-**ri**-a	Jo	**M'hau**-ri-a con-ver-**tit**				
Tu	**Et** con-ver-ti-**ri**-es	Tu	**T'hau**-ri-es con-ver-**tit**	Con.ver.**teix**-te		(Tu)	
Ell	**Es** con-ver-ti-**ri**-a	Ell	**S'hau**-ri-a con-ver-**tit**	**Es** con.ver.**tei**.xi		(Ell)	
Nos	**Ens** con-ver-ti-**rí**-em	Nos.	**Ens hau**-**rí**-em con-ver-**tit**	Con.ver.**tim**-nos		(Nos.)	
Vos.	**Us** con-ver-ti-**rí**-eu	Vos.	**Us hau**-**rí**-eu con-ver-**tit**	Con.ver.**tiu**-vos		(Vos.)	
Ells	**Es** con-ver-ti-**ri**-en	Ells	**S'hau**-ri-en con-ver-**tit**	**Es** con.ver.**tei**.xin		(Ells)	

IMPERSONAL		
	SIMPLE	**COMPOUND**
Infinitive	Con.ver.**tir**-se	Ha.**ver**-se con.ver.**tit**
Participle	Con.ver.**tit**	-
Gerund	Con.ver.**tint**-se	Ha.**vent**-se con.ver.**tit**

*Convertir-se is a reflexive verb, which means that the action takes places on the subject. It is build with the weak pronouns, EM, ET, ES, ENS, US, ES and their variations depending on the place they are written.
** When the pronoun goes behind the word it is attached to it by a hyphen. In this case the syllables are separated with dots, to appreciate the difference.
*** It is also correct to put the pronouns before the verb "to go", as in "Em vaig convertir".

TO BEGIN - COMENÇAR

<table>
<tr><th colspan="8">PERSONAL</th></tr>
<tr><th colspan="4">INDICATIVE</th><th colspan="4">SUBJUNCTIVE</th></tr>
<tr><th colspan="2">SIMPLE</th><th colspan="2">COMPOUND</th><th colspan="2">SIMPLE</th><th colspan="2">COMPOUND</th></tr>
<tr><td colspan="2">Present</td><td colspan="2">Past Indefinite</td><td colspan="2">Present</td><td colspan="2">Past Perfet</td></tr>
<tr><td>Jo</td><td>Co-men-ço</td><td>Jo</td><td>He co-men-çat</td><td>Jo</td><td>Co-men-ci</td><td>Jo</td><td>Ha-gi co-men-çat</td></tr>
<tr><td>Tu</td><td>Co-men-ces</td><td>Tu</td><td>Has co-men-çat</td><td>Tu</td><td>Co-men-cis</td><td>Tu</td><td>Ha-gis co-men-çat</td></tr>
<tr><td>Ell</td><td>Co-men-ça</td><td>Ell</td><td>Ha co-men-çat</td><td>Ell</td><td>Co-men-ci</td><td>Ell</td><td>Ha-gi co-men-çat</td></tr>
<tr><td>No.</td><td>Co-men-cem</td><td>Nos.</td><td>Hem co-men-çat</td><td>Nos.</td><td>Co-men-cem</td><td>Nos.</td><td>Hà-gim co-men-çat</td></tr>
<tr><td>Vos.</td><td>Co-men-ceu</td><td>Vos.</td><td>Heu co-men-çat</td><td>Vos.</td><td>Co-men-ceu</td><td>Vos.</td><td>Hà-giu co-men-çat</td></tr>
<tr><td>Ells</td><td>Co-men-cen</td><td>Ells</td><td>Han co-men-çat</td><td>Ells</td><td>Co-men-cin</td><td>Ells</td><td>Ha-gin co-men-çat</td></tr>
<tr><td colspan="2">Imperfet</td><td colspan="2">Past Plusquamperfet</td><td colspan="2">Imperfet past</td><td colspan="2">Plusquamperfet past</td></tr>
<tr><td>Jo</td><td>Co-men-ça-va</td><td>Jo</td><td>Ha-vi-a co-men-çat</td><td>Jo</td><td>Co-men-cés</td><td>Jo</td><td>Ha-gués co-men-çat</td></tr>
<tr><td>Tu</td><td>Co-men-ça-ves</td><td>Tu</td><td>Ha-vi-es co-men-çat</td><td>Tu</td><td>Co-men-ces-sis</td><td>Tu</td><td>Ha-gues-sis co-men-çat</td></tr>
<tr><td>Ell</td><td>Co-men-ça-va</td><td>Ell</td><td>Ha-vi-a co-men-çat</td><td>Ell</td><td>Co-men-cés</td><td>Ell</td><td>Ha-gués co-men-çat</td></tr>
<tr><td>No.</td><td>Co-men-çà-vem</td><td>Nos.</td><td>Ha-ví-em co-men-çat</td><td>Nos</td><td>Co-men-cés-sim</td><td>Nos.</td><td>Ha-gués-sim co-men-çat</td></tr>
<tr><td>Vos.</td><td>Co-men-çà-veu</td><td>Vos.</td><td>Ha-ví-eu co-men-çat</td><td>Vos.</td><td>Co-men-cés-siu</td><td>Vos.</td><td>Ha-gués-siu co-men-çat</td></tr>
<tr><td>Ells</td><td>Co-men-ça-ven</td><td>Ells</td><td>Ha-vi-en co-men-çat</td><td>Ells</td><td>Co-men-ces-sin</td><td>Ells</td><td>Ha-gues-sin co-men-çat</td></tr>
</table>

<table>
<tr><td colspan="2">Past Simple</td><td colspan="2">Past Perifrastic</td><td colspan="2">Past Anterior perifrastic</td></tr>
<tr><td>Jo</td><td>Co-men-cí</td><td>Jo</td><td>Vaig co-men-çar</td><td colspan="2">Vaig ha-ver co-men-çat</td></tr>
<tr><td>Tu</td><td>Co-men-ça-res</td><td>Tu</td><td>Vas co-men-çar</td><td colspan="2">Vas ha-ver co-men-çat</td></tr>
<tr><td>Ell</td><td>Co-men-çà</td><td>Ell</td><td>Va co-men-çar</td><td colspan="2">Va ha-ver co-men-çat</td></tr>
<tr><td>Nos</td><td>Co-men-çà-rem</td><td>Nos.</td><td>Vam co-men-çar</td><td colspan="2">Vam ha-ver co-men-çat</td></tr>
<tr><td>Vos.</td><td>Co-men-çà-reu</td><td>Vos.</td><td>Vau co-men-çar</td><td colspan="2">Vau ha-ver co-men-çat</td></tr>
<tr><td>Ells</td><td>Co-men-ça-ren</td><td>Ells</td><td>Van co-men-çar</td><td colspan="2">Van ha-ver co-men-çat</td></tr>
<tr><td colspan="2">Future Simple</td><td colspan="4">Future Compound</td></tr>
<tr><td>Jo</td><td>Co-men-ça-ré</td><td>Jo</td><td colspan="3">Hau-ré co-men-çat</td></tr>
<tr><td>Tu</td><td>Co-men-ça-ràs</td><td>Tu</td><td colspan="3">Hau-ràs co-men-çat</td></tr>
<tr><td>Ell</td><td>Co-men-ça-rà</td><td>Ell</td><td colspan="3">Hau-rà co-men-çat</td></tr>
<tr><td>Nos.</td><td>Co-men-ça-rem</td><td>Nos.</td><td colspan="3">Hau-rem co-men-çat</td></tr>
<tr><td>Vos.</td><td>Co-men-ça-reu</td><td>Vos.</td><td colspan="3">Hau-reu co-men-çat</td></tr>
<tr><td>Ells</td><td>Co-men-ça-ran</td><td>Ells</td><td colspan="3">Hau-ran co-men-çat</td></tr>
<tr><td colspan="2">Conditional Simple</td><td colspan="2">Conditional Compound</td><td colspan="2">IMPERATIVE</td></tr>
<tr><td>Jo</td><td>Co-men-ça-ri-a</td><td>Jo</td><td>Hau-ri-a co-men-çat</td><td></td><td></td></tr>
<tr><td>Tu</td><td>Co-men-ça-ri-es</td><td>Tu</td><td>Hau-ri-es co-men-çat</td><td>Co-men-ça</td><td>(Tu)</td></tr>
<tr><td>Ell</td><td>Co-men-ça-ri-a</td><td>Ell</td><td>Hau-ri-a co-men-çat</td><td>Co-men-ci</td><td>(Ell)</td></tr>
<tr><td>Nos</td><td>Co-men-ça-rí-em</td><td>Nos.</td><td>Hau-rí-em co-men-çat</td><td>Co-men-cem</td><td>(Nos.)</td></tr>
<tr><td>Vos.</td><td>Co-men-ça-rí-eu</td><td>Vos.</td><td>Hau-rí-eu co-men-çat</td><td>Co-men-ceu</td><td>(Vos.)</td></tr>
<tr><td>Ells</td><td>Co-men-ça-ri-en</td><td>Ells</td><td>Hau-ri-en co-men-çat</td><td>Co-men-cin</td><td>(Ells)</td></tr>
</table>

<table>
<tr><th colspan="3">IMPERSONAL</th></tr>
<tr><th></th><th>SIMPLE</th><th>COMPOUND</th></tr>
<tr><td>Infinitive</td><td>Co-men-çar</td><td>Ha-ver co-men-çat</td></tr>
<tr><td>Participle</td><td>Co-men-çat</td><td>-</td></tr>
<tr><td>Gerund</td><td>Co-men-çant</td><td>Ha-vent co-men-çat</td></tr>
</table>

TO BREAK - TRENCAR

PERSONAL				
INDICATIVE			**SUBJUNCTIVE**	
SIMPLE	**COMPOUND**		**SIMPLE**	**COMPOUND**

Present		*Past Indefinite*		*Present*		*Past Perfet*	
Jo	**Tren**-co	Jo	**He** tren-**cat**	Jo	**Tren**-qui	Jo	**Ha**-gi tren-**cat**
Tu	**Tren**-ques	Tu	**Has** tren-**cat**	Tu	**Tren**-quis	Tu	**Ha**-gis tren-**cat**
Ell	**Tren**-ca	Ell	**Ha** tren-**cat**	Ell	**Tren**-qui	Ell	**Ha**-gi tren-**cat**
No.	Tren-**quem**	Nos.	**Hem** tren-**cat**	Nos.	Tren-**quem**	Nos.	**Hà**-gim tren-**cat**
Vos.	Tren-**queu**	Vos.	**Heu** tren-**cat**	Vos.	Tren-**queu**	Vos.	**Hà**-giu tren-**cat**
Ells	**Tren**-quen	Ells	**Han** tren-**cat**	Ells	**Tren**-quin	Ells	**Ha**-gin tren-**cat**

Imperfet		*Past Plusquamperfet*		*Imperfet past*		*Plusquamperfet past*	
Jo	Tren-**ca**-va	Jo	Ha-**vi**-a tren-**cat**	Jo	Tren-**qués**	Jo	Ha-**gués** tren-**cat**
Tu	Tren-**ca**-ves	Tu	Ha-**vi**-es tren-**cat**	Tu	Tren-**ques**-sis	Tu	Ha-**gues**-sis tren-**cat**
Ell	Tren-**ca**-va	Ell	Ha-**vi**-a tren-**cat**	Ell	Tren-**qués**	Ell	Ha-**gués** tren-**cat**
No.	Tren-**cà**-vem	Nos.	Ha-**ví**-em tren-**cat**	Nos	Tren-**qués**-sim	Nos.	Ha-**gués**-sim tren-**cat**
Vos.	Tren-**cà**-veu	Vos.	Ha-**ví**-eu tren-**cat**	Vos.	Tren-**qués**-siu	Vos.	Ha-**gués**-siu tren-**cat**
Ells	Tren-**ca**-ven	Ells	Ha-**vi**-en tren-**cat**	Ells	Tren-**ques**-sin	Ells	Ha-**gues**-sin tren-**cat**

Past Simple		*Past Perifrastic*		*Past Anterior perifrastic*
Jo	Tren-**quí**	Jo	**Vaig** tren-**car**	**Vaig** ha-**ver** tren-**cat**
Tu	Tren-**ca**-res	Tu	**Vas** tren-**car**	**Vas** ha-**ver** tren-**cat**
Ell	Tren-**cà**	Ell	**Va** tren-**car**	**Va** ha-**ver** tren-**cat**
Nos	Tren-**cà**-rem	Nos.	**Vam** tren-**car**	**Vam** ha-**ver** tren-**cat**
Vos.	Tren-**cà**-reu	Vos.	**Vau** tren-**car**	**Vau** ha-**ver** tren-**cat**
Ells	Tren-**ca**-ren	Ells	**Van** tren-**car**	**Van** ha-**ver** tren-**cat**

Future Simple		*Future Compound*	
Jo	Tren-ca-**ré**	Jo	Hau-**ré** tren-**cat**
Tu	Tren-ca-**ràs**	Tu	Hau-**ràs** tren-**cat**
Ell	Tren-ca-**rà**	Ell	Hau-**rà** tren-**cat**
Nos.	Tren-ca-**rem**	Nos.	Hau-**rem** tren-**cat**
Vos.	Tren-ca-**reu**	Vos.	Hau-**reu** tren-**cat**
Ells	Tren-ca-**ran**	Ells	Hau-**ran** tren-**cat**

Conditional Simple		*Conditional Compound*		**IMPERATIVE**	
Jo	Tren-ca-**ri**-a	Jo	Hau-**ri**-a tren-**cat**		
Tu	Tren-ca-**ri**-es	Tu	Hau-**ri**-es tren-**cat**	**Tren**-ca	(Tu)
Ell	Tren-ca-**ri**-a	Ell	Hau-**ri**-a tren-**cat**	**Tren**-qui	(Ell)
Nos	Tren-ca-**rí**-em	Nos.	Hau-**rí**-em tren-**cat**	Tren-**quem**	(Nos.)
Vos.	Tren-ca-**rí**-eu	Vos.	Hau-**rí**-eu tren-**cat**	Tren-**queu**	(Vos.)
Ells	Tren-ca-**ri**-en	Ells	Hau-**ri**-en tren-**cat**	**Tren**-quin	(Ells)

IMPERSONAL		
	SIMPLE	**COMPOUND**
Infinitive	Tren-**car**	Ha-**ver** tren-**cat**
Participle	Tren-**cat**	-
Gerund	Tren-**cant**	Ha-**vent** tren-**cat**

TO BREATHE - RESPIRAR

PERSONAL							
INDICATIVE				**SUBJUNCTIVE**			
SIMPLE		**COMPOUND**		**SIMPLE**		**COMPOUND**	
Present		*Past Indefinite*		*Present*		*Past Perfet*	
Jo	Res-**pi**-ro	Jo	**He** res-pi-**rat**	Jo	Res-**pi**-ri	Jo	**Ha**-gi res-pi-**rat**
Tu	Res-**pi**-res	Tu	**Has** res-pi-**rat**	Tu	Res-**pi**-ris	Tu	**Ha**-gis res-pi-**rat**
Ell	Res-**pi**-ra	Ell	**Ha** res-pi-**rat**	Ell	Res-**pi**-ri	Ell	**Ha**-gi res-pi-**rat**
No.	Res-pi-**rem**	Nos.	**Hem** res-pi-**rat**	Nos.	Res-pi-**rem**	Nos.	**Hà**-gim res-pi-**rat**
Vos.	Res-pi-**reu**	Vos.	**Heu** res-pi-**rat**	Vos.	Res-pi-**reu**	Vos.	**Hà**-giu res-pi-**rat**
Ells	Res-**pi**-ren	Ells	**Han** res-pi-**rat**	Ells	Res-**pi**-rin	Ells	**Ha**-gin res-pi-**rat**
Imperfet		*Past Plusquamperfet*		*Imperfet past*		*Plusquamperfet past*	
Jo	Res-pi-**ra**-va	Jo	Ha-**vi**-a res-pi-**rat**	Jo	Res-pi-**rés**	Jo	Ha-**gués** res-pi-**rat**
Tu	Res-pi-**ra**-ves	Tu	Ha-**vi**-es res-pi-**rat**	Tu	Res-pi-**res**-sis	Tu	Ha-**gues**-sis res-pi-**rat**
Ell	Res-pi-**ra**-va	Ell	Ha-**vi**-a res-pi-**rat**	Ell	Res-pi-**rés**	Ell	Ha-**gués** res-pi-**rat**
No.	Res-pi-**rà**-vem	Nos.	Ha-**ví**-em res-pi-**rat**	Nos	Res-pi-**rés**-sim	Nos.	Ha-**gués**-sim res-pi-**rat**
Vos.	Res-pi-**rà**-veu	Vos.	Ha-**ví**-eu res-pi-**rat**	Vos.	Res-pi-**rés**-siu	Vos.	Ha-**gués**-siu res-pi-**rat**
Ells	Res-pi-**ra**-ven	Ells	Ha-**vi**-en res-pi-**rat**	Ells	Res-pi-**res**-sin	Ells	Ha-**gues**-sin res-pi-**rat**

Past Simple		*Past Perifrastic*		*Past Anterior perifrastic*
Jo	Res-pi-**rí**	Jo	**Vaig** res-pi-rar	**Vaig** ha-**ver** res-pi-**rat**
Tu	Res-pi-**ra**-res	Tu	**Vas** res-pi-rar	**Vas** ha-**ver** res-pi-**rat**
Ell	Res-pi-**rà**	Ell	**Va** res-pi-rar	**Va** ha-**ver** res-pi-**rat**
Nos	Res-pi-**rà**-rem	Nos.	**Vam** res-pi-rar	**Vam** ha-**ver** res-pi-**rat**
Vos.	Res-pi-**rà**-reu	Vos.	**Vau** res-pi-rar	**Vau** ha-**ver** res-pi-**rat**
Ells	Res-pi-**ra**-ren	Ells	**Van** res-pi-rar	**Van** ha-**ver** res-pi-**rat**

Future Simple		*Future Compound*	
Jo	Res-pi-ra-**ré**	Jo	Hau-**ré** res-pi-**rat**
Tu	Res-pi-ra-**ràs**	Tu	Hau-**ràs** res-pi-**rat**
Ell	Res-pi-ra-**rà**	Ell	Hau-**rà** res-pi-**rat**
Nos.	Res-pi-ra-**rem**	Nos.	Hau-**rem** res-pi-**rat**
Vos.	Res-pi-ra-**reu**	Vos.	Hau-**reu** res-pi-**rat**
Ells	Res-pi-ra-**ran**	Ells	Hau-**ran** res-pi-**rat**

Conditional Simple		*Conditional Compound*		**IMPERATIVE**	
Jo	Res-pi-ra-**ri**-a	Jo	Hau-**ri**-a res-pi-**rat**		
Tu	Res-pi-ra-**ri**-es	Tu	Hau-**ri**-es res-pi-**rat**	Res-**pi**-ra	*(Tu)*
Ell	Res-pi-ra-**ri**-a	Ell	Hau-**ri**-a res-pi-**rat**	Res-**pi**-ri	*(Ell)*
Nos	Res-pi-ra-**rí**-em	Nos.	Hau-**rí**-em res-pi-**rat**	Res-pi-**rem**	*(Nos.)*
Vos.	Res-pi-ra-**rí**-eu	Vos.	Hau-**rí**-eu res-pi-**rat**	Res-pi-**reu**	*(Vos.)*
Ells	Res-pi-ra-**ri**-en	Ells	Hau-**ri**-en res-pi-**rat**	Res-**pi**-rin	*(Ells)*

IMPERSONAL		
	SIMPLE	**COMPOUND**
Infinitive	Res-pi-**rar**	Ha-**ver** res-pi-**rat**
Participle	Res-pi-**rat**	-
Gerund	Res-pi-**rant**	Ha-**vent** res-pi-**rat**

TO BUY - COMPRAR

PERSONAL			
INDICATIVE		**SUBJUNCTIVE**	
SIMPLE	**COMPOUND**	**SIMPLE**	**COMPOUND**
Present	*Past Indefinite*	*Present*	*Past Perfet*
Jo **Com**-pro	Jo **He** com-**prat**	Jo **Com**-pri	Jo **Ha**-gi com-**prat**
Tu **Com**-pres	Tu **Has** com-**prat**	Tu **Com**-pris	Tu **Ha**-gis com-**prat**
Ell **Com**-pra	Ell **Ha** com-**prat**	Ell **Com**-pri	Ell **Ha**-gi com-**prat**
No. Com-**prem**	Nos. **Hem** com-**prat**	Nos. Com-**prem**	Nos. **Hà**-gim com-**prat**
Vos. Com-**preu**	Vos. **Heu** com-**prat**	Vos. Com-**preu**	Vos. **Hà**-giu com-**prat**
Ells **Com**-pren	Ells **Han** com-**prat**	Ells **Com**-prin	Ells **Ha**-gin com-**prat**
Imperfet	*Past Plusquamperfet*	*Imperfet past*	*Plusquamperfet past*
Jo Com-**pra**-va	Jo Ha-**vi**-a com-**prat**	Jo Com-**prés**	Jo Ha-**gués** com-**prat**
Tu Com-**pra**-ves	Tu Ha-**vi**-es com-**prat**	Tu Com-**pres**-sis	Tu Ha-**gues**-sis com-**prat**
Ell Com-**pra**-va	Ell Ha-**vi**-a com-**prat**	Ell Com-**prés**	Ell Ha-**gués** com-**prat**
No. Com-**prà**-vem	Nos. Ha-**ví**-em com-**prat**	Nos Com-**prés**-sim	Nos. Ha-**gués**-sim com-**prat**
Vos. Com-**prà**-veu	Vos. Ha-**ví**-eu com-**prat**	Vos. Com-**prés**-siu	Vos. Ha-**gués**-siu com-**prat**
Ells Com-**pra**-ven	Ells Ha-**vi**-en com-**prat**	Ells Com-**pres**-sin	Ells Ha-**gues**-sin com-**prat**

Past Simple	*Past Perifrastic*	*Past Anterior perifrastic*	
Jo Com-**prí**	Jo **Vaig** com-**prar**	**Vaig** ha-**ver** com-**prat**	
Tu Com-**pra**-res	Tu **Vas** com-**prar**	**Vas** ha-**ver** com-**prat**	
Ell Com-**prà**	Ell **Va** com-**prar**	**Va** ha-**ver** com-**prat**	
Nos Com-**prà**-rem	Nos. **Vam** com-**prar**	**Vam** ha-**ver** com-**prat**	
Vos. Com-**prà**-reu	Vos. **Vau** com-**prar**	**Vau** ha-**ver** com-**prat**	
Ells Com-**pra**-ren	Ells **Van** com-**prar**	**Van** ha-**ver** com-**prat**	

Future Simple	*Future Compound*
Jo Com-pra-**ré**	Jo Hau-**ré** com-**prat**
Tu Com-pra-**ràs**	Tu Hau-**ràs** com-**prat**
Ell Com-pra-**rà**	Ell Hau-**rà** com-**prat**
Nos. Com-pra-**rem**	Nos. Hau-**rem** com-**prat**
Vos. Com-pra-**reu**	Vos. Hau-**reu** com-**prat**
Ells Com-pra-**ran**	Ells Hau-**ran** com-**prat**

Conditional Simple	*Conditional Compound*	IMPERATIVE	
Jo Com-pra-**ri**-a	Jo Hau-**ri**-a com-**prat**		
Tu Com-pra-**ri**-es	Tu Hau-**ri**-es com-**prat**	**Com**-pra	*(Tu)*
Ell Com-pra-**ri**-a	Ell Hau-**ri**-a com-**prat**	**Com**-pri	*(Ell)*
Nos. Com-pra-**rí**-em	Nos. Hau-**rí**-em com-**prat**	Com-**prem**	*(Nos.)*
Vos. Com-pra-**rí**-eu	Vos. Hau-**rí**-eu com-**prat**	Com-**preu**	*(Vos.)*
Ells Com-pra-**ri**-en	Ells Hau-**ri**-en com-**prat**	**Com**-prin	*(Ells)*

IMPERSONAL		
	SIMPLE	**COMPOUND**
Infinitive	Com-**prar**	Ha-**ver** com-**prat**
Participle	Com-**prat**	-
Gerund	Com-pr**ant**	Ha-**vent** com-**prat**

TO CALL - TRUCAR

PERSONAL								
INDICATIVE					**SUBJUNCTIVE**			
SIMPLE		**COMPOUND**			**SIMPLE**		**COMPOUND**	
Present		*Past Indefinite*			*Present*		*Past Perfet*	
Jo	**Tru**-co	Jo	**He** tru-**cat**		Jo	**Tru**-qui	Jo	**Ha**-gi tru-**cat**
Tu	**Tru**-ques	Tu	**Has** tru-**cat**		Tu	**Tru**-quis	Tu	**Ha**-gis tru-**cat**
Ell	**Tru**-ca	Ell	**Ha** tru-**cat**		Ell	**Tru**-qui	Ell	**Ha**-gi tru-**cat**
No.	Tru-**quem**	Nos.	**Hem** tru-**cat**		Nos.	Tru-**quem**	Nos.	**Hà**-gim tru-**cat**
Vos.	Tru-**queu**	Vos.	**Heu** tru-**cat**		Vos.	Tru-**queu**	Vos.	**Hà**-giu tru-**cat**
Ells	**Tru**-quen	Ells	**Han** tru-**cat**		Ells	**Tru**-quin	Ells	**Ha**-gin tru-**cat**
Imperfet		*Past Plusquamperfet*			*Imperfet past*		*Plusquamperfet past*	
Jo	Tru-**ca**-va	Jo	Ha-**vi**-a tru-**cat**		Jo	Tru-**qués**	Jo	Ha-**gués** tru-**cat**
Tu	Tru-**ca**-ves	Tu	Ha-**vi**-es tru-**cat**		Tu	Tru-**ques**-sis	Tu	Ha-**gues**-sis tru-**cat**
Ell	Tru-**ca**-va	Ell	Ha-**vi**-a tru-**cat**		Ell	Tru-**qués**	Ell	Ha-**gués** tru-**cat**
No.	Tru-**cà**-vem	Nos.	Ha-**ví**-em tru-**cat**		Nos	Tru-**qués**-sim	Nos.	Ha-**gués**-sim tru-**cat**
Vos.	Tru-**cà**-veu	Vos.	Ha-**ví**-eu tru-**cat**		Vos.	Tru-**qués**-siu	Vos.	Ha-**gués**-siu tru-**cat**
Ells	Tru-**ca**-ven	Ells	Ha-**vi**-en tru-**cat**		Ells	Tru-**ques**-sin	Ells	Ha-**gues**-sin tru-**cat**

Past Simple		*Past Perifrastic*		*Past Anterior perifrastic*
Jo	Tru-**quí**	Jo	**Vaig** tru-**car**	**Vaig** ha-**ver** tru-**cat**
Tu	Tru-**ca**-res	Tu	**Vas** tru-**car**	**Vas** ha-**ver** tru-**cat**
Ell	Tru-**cà**	Ell	**Va** tru-**car**	**Va** ha-**ver** tru-**cat**
Nos	Tru-**cà**-rem	Nos.	**Vam** tru-**car**	**Vam** ha-**ver** tru-**cat**
Vos.	Tru-**cà**-reu	Vos.	**Vau** tru-**car**	**Vau** ha-**ver** tru-**cat**
Ells	Tru-**ca**-ren	Ells	**Van** tru-**car**	**Van** ha-**ver** tru-**cat**

Future Simple		*Future Compound*	
Jo	Tru-ca-**ré**	Jo	Hau-**ré** tru-**cat**
Tu	Tru-ca-**ràs**	Tu	Hau-**ràs** tru-**cat**
Ell	Tru-ca-**rà**	Ell	Hau-**rà** tru-**cat**
Nos.	Tru-ca-**rem**	Nos.	Hau-**rem** tru-**cat**
Vos.	Tru-ca-**reu**	Vos.	Hau-**reu** tru-**cat**
Ells	Tru-ca-**ran**	Ells	Hau-**ran** tru-**cat**

Conditional Simple		*Conditional Compound*		**IMPERATIVE**	
Jo	Tru-ca-**ri**-a	Jo	Hau-**ri**-a tru-**cat**		
Tu	Tru-ca-**ri**-es	Tu	Hau-**ri**-es tru-**cat**	**Tru**-ca	*(Tu)*
Ell	Tru-ca-**ri**-a	Ell	Hau-**ri**-a tru-**cat**	**Tru**-qui	*(Ell)*
Nos	Tru-ca-**rí**-em	Nos.	Hau-**rí**-em tru-**cat**	Tru-**quem**	*(Nos.)*
Vos.	Tru-ca-**rí**-eu	Vos.	Hau-**rí**-eu tru-**cat**	Tru-**queu**	*(Vos.)*
Ells	Tru-ca-**ri**-en	Ells	Hau-**ri**-en tru-**cat**	**Tru**-quin	*(Ells)*

IMPERSONAL		
	SIMPLE	**COMPOUND**
Infinitive	Tru-**car**	Ha-**ver** tru-**cat**
Participle	Tru-**cat**	-
Gerund	Tru-**cant**	Ha-**vent** tru-**cat**

TO CAN - PODER

PERSONAL				
INDICATIVE			**SUBJUNCTIVE**	
SIMPLE	**COMPOUND**		**SIMPLE**	**COMPOUND**

Present		*Past Indefinite*			*Present*		*Past Perfet*	
Jo	**Puc**	Jo	**He** po-**gut**		Jo	**Pu**-gui	Jo	**Ha**-gi po-**gut**
Tu	**Pots**	Tu	**Has** po-**gut**		Tu	**Pu**-guis	Tu	**Ha**-gis po-**gut**
Ell	**Pot**	Ell	**Ha** po-**gut**		Ell	**Pu**-gui	Ell	**Ha**-gi po-**gut**
No.	Po-**dem**	Nos.	**Hem** po-**gut**		Nos.	Pu-**guem**	Nos.	**Hà**-gim po-**gut**
Vos.	Po-**deu**	Vos.	**Heu** po-**gut**		Vos.	Pu-**gueu**	Vos.	**Hà**-giu po-**gut**
Ells	**Po**-den	Ells	**Han** po-**gut**		Ells	**Pu**-guin	Ells	**Ha**-gin po-**gut**

Imperfet		*Past Plusquamperfet*			*Imperfet past*		*Plusquamperfet past*	
Jo	Po-**di**-a	Jo	Ha-**vi**-a po-**gut**		Jo	Po-**gués**	Jo	Ha-**gués** po-**gut**
Tu	Po-**di**-es	Tu	Ha-**vi**-es po-**gut**		Tu	Po-**gues**-sis	Tu	Ha-**gues**-sis po-**gut**
Ell	Po-**di**-a	Ell	Ha-**vi**-a po-**gut**		Ell	Po-**gués**	Ell	Ha-**gués** po-**gut**
No.	Po-**dí**-em	Nos.	Ha-**ví**-em po-**gut**		Nos	Po-**gués**-sim	Nos.	Ha-**gués**-sim po-**gut**
Vos.	Po-**dí**-eu	Vos.	Ha-**ví**-eu po-**gut**		Vos.	Po-**gués**-siu	Vos.	Ha-**gués**-siu po-**gut**
Ells	Po-**di**-en	Ells	Ha-**vi**-en po-**gut**		Ells	Po-**gues**-sin	Ells	Ha-**gues**-sin po-**gut**

Past Simple		*Past Perifrastic*		*Past Anterior perifrastic*
Jo	Po-**guí**	Jo	**Vaig** po-**der**	**Vaig** ha-**ver** po-**gut**
Tu	Po-**gue**-res	Tu	**Vas** po-**der**	**Vas** ha-**ver** po-**gut**
Ell	Po-**gué**	Ell	**Va** po-**der**	**Va** ha-**ver** po-**gut**
Nos	Po-**gué**-rem	Nos.	**Vam** po-**der**	**Vam** ha-**ver** po-**gut**
Vos.	Po-**gué**-reu	Vos.	**Vau** po-**der**	**Vau** ha-**ver** po-**gut**
Ells	Po-**gue**-ren	Ells	**Van** po-**der**	**Van** ha-**ver** po-**gut**

Future Simple		*Future Compound*	
Jo	Po-**dré**	Jo	Hau-**ré** po-**gut**
Tu	Po-**dràs**	Tu	Hau-**ràs** po-**gut**
Ell	Po-**drà**	Ell	Hau-**rà** po-**gut**
Nos.	Po-**drem**	Nos.	Hau-**rem** po-**gut**
Vos.	Po-**dreu**	Vos.	Hau-**reu** po-**gut**
Ells	Po-**dran**	Ells	Hau-**ran** po-**gut**

Conditional Simple		*Conditional Compound*		**IMPERATIVE**	
Jo	Po-**dri**-a	Jo	Hau-**ri**-a po-**gut**		
Tu	Po-**dri**-es	Tu	Hau-**ri**-es po-**gut**	**Pu**-gues	(Tu)
Ell	Po-**dri**-a	Ell	Hau-**ri**-a po-**gut**	**Pu**-gui	(Ell)
Nos	Po-**drí**-em	Nos.	Hau-**rí**-em po-**gut**	Pu-**guem**	(Nos.)
Vos.	Po-**drí**-eu	Vos.	Hau-**rí**-eu po-**gut**	Pu-**gueu**	(Vos.)
Ells	Po-**dri**-en	Ells	Hau-**ri**-en po-**gut**	**Pu**-guin	(Ells)

IMPERSONAL		
	SIMPLE	**COMPOUND**
Infinitive	Po-**der**	Ha-**ver** po-**gut**
Participle	Po-**gut**	-
Gerund	Po-**dent**	Ha-**vent** po-**gut**

TO CHOOSE - ESCOLLIR

PERSONAL			
INDICATIVE		**SUBJUNCTIVE**	
SIMPLE	**COMPOUND**	**SIMPLE**	**COMPOUND**

Present		*Past Indefinite*		*Present*		*Past Perfet*	
Jo	Es-**cu**-llo	Jo	**He** es-co-**llit**	Jo	Es-**cu**-lli	Jo	**Ha**-gi es-co-**llit**
Tu	Es-**culls**	Tu	**Has** es-co-**llit**	Tu	Es-**cu**-llis	Tu	**Ha**-gis es-co-**llit**
Ell	Es-**cull**	Ell	**Ha** es-co-**llit**	Ell	Es-**cu**-lli	Ell	**Ha**-gi es-co-**llit**
No.	Es-co-**llim**	Nos.	**Hem** es-co-**llit**	Nos.	Es-co-**llim**	Nos.	**Hà**-gim es-co-**llit**
Vos.	Es-co-**lliu**	Vos.	**Heu** es-co-**llit**	Vos.	Es-co-**lliu**	Vos.	**Hà**-giu es-co-**llit**
Ells	Es-**cu**-llen	Ells	**Han** es-co-**llit**	Ells	Es-**cu**-llin	Ells	**Ha**-gin es-co-**llit**

Imperfet		*Past Plusquamperfet*		*Imperfet past*		*Plusquamperfet past*	
Jo	Es-co-**lli**-a	Jo	Ha-**vi**-a es-co-**llit**	Jo	Es-co-**llís**	Jo	Ha-**gués** es-co-**llit**
Tu	Es-co-**lli**-es	Tu	Ha-**vi**-es es-co-**llit**	Tu	Es-co-**llis**-sis	Tu	Ha-**gues**-sis es-co-**llit**
Ell	Es-co-**lli**-a	Ell	Ha-**vi**-a es-co-**llit**	Ell	Es-co-**llís**	Ell	Ha-**gués** es-co-**llit**
No.	Es-co-**llí**-em	Nos.	Ha-**ví**-em es-co-**llit**	Nos	Es-co-**llís**-sim	Nos.	Ha-**gués**-sim es-co-**llit**
Vos.	Es-co-**llí**-eu	Vos.	Ha-**ví**-eu es-co-**llit**	Vos.	Es-co-**llís**-siu	Vos.	Ha-**gués**-siu es-co-**llit**
Ells	Es-co-**lli**-en	Ells	Ha-**vi**-en es-co-**llit**	Ells	Es-co-**llis**-sin	Ells	Ha-**gues**-sin es-co-**llit**

Past Simple		*Past Perifrastic*		*Past Anterior perifrastic*
Jo	Es-co-**llí**	Jo	**Vaig** es-co-llir	**Vaig** ha-**ver** es-co-**llit**
Tu	Es-co-**lli**-res	Tu	**Vas** es-co-llir	**Vas** ha-**ver** es-co-**llit**
Ell	Es-co-**llí**	Ell	**Va** es-co-llir	**Va** ha-**ver** es-co-**llit**
Nos	Es-co-**llí**-rem	Nos.	**Vam** es-co-llir	**Vam** ha-**ver** es-co-**llit**
Vos.	Es-co-**llí**-reu	Vos.	**Vau** es-co-llir	**Vau** ha-**ver** es-co-**llit**
Ells	Es-co-**lli**-ren	Ells	**Van** es-co-llir	**Van** ha-**ver** es-co-**llit**

Future Simple		*Future Compound*	
Jo	Es-co-lli-**ré**	Jo	Hau-**ré** es-co-**llit**
Tu	Es-co-lli-**ràs**	Tu	Hau-**ràs** es-co-**llit**
Ell	Es-co-lli-**rà**	Ell	Hau-**rà** es-co-**llit**
Nos.	Es-colli-**rem**	Nos.	Hau-**rem** es-co-**llit**
Vos.	Es-co-lli-**reu**	Vos.	Hau-**reu** es-co-**llit**
Ells	Es-co-lli-**ran**	Ells	Hau-**ran** es-co-**llit**

Conditional Simple		*Conditional Compound*		**IMPERATIVE**	
Jo	Es-co-lli-**ri**-a	Jo	Hau-**ri**-a es-co-**llit**		
Tu	Es-co-lli-**ri**-es	Tu	Hau-**ri**-es es-co-**llit**	Es-**cull**	(Tu)
Ell	Es-co-lli-**ri**-a	Ell	Hau-**ri**-a es-co-**llit**	Es-**cu**-lli	(Ell)
Nos	Es-co-lli-**rí**-em	Nos.	Hau-**rí**-em es-co-**llit**	Es-co-**llim**	(Nos.)
Vos.	Es-co-lli-**rí**-eu	Vos.	Hau-**rí**-eu es-co-**llit**	Es-co-**lliu**	(Vos.)
Ells	Es-co-lli-**ri**-en	Ells	Hau-**ri**-en es-co-**llit**	Es-**cu**-llin	(Ells)

IMPERSONAL		
	SIMPLE	**COMPOUND**
Infinitive	Es-co-**llir**	Ha-**ver** es-co-**llit**
Participle	Es-co-**llit**	-
Gerund	Es-co-**llint**	Ha-**vent** es-co-**llit**

TO CLOSE - TANCAR

PERSONAL							
INDICATIVE				**SUBJUNCTIVE**			
SIMPLE		**COMPOUND**		**SIMPLE**		**COMPOUND**	
Present		*Past Indefinite*		*Present*		*Past Perfet*	
Jo	**Tan**-co	Jo	**He** tan-**cat**	Jo	**Tan**-qui	Jo	**Ha**-gi tan-**cat**
Tu	**Tan**-ques	Tu	**Has** tan-**cat**	Tu	**Tan**-quis	Tu	**Ha**-gis tan-**cat**
Ell	**Tan**-ca	Ell	**Ha** tan-**cat**	Ell	**Tan**-qui	Ell	**Ha**-gi tan-**cat**
No.	Tan-**quem**	Nos.	**Hem** tan-**cat**	Nos.	Tan-**quem**	Nos.	**Hà**-gim tan-**cat**
Vos.	Tan-**queu**	Vos.	**Heu** tan-**cat**	Vos.	Tan-**queu**	Vos.	**Hà**-giu tan-**cat**
Ells	**Tan**-quen	Ells	**Han** tan-**cat**	Ells	**Tan**-quin	Ells	**Ha**-gin tan-**cat**
Imperfet		*Past Plusquamperfet*		*Imperfet past*		*Plusquamperfet past*	
Jo	Tan-**ca**-va	Jo	Ha-**vi**-a tan-**cat**	Jo	Tan-**qués**	Jo	Ha-**gués** tan-**cat**
Tu	Tan-**ca**-ves	Tu	Ha-**vi**-es tan-**cat**	Tu	Tan-**ques**-sis	Tu	Ha-**gues**-sis tan-**cat**
Ell	Tan-**ca**-va	Ell	Ha-**vi**-a tan-**cat**	Ell	Tan-**qués**	Ell	Ha-**gués** tan-**cat**
No.	Tan-**cà**-vem	Nos.	Ha-**ví**-em tan-**cat**	Nos	Tan-**qués**-sim	Nos.	Ha-**gués**-sim tan-**cat**
Vos.	Tan-**cà**-veu	Vos.	Ha-**ví**-eu tan-**cat**	Vos.	Tan-**qués**-siu	Vos.	Ha-**gués**-siu tan-**cat**
Ells	Tan-**ca**-ven	Ells	Ha-**vi**-en tan-**cat**	Ells	Tan-**ques**-sin	Ells	Ha-**gues**-sin tan-**cat**

Past Simple		*Past Perifrastic*		*Past Anterior perifrastic*			
Jo	Tan-**quí**	Jo	**Vaig** tan-**car**	**Vaig** ha-**ver** tan-**cat**			
Tu	Tan-**ca**-res	Tu	**Vas** tan-**car**	**Vas** ha-**ver** tan-**cat**			
Ell	Tan-**cà**	Ell	**Va** tan-**car**	**Va** ha-**ver** tan-**cat**			
Nos	Tan-**cà**-rem	Nos.	**Vam** tan-**car**	**Vam** ha-**ver** tan-**cat**			
Vos.	Tan-**cà**-reu	Vos.	**Vau** tan-**car**	**Vau** ha-**ver** tan-**cat**			
Ells	Tan-**ca**-ren	Ells	**Van** tan-**car**	**Van** ha-**ver** tan-**cat**			

Future Simple		*Future Compound*					
Jo	Tan-ca-**ré**	Jo	Hau-**ré** tan-**cat**				
Tu	Tan-ca-**ràs**	Tu	Hau-**ràs** tan-**cat**				
Ell	Tan-ca-**rà**	Ell	Hau-**rà** tan-**cat**				
Nos.	Tan-ca-**rem**	Nos.	Hau-**rem** tan-**cat**				
Vos.	Tan-ca-**reu**	Vos.	Hau-**reu** tan-**cat**				
Ells	Tan-ca-**ran**	Ells	Hau-**ran** tan-**cat**				

Conditional Simple		*Conditional Compound*		**IMPERATIVE**			
Jo	Tan-ca-**ri**-a	Jo	Hau-**ri**-a tan-**cat**				
Tu	Tan-ca-**ri**-es	Tu	Hau-**ri**-es tan-**cat**	**Tan**-ca		(Tu)	
Ell	Tan-ca-**ri**-a	Ell	Hau-**ri**-a tan-**cat**	**Tan**-qui		(Ell)	
Nos	Tan-ca-**rí**-em	Nos.	Hau-**rí**-em tan-**cat**	Tan-**quem**		(Nos.)	
Vos.	Tan-ca-**rí**-eu	Vos.	Hau-**rí**-eu tan-**cat**	Tan-**queu**		(Vos.)	
Ells	Tan-ca-**ri**-en	Ells	Hau-**ri**-en tan-**cat**	**Tan**-quin		(Ells)	

IMPERSONAL		
	SIMPLE	**COMPOUND**
Infinitive	Tan-**car**	Ha-**ver** tan-**cat**
Participle	Tan-**cat**	-
Gerund	Tan-**cant**	Ha-**vent** tan-**cat**

TO COME - VENIR

PERSONAL			
INDICATIVE		**SUBJUNCTIVE**	
SIMPLE	**COMPOUND**	**SIMPLE**	**COMPOUND**

Present		*Past Indefinite*		*Present*		*Past Perfet*	
Jo	**Vinc**	Jo	**He** vin-**gut**	Jo	**Vin**-gui	Jo	**Ha**-gi vin-**gut**
Tu	**Véns**	Tu	**Has** vin-**gut**	Tu	**Vin**-guis	Tu	**Ha**-gis vin-**gut**
Ell	**Ve**	Ell	**Ha** vin-**gut**	Ell	**Vin**-gui	Ell	**Ha**-gi vin-**gut**
No.	Ve-**nim**	Nos.	**Hem** vin-**gut**	Nos.	**Vin**-guem	Nos.	**Hà**-gim vin-**gut**
Vos.	Ve-**niu**	Vos.	**Heu** vin-**gut**	Vos.	**Vin**-gueu	Vos.	**Hà**-giu vin-**gut**
Ells	**Vé**-nen	Ells	**Han** vin-**gut**	Ells	**Vin**-guin	Ells	**Ha**-gin vin-**gut**

Imperfet		*Past Plusquamperfet*		*Imperfet past*		*Plusquamperfet past*	
Jo	Ve-**ni**-a	Jo	Ha-**vi**-a vin-**gut**	Jo	Vin-**gués**	Jo	Ha-**gués** vin-**gut**
Tu	Ve-**ni**-es	Tu	Ha-**vi**-es vin-**gut**	Tu	Vin-**gues**-sis	Tu	Ha-**gues**-sis vin-**gut**
Ell	Ve-**ni**-a	Ell	Ha-**vi**-a vin-**gut**	Ell	Vin-**gués**	Ell	Ha-**gués** vin-**gut**
No.	Ve-**ní**-em	Nos.	Ha-**ví**-em vin-**gut**	Nos	Vin-**gués**-sim	Nos.	Ha-**gués**-sim vin-**gut**
Vos.	Ve-**ní**-eu	Vos.	Ha-**ví**-eu vin-**gut**	Vos.	Vin-**gués**-siu	Vos.	Ha-**gués**-siu vin-**gut**
Ells	Ve-**ni**-en	Ells	Ha-**vi**-en vin-**gut**	Ells	Vin-**gues**-sin	Ells	Ha-**gues**-sin vin-**gut**

Past Simple		*Past Perifrastic*		*Past Anterior perifrastic*
Jo	Vin-**guí**	Jo	**Vaig** ve-**nir**	**Vaig** ha-**ver** vin-**gut**
Tu	Vin-**gue**-res	Tu	**Vas** ve-**nir**	**Vas** ha-**ver** vin-**gut**
Ell	Vin-**gué**	Ell	**Va** ve-**nir**	**Va** ha-**ver** vin-**gut**
Nos	Vin-**gué**-rem	Nos.	**Vam** ve-**nir**	**Vam** ha-**ver** vin-**gut**
Vos.	Vin-**gué**-reu	Vos.	**Vau** ve-**nir**	**Vau** ha-**ver** vin-**gut**
Ells	Vin-**gue**-ren	Ells	**Van** ve-**nir**	**Van** ha-**ver** vin-**gut**

Future Simple		*Future Compound*	
Jo	Vin-**dré**	Jo	Hau-**ré** vin-**gut**
Tu	Vin-**dràs**	Tu	Hau-**ràs** vin-**gut**
Ell	Vin-**drà**	Ell	Hau-**rà** vin-**gut**
Nos.	Vin-**drem**	Nos.	Hau-**rem** vin-**gut**
Vos.	Vin-**dreu**	Vos.	Hau-**reu** vin-**gut**
Ells	Vin-**dran**	Ells	Hau-**ran** vin-**gut**

Conditional Simple		*Conditional Compound*		**IMPERATIVE**	
Jo	Vin-**dri**-a	Jo	Hau-**ri**-a vin-**gut**		
Tu	Vin-**dri**-es	Tu	Hau-**ri**-es vin-**gut**	**Vi**-ne	*(Tu)*
Ell	Vin-**dri**-a	Ell	Hau-**ri**-a vin-**gut**	**Vin**-gui	*(Ell)*
Nos	Vin-**drí**-em	Nos.	Hau-**rí**-em vin-**gut**	Vin-**guem**	*(Nos.)*
Vos.	Vin-**drí**-eu	Vos.	Hau-**rí**-eu vin-**gut**	Ve-**niu**	*(Vos.)*
Ells	Vin-**dri**-en	Ells	Hau-**ri**-en vin-**gut**	**Vin**-guin	*(Ells)*

IMPERSONAL		
	SIMPLE	**COMPOUND**
Infinitive	Ve-**nir**	Ha-**ver** vin **gut**
Participle	Vin-**gut**	-
Gerund	Ve-**nint**	Ha-**vent** vin-**gut**

TO COOK - CUINAR

PERSONAL							
INDICATIVE				**SUBJUNCTIVE**			
SIMPLE		**COMPOUND**		**SIMPLE**		**COMPOUND**	
Present		*Past Indefinite*		*Present*		*Past Perfet*	
Jo	**Cui**-no	Jo	**He** cui-**nat**	Jo	**Cui**-ni	Jo	**Ha**-gi cui-**nat**
Tu	**Cui**-nes	Tu	**Has** cui-**nat**	Tu	**Cui**-nis	Tu	**Ha**-gis cui-**nat**
Ell	**Cui**-na	Ell	**Ha** cui-**nat**	Ell	**Cui**-ni	Ell	**Ha**-gi cui-**nat**
No.	Cui-**nem**	Nos.	**Hem** cui-**nat**	Nos.	Cui-**nem**	Nos.	**Hà**-gim cui-**nat**
Vos.	Cui-**neu**	Vos.	**Heu** cui-**nat**	Vos.	Cui-**neu**	Vos.	**Hà**-giu cui-**nat**
Ells	**Cui**-nen	Ells	**Han** cui-**nat**	Ells	**Cui**-nin	Ells	**Ha**-gin cui-**nat**
Imperfet		*Past Plusquamperfet*		*Imperfet past*		*Plusquamperfet past*	
Jo	Cui-**na**-va	Jo	Ha-**vi**-a cui-**nat**	Jo	Cui-**nés**	Jo	Ha-**gués** cui-**nat**
Tu	Cui-**na**-ves	Tu	Ha-**vi**-es cui-**nat**	Tu	Cui-**nes**-sis	Tu	Ha-**gues**-sis cui-**nat**
Ell	Cui-**na**-va	Ell	Ha-**vi**-a cui-**nat**	Ell	Cui-**nés**	Ell	Ha-**gués** cui-**nat**
No.	Cui-**nà**-vem	Nos.	Ha-**ví**-em cui-**nat**	Nos	Cui-**nés**-sim	Nos.	Ha-**gués**-sim cui-**nat**
Vos.	Cui-**nà**-veu	Vos.	Ha-**ví**-eu cui-**nat**	Vos.	Cui-**nés**-siu	Vos.	Ha-**gués**-siu cui-**nat**
Ells	Cui-**na**-ven	Ells	Ha-**vi**-en cui-**nat**	Ells	Cui-**nes**-sin	Ells	Ha-**gues**-sin cui-**nat**

Past Simple		*Past Perifrastic*		*Past Anterior perifrastic*
Jo	Cui-**ní**	Jo	**Vaig** cui-**nar**	**Vaig** ha-**ver** cui-**nat**
Tu	Cui-**na**-res	Tu	**Vas** cui-**nar**	**Vas** ha-**ver** cui-**nat**
Ell	Cui-**nà**	Ell	**Va** cui-**nar**	**Va** ha-**ver** cui-**nat**
Nos	Cui-**nà**-rem	Nos.	**Vam** cui-**nar**	**Vam** ha-**ver** cui-**nat**
Vos.	Cui-**nà**-reu	Vos.	**Vau** cui-**nar**	**Vau** ha-**ver** cui-**nat**
Ells	Cui-**na**-ren	Ells	**Van** cui-**nar**	**Van** ha-**ver** cui-**nat**

Future Simple		*Future Compound*	
Jo	Cui-na-**ré**	Jo	Hau-**ré** cui-**nat**
Tu	Cui-na-**ràs**	Tu	Hau-**ràs** cui-**nat**
Ell	Cui-na-**rà**	Ell	Hau-**rà** cui-**nat**
Nos.	Cui-na-**rem**	Nos.	Hau-**rem** cui-**nat**
Vos.	Cui-na-**reu**	Vos.	Hau-**reu** cui-**nat**
Ells	Cui-na-**ran**	Ells	Hau-**ran** cui-**nat**

Conditional Simple		*Conditional Compound*		**IMPERATIVE**		
Jo	Cui-na-**ri**-a	Jo	Hau-**ri**-a cui-**nat**			
Tu	Cui-na-**ri**-es	Tu	Hau-**ri**-es cui-**nat**	**Cui**-na	(Tu)	
Ell	Cui-na-**ri**-a	Ell	Hau-**ri**-a cui-**nat**	**Cui**-ni	(Ell)	
Nos	Cui-na-**rí**-em	Nos.	Hau-**rí**-em cui-**nat**	Cui-**nem**	(Nos.)	
Vos.	Cui-na-**rí**-eu	Vos.	Hau-**rí**-eu cui-**nat**	Cui-**neu**	(Vos.)	
Ells	Cui-na-**ri**-en	Ells	Hau-**ri**-en cui-**nat**	**Cui**-nin	(Ells)	

IMPERSONAL		
	SIMPLE	**COMPOUND**
Infinitive	Cui-**nar**	Ha-**ver** cui-**nat**
Participle	Cui-**nat**	-
Gerund	Cui-**nant**	Ha-**vent** cui-**nat**

TO CRY - PLORAR

PERSONAL				
INDICATIVE			**SUBJUNCTIVE**	
SIMPLE	**COMPOUND**		**SIMPLE**	**COMPOUND**

Present		*Past Indefinite*			*Present*		*Past Perfet*	
Jo	**Plo**-ro	Jo	**He** plo-**rat**		Jo	**Plo**-ri	Jo	**Ha**-gi plo-**rat**
Tu	**Plo**-res	Tu	**Has** plo-**rat**		Tu	**Plo**-ris	Tu	**Ha**-gis plo-**rat**
Ell	**Plo**-ra	Ell	**Ha** plo-**rat**		Ell	**Plo**-ri	Ell	**Ha**-gi plo-**rat**
No.	Plo-**rem**	Nos.	**Hem** plo-**rat**		Nos.	Plo-**rem**	Nos.	**Hà**-gim plo-**rat**
Vos.	Plo-**reu**	Vos.	**Heu** plo-**rat**		Vos.	Plo-**reu**	Vos.	**Hà**-giu plo-**rat**
Ells	**Plo**-ren	Ells	**Han** plo-**rat**		Ells	**Plo**-rin	Ells	**Ha**-gin plo-**rat**

Imperfet		*Past Plusquamperfet*			*Imperfet past*		*Plusquamperfet past*	
Jo	Plo-**ra**-va	Jo	**Ha**-**vi**-a plo-**rat**		Jo	Plo-**rés**	Jo	**Ha**-**gués** plo-**rat**
Tu	Plo-**ra**-ves	Tu	**Ha**-**vi**-es plo-**rat**		Tu	Plo-**res**-sis	Tu	**Ha**-**gues**-sis plo-**rat**
Ell	Plo-**ra**-va	Ell	**Ha**-**vi**-a plo-**rat**		Ell	Plo-**rés**	Ell	**Ha**-**gués** plo-**rat**
No.	Plo-**rà**-vem	Nos.	**Ha**-**ví**-em plo-**rat**		Nos	Plo-**rés**-sim	Nos.	**Ha**-**gués**-sim plo-**rat**
Vos.	Plo-**rà**-veu	Vos.	**Ha**-**ví**-eu plo-**rat**		Vos.	Plo-**rés**-siu	Vos.	**Ha**-**gués**-siu plo-**rat**
Ells	Plo-**ra**-ven	Ells	**Ha**-**vi**-en plo-**rat**		Ells	Plo-**res**-sin	Ells	**Ha**-**gues**-sin plo-**rat**

Past Simple		*Past Perifrastic*		*Past Anterior perifrastic*
Jo	Plo-**rí**	Jo	**Vaig** plo-rar	**Vaig** ha-**ver** plo-**rat**
Tu	Plo-**ra**-res	Tu	**Vas** plo-rar	**Vas** ha-**ver** plo-**rat**
Ell	Plo-**rà**	Ell	**Va** plo-rar	**Va** ha-**ver** plo-**rat**
Nos	Plo-**rà**-rem	Nos.	**Vam** plo-rar	**Vam** ha-**ver** plo-**rat**
Vos.	Plo-**rà**-reu	Vos.	**Vau** plo-rar	**Vau** ha-**ver** plo-**rat**
Ells	Plo-**ra**-ren	Ells	**Van** plo-rar	**Van** ha-**ver** plo-**rat**

Future Simple		*Future Compound*	
Jo	Plo-ra-**ré**	Jo	**Hau**-**ré** plo-**rat**
Tu	Plo-ra-**ràs**	Tu	**Hau**-**ràs** plo-**rat**
Ell	Plo-ra-**rà**	Ell	**Hau**-**rà** plo-**rat**
Nos.	Plo-ra-**rem**	Nos.	**Hau**-**rem** plo-**rat**
Vos.	Plo-ra-**reu**	Vos.	**Hau**-**reu** plo-**rat**
Ells	Plo-ra-**ran**	Ells	**Hau**-**ran** plo-**rat**

Conditional Simple		*Conditional Compound*		**IMPERATIVE**	
Jo	Plo-ra-**ri**-a	Jo	**Hau**-**ri**-a plo-**rat**		
Tu	Plo-ra-**ri**-es	Tu	**Hau**-**ri**-es plo-**rat**	**Plo**-ra	*(Tu)*
Ell	Plo-ra-**ri**-a	Ell	**Hau**-**ri**-a plo-**rat**	**Plo**-ri	*(Ell)*
Nos	Plo-ra-**rí**-em	Nos.	**Hau**-**rí**-em plo-**rat**	Plo-**rem**	*(Nos.)*
Vos.	Plo-ra-**rí**-eu	Vos.	**Hau**-**rí**-eu plo-**rat**	Plo-**reu**	*(Vos.)*
Ells	Plo-ra-**ri**-en	Ells	**Hau**-**ri**-en plo-**rat**	**Plo**-rin	*(Ells)*

IMPERSONAL		
	SIMPLE	**COMPOUND**
Infinitive	Plo-**rar**	Ha-**ver** plo-**rat**
Participle	Plo-**rat**	-
Gerund	Plo-r**ant**	Ha-**vent** plo-**rat**

TO DANCE - BALLAR

PERSONAL							
INDICATIVE				**SUBJUNCTIVE**			
SIMPLE		**COMPOUND**		**SIMPLE**		**COMPOUND**	
Present		*Past Indefinite*		*Present*		*Past Perfet*	
Jo	**Ba**-llo	Jo	**He** ba-**llat**	Jo	**Ba**-lli	Jo	**Ha**-gi ba-**llat**
Tu	**Ba**-lles	Tu	**Has** ba-**llat**	Tu	**Ba**-llis	Tu	**Ha**-gis ba-**llat**
Ell	**Ba**-lla	Ell	**Ha** ba-**llat**	Ell	**Ba**-lli	Ell	**Ha**-gi ba-**llat**
No.	Ba-**llem**	Nos.	**Hem** ba-**llat**	Nos.	Ba-**llem**	Nos.	**Hà**-gim ba-**llat**
Vos.	Ba-**lleu**	Vos.	**Heu** ba-**llat**	Vos.	Ba-**lleu**	Vos.	**Hà**-giu ba-**llat**
Ells	**Ba**-llen	Ells	**Han** ba-**llat**	Ells	**Ba**-llin	Ells	**Ha**-gin ba-**llat**
Imperfet		*Past Plusquamperfet*		*Imperfet past*		*Plusquamperfet past*	
Jo	Ba-**lla**-va	Jo	Ha-**vi**-a ba-**llat**	Jo	Ba-**llés**	Jo	Ha-**gués** ba-**llat**
Tu	Ba-**lla**-ves	Tu	Ha-**vi**-es ba-**llat**	Tu	Ba-**lles**-sis	Tu	Ha-**gues**-sis ba-**llat**
Ell	Ba-**lla**-va	Ell	Ha-**vi**-a ba-**llat**	Ell	Ba-**llés**	Ell	Ha-**gués** ba-**llat**
No.	Ba-**llà**-vem	Nos.	Ha-**ví**-em ba-**llat**	Nos	Ba-**llés**-sim	Nos.	Ha-**gués**-sim ba-**llat**
Vos.	Ba-**llà**-veu	Vos.	Ha-**ví**-eu ba-**llat**	Vos.	Ba-**llés**-siu	Vos.	Ha-**gués**-siu ba-**llat**
Ells	Ba-**lla**-ven	Ells	Ha-**vi**-en ba-**llat**	Ells	Ba-**lles**-sin	Ells	Ha-**gues**-sin ba-**llat**
Past Simple		*Past Perifrastic*	*Past Anterior perifrastic*				
Jo	Ba-**llí**	Jo	**Vaig** ba-**llar**	**Vaig** ha-**ver** ba-**llat**			
Tu	Ba-**lla**-res	Tu	**Vas** ba-**llar**	**Vas** ha-**ver** ba-**llat**			
Ell	Ba-**llà**	Ell	**Va** ba-**llar**	**Va** ha-**ver** ba-**llat**			
Nos	Ba-**llà**-rem	Nos.	**Vam** ba-**llar**	**Vam** ha-**ver** ba-**llat**			
Vos.	Ba-**llà**-reu	Vos.	**Vau** ba-**llar**	**Vau** ha-**ver** ba-**llat**			
Ells	Ba-**lla**-ren	Ells	**Van** ba-**llar**	**Van** ha-**ver** ba-**llat**			
Future Simple		*Future Compound*					
Jo	Ba-lla-**ré**	Jo	Hau-**ré** ba-**llat**				
Tu	Ba-lla-**ràs**	Tu	Hau-**ràs** ba-**llat**				
Ell	Ba-lla-**rà**	Ell	Hau-**rà** ba-**llat**				
Nos.	Ba-lla-**rem**	Nos.	Hau-**rem** ba-**llat**				
Vos.	Ba-lla-**reu**	Vos.	Hau-**reu** ba-**llat**				
Ells	Ba-lla-**ran**	Ells	Hau-**ran** ba-**llat**				
Conditional Simple		*Conditional Compound*		**IMPERATIVE**			
Jo	Ba-lla-**ri**-a	Jo	Hau-**ri**-a ba-**llat**				
Tu	Ba-lla-**ri**-es	Tu	Hau-**ri**-es ba-**llat**	**Ba**-lla		(Tu)	
Ell	Ba-lla-**ri**-a	Ell	Hau-**ri**-a ba-**llat**	**Ba**-lli		(Ell)	
Nos	Ba-lla-**rí**-em	Nos.	Hau-**rí**-em ba-**llat**	Ba-**llem**		(Nos.)	
Vos.	Ba-lla-**rí**-eu	Vos.	Hau-**rí**-eu ba-**llat**	Ba-**lleu**		(Vos.)	
Ells	Ba-lla-**ri**-en	Ells	Hau-**ri**-en ba-**llat**	**Ba**-llin		(Ells)	

IMPERSONAL		
	SIMPLE	**COMPOUND**
Infinitive	Ba-**llar**	Ha-**ver** ba-**llat**
Participle	Ba-**llat**	-
Gerund	Ba-**llant**	Ha-**vent** ba-**llat**

TO DECIDE - DECIDIR

PERSONAL							
INDICATIVE				**SUBJUNCTIVE**			
SIMPLE		**COMPOUND**		**SIMPLE**		**COMPOUND**	
Present		*Past Indefinite*		*Present*		*Past Perfet*	
Jo	De-ci-**dei**-xo	Jo	**He** de-ci-**dit**	Jo	De-ci-**dei**-xi	Jo	**Ha**-gi de-ci-**dit**
Tu	De-ci-**dei**-xes	Tu	**Has** de-ci-**dit**	Tu	De-ci-**dei**-xis	Tu	**Ha**-gis de-ci-**dit**
Ell	De-ci-**deix**	Ell	**Ha** de-ci-**dit**	Ell	De-ci-**dei**-xi	Ell	**Ha**-gi de-ci-**dit**
No.	De-ci-**dim**	Nos.	**Hem** de-ci-**dit**	Nos.	De-ci-**dim**	Nos.	**Hà**-gim de-ci-**dit**
Vos.	De-ci-**diu**	Vos.	**Heu** de-ci-**dit**	Vos.	De-ci-**diu**	Vos.	**Hà**-giu de-ci-**dit**
Ells	De-ci-**dei**-xen	Ells	**Han** de-ci-**dit**	Ells	De-ci-**dei**-xin	Ells	**Ha**-gin de-ci-**dit**
Imperfet		*Past Plusquamperfet*		*Imperfet past*		*Plusquamperfet past*	
Jo	De-ci-**di**-a	Jo	Ha-**vi**-a de-ci-**dit**	Jo	De-ci-**dís**	Jo	Ha-**gués** de-ci-**dit**
Tu	De-ci-**di**-es	Tu	Ha-**vi**-es de-ci-**dit**	Tu	De-ci-**dis**-sis	Tu	Ha-**gues**-sis de-ci-**dit**
Ell	De-ci-**di**-a	Ell	Ha-**vi**-a de-ci-**dit**	Ell	De-ci-**dís**	Ell	Ha-**gués** de-ci-**dit**
No.	De-ci-**dí**-em	Nos.	Ha-**ví**-em de-ci-**dit**	Nos	De-ci-**dís**-sim	Nos.	Ha-**gués**-sim de-ci-**dit**
Vos.	De-ci-**dí**-eu	Vos.	Ha-**ví**-eu de-ci-**dit**	Vos.	De-ci-**dís**-siu	Vos.	Ha-**gués**-siu de-ci-**dit**
Ells	De-ci-**di**-en	Ells	Ha-**vi**-en de-ci-**dit**	Ells	De-ci-**dis**-sin	Ells	Ha-**gues**-sin de-ci-**dit**

Past Simple		*Past Perifrastic*		*Past Anterior perifrastic*		
Jo	De-ci-**dí**	Jo	**Vaig** de-ci-**dir**	**Vaig** ha-**ver** de-ci-**dit**		
Tu	De-ci-**di**-res	Tu	**Vas** de-ci-**dir**	**Vas** ha-**ver** de-ci-**dit**		
Ell	De-ci-**dí**	Ell	**Va** de-ci-**dir**	**Va** ha-**ver** de-ci-**dit**		
Nos	De-ci-**dí**-rem	Nos.	**Vam** de-ci-**dir**	**Vam** ha-**ver** de-ci-**dit**		
Vos.	De-ci-**dí**-reu	Vos.	**Vau** de-ci-**dir**	**Vau** ha-**ver** de-ci-**dit**		
Ells	De-ci-**dí**-ren	Ells	**Van** de-ci-**dir**	**Van** ha-**ver** de-ci-**dit**		

Future Simple		*Future Compound*		
Jo	De-ci-di-**ré**	Jo	Hau-**ré** de-ci-**dit**	
Tu	De-ci-di-**ràs**	Tu	Hau-**ràs** de-ci-**dit**	
Ell	De-ci-di-**rà**	Ell	Hau-**rà** de-ci-**dit**	
Nos.	De-ci-di-**rem**	Nos.	Hau-**rem** de-ci-**dit**	
Vos.	De-ci-di-**reu**	Vos.	Hau-**reu** de-ci-**dit**	
Ells	De-ci-di-**ran**	Ells	Hau-**ran** de-ci-**dit**	

Conditional Simple		*Conditional Compound*		**IMPERATIVE**	
Jo	De-ci-di-**ri**-a	Jo	Hau-**ri**-a de-ci-**dit**		
Tu	De-ci-di-**ri**-es	Tu	Hau-**ri**-es de-ci-**dit**	De-ci-**deix**	(Tu)
Ell	De-ci-di-**ri**-a	Ell	Hau-**ri**-a de-ci-**dit**	De-ci-**dei**-xi	(Ell)
Nos	De-ci-di-**rí**-em	Nos.	Hau-**rí**-em de-ci-**dit**	De-ci-**dim**	(Nos.)
Vos.	De-ci-di-**rí**-eu	Vos.	Hau-**rí**-eu de-ci-**dit**	De-ci-**diu**	(Vos.)
Ells	De-ci-di-**ri**-en	Ells	Hau-**ri**-en de-ci-**dit**	De-ci-**dei**-xin	(Ells)

IMPERSONAL		
	SIMPLE	**COMPOUND**
Infinitive	De-ci-**dir**	Ha-**ver** de-ci-**dit**
Participle	De-ci-**dit**	-
Gerund	De-ci-**dint**	Ha-**vent** de-ci-**dit**

TO DECREASE - DISMINUIR

PERSONAL							
INDICATIVE				**SUBJUNCTIVE**			
SIMPLE		**COMPOUND**		**SIMPLE**		**COMPOUND**	
Present		*Past Indefinite*		*Present*		*Past Perfet*	
Jo	Dis-mi-nu-**ei**-xo	Jo	**He** dis-mi-nu-**ït**	Jo	Dis-mi-nu-**ei**-xi	Jo	**Ha**-gi dis-mi-nu-**ït**
Tu	Dis-mi-nu-**ei**-xes	Tu	**Has** dis-mi-nu-**ït**	Tu	Dis-mi-nu-**ei**-xis	Tu	**Ha**-gis dis-mi-nu-**ït**
Ell	Dis-mi-nu-**eix**	Ell	**Ha** dis-mi-nu-**ït**	Ell	Dis-mi-nu-**ei**-xi	Ell	**Ha**-gi dis-mi-nu-**ït**
No.	Dis-mi-nu-**ïm**	Nos	**Hem** dis-mi-nu-**ït**	Nos	Dis-mi-nu-**ïm**	Nos	**Hà**-gim dis-mi-nu-**ït**
Vos.	Dis-mi-nu-**ïu**	Vos.	**Heu** dis-mi-nu-**ït**	Vos.	Dis-mi-nu-**ïu**	Vos.	**Hà**-giu dis-mi-nu-**ït**
Ells	Dis-mi-nu-**ei**-xen	Ells	**Han** dis-mi-nu-**ït**	Ells	Dis-mi-nu-**ei**-xin	Ells	**Ha**-gin dis-mi-nu-**ït**
Imperfet		*Past Plusquamperfet*		*Imperfet past*		*Plusquamperfet past*	
Jo	Dis-mi-nu-**ï**-a	Jo	Ha-**vi**-a dis-mi-nu-**ït**	Jo	Dis-mi-nu-**ís**	Jo	Ha-**gués** dis-mi-nu-**ït**
Tu	Dis-mi-nu-**ï**-es	Tu	Ha-**vi**-es dis-mi-nu-**ït**	Tu	Dis-mi-nu-**ïs**-sis	Tu	Ha-**gues**-sis dis-mi-nu-**ït**
Ell	Dis-mi-nu-**ï**-a	Ell	Ha-**vi**-a dis-mi-nu-**ït**	Ell	Dis-mi-nu-**ís**	Ell	Ha-**gués** dis-mi-nu-**ït**
No.	Dis-mi-nu-**í**-em	Nos	Ha-**ví**-em dis-mi-nu-**ït**	Nos	Dis-mi-nu-**ís**-sim	Nos	Ha-**gués**-sim dis-mi-nu-**ït**
Vos.	Dis-mi-nu-**í**-eu	Vos.	Ha-**ví**-eu dis-mi-nu-**ït**	Vos.	Dis-mi-nu-**ís**-siu	Vos.	Ha-**gués**-siu dis-mi-nu-**ït**
Ells	Dis-mi-nu-**ï**-en	Ells	Ha-**vi**-en dis-mi-nu-**ït**	Ells	Dis-mi-nu-**ïs**-sin	Ells	Ha-**gues**-sin dis-mi-nu-**ït**

Past Simple		*Past Perifrastic*		*Past Anterior perifrastic*			
Jo	Dis-mi-nu-**í**	Jo	**Vaig** dis-mi-nu-**ir**	**Vaig** ha-**ver** dis-mi-nu-**ït**			
Tu	Dis-mi-nu-**í**-res	Tu	**Vas** dis-mi-nu-**ir**	**Vas** ha-**ver** dis-mi-nu-**ït**			
Ell	Dis-mi-nu-**í**	Ell	**Va** dis-mi-nu-**ir**	**Va** ha-**ver** dis-mi-nu-**ït**			
Nos	Dis-mi-nu-**í**-rem	Nos.	**Vam** dis-mi-nu-**ir**	**Vam** ha-**ver** dis-mi-nu-**ït**			
Vos.	Dis-mi-nu-**í**-reu	Vos.	**Vau** dis-mi-nu-**ir**	**Vau** ha-**ver** dis-mi-nu-**ït**			
Ells	Dis-mi-nu-**i**-ren	Ells	**Van** dis-mi-nu-**ir**	**Van** ha-**ver** dis-mi-nu-**ït**			

Future Simple		*Future Compound*					
Jo	Dis-mi-nu-i-**ré**	Jo	Hau-**ré** dis-mi-nu-**ït**				
Tu	Dis-mi-nu-i-**ràs**	Tu	Hau-**ràs** dis-mi-nu-**ït**				
Ell	Dis-mi-nu-i-**rà**	Ell	Hau-**rà** dis-mi-nu-**ït**				
Nos.	Dis-mi-nu-i-**rem**	Nos.	Hau-**rem** dis-mi-nu-**ït**				
Vos.	Dis-mi-nu-i-**reu**	Vos.	Hau-**reu** dis-mi-nu-**ït**				
Ells	Dis-mi-nu-i-**ran**	Ells	Hau-**ran** dis-mi-nu-**ït**				

Conditional Simple		*Conditional Compound*		**IMPERATIVE**			
Jo	Dis-mi-nu-i-**ri**-a	Jo	Hau-**ri**-a dis-mi-nu-**ït**				
Tu	Dis-mi-nu-i-**ri**-es	Tu	Hau-**ri**-es dis-mi-nu-**ït**	Dis-mi-nu-**eix**		*(Tu)*	
Ell	Dis-mi-nu-i-**ri**-a	Ell	Hau-**ri**-a dis-mi-nu-**ït**	Dis-mi-nu-**ei**-xi		*(Ell)*	
Nos	Dis-mi-nu-i-**rí**-em	Nos.	Hau-**rí**-em dis-mi-nu-**ït**	Dis-mi-nu-**ïm**		*(Nos.)*	
Vos.	Dis-mi-nu-i-**rí**-eu	Vos.	Hau-**rí**-eu dis-mi-nu-**ït**	Dis-mi-nu-**ïu**		*(Vos.)*	
Ells	Dis-mi-nu-i-**ri**-en	Ells	Hau-**ri**-en dis-mi-nu-**ït**	Dis-mi-nu-**ei**-xin		*(Ells)*	

IMPERSONAL		
	SIMPLE	**COMPOUND**
Infinitive	Dis-mi-nu-**ir**	Ha-**ver** dis-mi-nu-**ir**
Participle	Dis-mi-nu-**ït**	-
Gerund	Dis-mi-nu-**int**	Ha-**vent** dis-mi-nu-**ir**

TO DIE - MORIR

PERSONAL				
INDICATIVE		**SUBJUNCTIVE**		
SIMPLE	**COMPOUND**	**SIMPLE**	**COMPOUND**	

Present		*Past Indefinite*		*Present*		*Past Perfet*	
Jo	**Mo**-ro	Jo	**He mort**	Jo	**Mo**-ri	Jo	**Ha**-gi **mort**
Tu	**Mors**	Tu	**Has mort**	Tu	**Mo**-ris	Tu	**Ha**-gis **mort**
Ell	**Mor**	Ell	**Ha mort**	Ell	**Mo**-ri	Ell	**Ha**-gi **mort**
No.	Mo-**rim**	Nos.	**Hem mort**	Nos.	Mo-**rim**	Nos.	**Hà**-gim **mort**
Vos.	Mo-**riu**	Vos.	**Heu mort**	Vos.	Mo-**riu**	Vos.	**Hà**-giu **mort**
Ells	**Mo**-ren	Ells	**Han mort**	Ells	**Mo**-rin	Ells	**Ha**-gin **mort**
Imperfet		*Past Plusquamperfet*		*Imperfet past*		*Plusquamperfet past*	
Jo	Mo-**ri**-a	Jo	Ha-**vi**-a **mort**	Jo	Mo-**rís**	Jo	Ha-**gués mort**
Tu	Mo-**ri**-es	Tu	Ha-**vi**-es **mort**	Tu	Mo-**ris**-sis	Tu	Ha-**gues**-sis **mort**
Ell	Mo-**ri**-a	Ell	Ha-**vi**-a **mort**	Ell	Mo-**rís**	Ell	Ha-**gués mort**
No.	Mo-**rí**-em	Nos.	Ha-**ví**-em **mort**	Nos	Mo-**rís**-sim	Nos.	Ha-**gués**-sim **mort**
Vos.	Mo-**rí**-eu	Vos.	Ha-**ví**-eu **mort**	Vos.	Mo-**rís**-siu	Vos.	Ha-**gués**-siu **mort**
Ells	Mo-**ri**-en	Ells	Ha-**vi**-en **mort**	Ells	Mo-**ris**-sin	Ells	Ha-**gues**-sin **mort**

Past Simple		*Past Perifrastic*		*Past Anterior perifrastic*	
Jo	Mo-**rí**	Jo	**Vaig** mor-**rir**	**Vaig** ha-**ver mort**	
Tu	Mo-**ri**-res	Tu	**Vas** mor-**rir**	**Vas** ha-**ver mort**	
Ell	Mo-**rí**	Ell	**Va** mor-**rir**	**Va** ha-**ver mort**	
Nos	Mo-**rí**-rem	Nos.	**Vam** mor-**rir**	**Vam** ha-**ver mort**	
Vos	Mo-**rí**-reu	Vos.	**Vau** mor-**rir**	**Vau** ha-**ver mort**	
Ells	Mo-**ri**-ren	Ells	**Van** mor-**rir**	**Van** ha-**ver mort**	

Future Simple		*Future Compound*		
Jo	Mo-ri-**ré**	Jo	Hau-**ré mort**	
Tu	Mo-ri-**ràs**	Tu	Hau-**ràs mort**	
Ell	Mo-ri-**rà**	Ell	Hau-**rà mort**	
Nos.	Mo-ri-**rem**	Nos.	Hau-**rem mort**	
Vos.	Mo-ri-**reu**	Vos.	Hau-**reu mort**	
Ells	Mo-ri-**ran**	Ells	Hau-**ran mort**	

Conditional Simple		*Conditional Compound*		**IMPERATIVE**	
Jo	Mo-ri-**ri**-a	Jo	Hau-**ri**-a **mort**		
Tu	Mo-ri-**ri**-es	Tu	Hau-**ri**-es **mort**	**Mor**	*(Tu)*
Ell	Mo-ri-**ri**-a	Ell	Hau-**ri**-a **mort**	**Mo**-ri	*(Ell)*
Nos	Mo-ri-**rí**-em	Nos.	Hau-**rí**-em **mort**	Mo-**rim**	*(Nos.)*
Vos	Mo-ri-**rí**-eu	Vos.	Hau-**rí**-eu **mort**	Mo-**riu**	*(Vos.)*
Ells	Mo-ri-**ri**-en	Ells	Hau-**ri**-en **mort**	**Mo**-rin	*(Ells)*

IMPERSONAL		
	SIMPLE	**COMPOUND**
Infinitive	Mo-**rir**	Ha-**ver mort**
Participle	**Mort**	-
Gerund	Mo-**rint**	Ha-**vent mort**

TO DO - FER

PERSONAL							
INDICATIVE				**SUBJUNCTIVE**			
SIMPLE		**COMPOUND**		**SIMPLE**		**COMPOUND**	
Present		*Past Indefinite*		*Present*		*Past Perfet*	
Jo	**Faig**	Jo	**He fet**	Jo	**Fa**-ci	Jo	**Ha**-gi **fet**
Tu	**Fas**	Tu	**Has fet**	Tu	**Fa**-cis	Tu	**Ha**-gis **fet**
Ell	**Fa**	Ell	**Ha fet**	Ell	**Fa**-ci	Ell	**Ha**-gi **fet**
No.	**Fem**	Nos.	**Hem fet**	Nos.	**Fem**	Nos.	**Hà**-gim **fet**
Vos.	**Feu**	Vos.	**Heu fet**	Vos.	**Feu**	Vos.	**Hà**-giu **fet**
Ells	**Fan**	Ells	**Han fet**	Ells	**Fa**-cin	Ells	**Ha**-gin **fet**
Imperfet		*Past Plusquamperfet*		*Imperfet past*		*Plusquamperfet past*	
Jo	**Fe**-ia	Jo	Ha-**vi**-a **fet**	Jo	**Fes**	Jo	Ha-**gués fet**
Tu	**Fe**-ies	Tu	Ha-**vi**-es **fet**	Tu	**Fes**-sis	Tu	Ha-**gues**-sis **fet**
Ell	**Fe**-ia	Ell	Ha-**vi**-a **fet**	Ell	**Fes**	Ell	Ha-**gués fet**
No.	**Fè**-iem	Nos.	Ha-**ví**-em **fet**	Nos	**Fés**-sim	Nos.	Ha-**gués**-sim **fet**
Vos.	**Fè**-ieu	Vos.	Ha-**ví**-eu **fet**	Vos.	**Fés**-siu	Vos.	Ha-**gués**-siu **fet**
Ells	**Fe**-ien	Ells	Ha-**vi**-en **fet**	Ells	**Fes**-sin	Ells	Ha-**gues**-sin **fet**

Past Simple		*Past Perifrastic*		*Past Anterior perifrastic*	
Jo	**Fiu**	Jo	**Vaig fer**	**Vaig** ha-**ver fet**	
Tu	**Fe**-res	Tu	**Vas fer**	**Vas** ha-**ver fet**	
Ell	**Féu**	Ell	**Va fer**	**Va** ha-**ver fet**	
Nos	**Fé**-rem	Nos.	**Vam fer**	**Vam** ha-**ver fet**	
Vos.	**Fé**-reu	Vos.	**Vau fer**	**Vau** ha-**ver fet**	
Ells	**Fe**-ren	Ells	**Van fer**	**Van** ha-**ver fet**	

Future Simple		*Future Compound*	
Jo	Fa-**ré**	Jo	Hau-**ré fet**
Tu	Fa-**ràs**	Tu	Hau-**ràs fet**
Ell	Fa-**rà**	Ell	Hau-**rà fet**
Nos.	Fa-**rem**	Nos.	Hau-**rem fet**
Vos.	Fa-**reu**	Vos.	Hau-**reu fet**
Ells	Fa-**ran**	Ells	Hau-**ran fet**

Conditional Simple		*Conditional Compound*		**IMPERATIVE**	
Jo	Fa-**ri**-a	Jo	Hau-**ri**-a **fet**		
Tu	Fa-**ri**-es	Tu	Hau-**ri**-es **fet**	**Fes**	(Tu)
Ell	Fa-**ri**-a	Ell	Hau-**ri**-a **fet**	**Fa**-ci	(Ell)
Nos	Fa-**rí**-em	Nos.	Hau-**rí**-em **fet**	**Fem**	(Nos.)
Vos.	Fa-**rí**-eu	Vos.	Hau-**rí**-eu **fet**	**Feu**	(Vos.)
Ells	Fa-**ri**-en	Ells	Hau-**ri**-en **fet**	**Fa**-cin	(Ells)

IMPERSONAL		
	SIMPLE	**COMPOUND**
Infinitive	**Fer**	Ha-**ver fet**
Participle	**Fet**	-
Gerund	**Fent**	Ha-**vent fet**

TO DRINK - BEURE

PERSONAL			
INDICATIVE		**SUBJUNCTIVE**	
SIMPLE	**COMPOUND**	**SIMPLE**	**COMPOUND**

Present		*Past Indefinite*		*Present*		*Past Perfet*	
Jo	**Bec**	Jo	**He** be-**gut**	Jo	**Be**-gui	Jo	**Ha**-gi be-**gut**
Tu	**Beus**	Tu	**Has** be-**gut**	Tu	**Be**-guis	Tu	**Ha**-gis be-**gut**
Ell	**Beu**	Ell	**Ha** be-**gut**	Ell	**Be**-gui	Ell	**Ha**-gi be-**gut**
No.	Be-**vem**	Nos.	**Hem** be-**gut**	Nos.	Be-**guem**	Nos.	**Hà**-gim be-**gut**
Vos.	Be-**veu**	Vos.	**Heu** be-**gut**	Vos.	Be-**gueu**	Vos.	**Hà**-giu be-**gut**
Ells	**Be**-uen	Ells	**Han** be-**gut**	Ells	**Be**-guin	Ells	**Ha**-gin be-**gut**

Imperfet		*Past Plusquamperfet*		*Imperfet past*		*Plusquamperfet past*	
Jo	Be-**vi**-a	Jo	Ha-**vi**-a be-**gut**	Jo	Be-**gués**	Jo	Ha-**gués** be-**gut**
Tu	Be-**vi**-es	Tu	Ha-**vi**-es be-**gut**	Tu	Be-**gues**-sis	Tu	Ha-**gues**-sis be-**gut**
Ell	Be-**vi**-a	Ell	Ha-**vi**-a be-**gut**	Ell	Be-**gués**	Ell	Ha-**gués** be-**gut**
No.	Be-**ví**-em	Nos.	Ha-**ví**-em be-**gut**	Nos.	Be-**gués**-sim	Nos.	Ha-**gués**-sim be-**gut**
Vos.	Be-**ví**-eu	Vos.	Ha-**ví**-eu be-**gut**	Vos.	Be-**gués**-siu	Vos.	Ha-**gués**-siu be-**gut**
Ells	Be-**vi**-en	Ells	Ha-**vi**-en be-**gut**	Ells	Be-**gues**-sin	Ells	Ha-**gues**-sin be-**gut**

Past Simple		*Past Perifrastic*		*Past Anterior perifrastic*
Jo	Be-**guí**	Jo	**Vaig beu**-re	**Vaig** ha-**ver** be-**gut**
Tu	Be-**gue**-res	Tu	**Vas beu**-re	**Vas** ha-**ver** be-**gut**
Ell	Be-**gué**	Ell	**Va beu**-re	**Va** ha-**ver** be-**gut**
Nos.	Be-**gué**-rem	Nos.	**Vam beu**-re	**Vam** ha-**ver** be-**gut**
Vos.	Be-**gué**-reu	Vos.	**Vau beu**-re	**Vau** ha-**ver** be-**gut**
Ells	Be-**gue**-ren	Ells	**Van beu**-re	**Van** ha-**ver** be-**gut**

Future Simple		*Future Compound*	
Jo	Beu-**ré**	Jo	Hau-**ré** be-**gut**
Tu	Beu-**ràs**	Tu	Hau-**ràs** be-**gut**
Ell	Beu-**rà**	Ell	Hau-**rà** be-**gut**
Nos.	Beu-**rem**	Nos.	Hau-**rem** be-**gut**
Vos.	Beu-**reu**	Vos.	Hau-**reu** be-**gut**
Ells	Beu-**ran**	Ells	Hau-**ran** be-**gut**

Conditional Simple		*Conditional Compound*		**IMPERATIVE**	
Jo	Beu-**ri**-a	Jo	Hau-**ri**-a be-**gut**		
Tu	Beu-**ri**-es	Tu	Hau-**ri**-es be-**gut**	**Beu**	*(Tu)*
Ell	Beu-**ri**-a	Ell	Hau-**ri**-a be-**gut**	**Be**-gui	*(Ell)*
Nos.	Beu-**rí**-em	Nos.	Hau-**rí**-em be-**gut**	Be-**guem**	*(Nos.)*
Vos.	Beu-**rí**-eu	Vos.	Hau-**rí**-eu be-**gut**	Be-**veu**	*(Vos.)*
Ells	Beu-**ri**-en	Ells	Hau-**ri**-en be-**gut**	**Be**-guin	*(Ells)*

IMPERSONAL		
	SIMPLE	**COMPOUND**
Infinitive	**Beu**-re	Ha-**ver** be-**gut**
Participle	Be-**gut**	-
Gerund	Be-**vent**	Ha-**vent** be-**gut**

TO DRIVE - CONDUIR

PERSONAL								
INDICATIVE				**SUBJUNCTIVE**				
SIMPLE		**COMPOUND**			**SIMPLE**		**COMPOUND**	
Present		*Past Indefinite*			*Present*		*Past Perfet*	
Jo	Con-du-**ei**-xo	Jo	**He** con-du-**ït**		Jo	Con-du-**ei**-xi	Jo	**Ha**-gi con-du-**ït**
Tu	Con-du-**ei**-xes	Tu	**Has** con-du-**ït**		Tu	Con-du-**ei**-xis	Tu	**Ha**-gis con-du-**ït**
Ell	Con-du-**eix**	Ell	**Ha** con-du-**ït**		Ell	Con-du-**ei**-xi	Ell	**Ha**-gi con-du-**ït**
No.	Con-du-**ïm**	Nos	**Hem** con-du-**ït**		Nos	Con-du-**ïm**	Nos	**Hà**-gim con-du-**ït**
Vos.	Con-du-**ïu**	Vos.	**Heu** con-du-**ït**		Vos.	Con-du-**ïu**	Vos.	**Hà**-giu con-du-**ït**
Ells	Con-du-**ei**-xen	Ells	**Han** con-du-**ït**		Ells	Con-du-**ei**-xin	Ells	**Ha**-gin con-du-**ït**
Imperfet		*Past Plusquamperfet*			*Imperfet past*		*Plusquamperfet past*	
Jo	Con-du-**ï**-a	Jo	Ha-**vi**-a con-du-**ït**		Jo	Con-du-**ís**	Jo	Ha-**gués** con-du-**ït**
Tu	Con-du-**ï**-es	Tu	Ha-**vi**-es con-du-**ït**		Tu	Con-du-**ïs**-sis	Tu	Ha-**gues**-sis con-du-**ït**
Ell	Con-du-**ï**-a	Ell	Ha-**vi**-a con-du-**ït**		Ell	Con-du-**ís**	Ell	Ha-**gués** con-du-**ït**
No.	Con-du-**í**-em	Nos	Ha-**ví**-em con-du-**ït**		Nos	Con-du-**ís**-sim	Nos	Ha-**gués**-sim con-du-**ït**
Vos.	Con-du-**í**-eu	Vos.	Ha-**ví**-eu con-du-**ït**		Vos.	Con-du-**ís**-siu	Vos.	Ha-**gués**-siu con-du-**ït**
Ells	Con-du-**ï**-en	Ells	Ha-**vi**-en con-du-**ït**		Ells	Con-du-**ïs**-sin	Ells	Ha-**gues**-sin con-du-**ït**

Past Simple		*Past Perifrastic*		*Past Anterior perifrastic*
Jo	Con-du-**í**	Jo	**Vaig** con-du-**ir**	**Vaig** ha-**ver** con-du-**ït**
Tu	Con-du-**ï**-res	Tu	**Vas** con-du-**ir**	**Vas** ha-**ver** con-du-**ït**
Ell	Con-du-**í**	Ell	**Va** con-du-**ir**	**Va** ha-**ver** con-du-**ït**
Nos	Con-du-**í**-rem	Nos.	**Vam** con-du-**ir**	**Vam** ha-**ver** con-du-**ït**
Vos.	Con-du-**í**-reu	Vos.	**Vau** con-du-**ir**	**Vau** ha-**ver** con-du-**ït**
Ells	Con-du-**i**-ren	Ells	**Van** con-du-**ir**	**Van** ha-**ver** con-du-**ït**

Future Simple		*Future Compound*	
Jo	Con-du-i-**ré**	Jo	Hau-**ré** con-du-**ït**
Tu	Con-du-i-**ràs**	Tu	Hau-**ràs** con-du-**ït**
Ell	Con-du-i-**rà**	Ell	Hau-**rà** con-du-**ït**
Nos.	Con-du-i-**rem**	Nos.	Hau-**rem** con-du-**ït**
Vos.	Con-du-i-**reu**	Vos.	Hau-**reu** con-du-**ït**
Ells	Con-du-i-**ran**	Ells	Hau-**ran** con-du-**ït**

Conditional Simple		*Conditional Compound*		**IMPERATIVE**	
Jo	Con-du-i-**ri**-a	Jo	Hau-**ri**-a con-du-**ït**		
Tu	Con-du-i-**ri**-es	Tu	Hau-**ri**-es con-du-**ït**	Con-du-**eix**	*(Tu)*
Ell	Con-du-i-**ri**-a	Ell	Hau-**ri**-a con-du-**ït**	Con-du-**ei**-xi	*(Ell)*
Nos	Con-du-i-**rí**-em	Nos.	Hau-**rí**-em con-du-**ït**	Con-du-**ïm**	*(Nos.)*
Vos.	Con-du-i-**rí**-eu	Vos.	Hau-**rí**-eu con-du-**ït**	Con-du-**ïu**	*(Vos.)*
Ells	Con-du-i-**ri**-en	Ells	Hau-**ri**-en con-du-**ït**	Con-du-**ei**-xin	*(Ells)*

IMPERSONAL		
	SIMPLE	**COMPOUND**
Infinitive	Con-du-**ir**	Ha-**ver** con-du-**ir**
Participle	Con-du-**ït**	-
Gerund	Con-du-**int**	Ha-**vent** con-du-**ir**

TO EAT – MENJAR

PERSONAL							
INDICATIVE				SUBJUNCTIVE			
SIMPLE		COMPOUND		SIMPLE		COMPOUND	
Present		*Past Indefinite*		*Present*		*Past Perfet*	
Jo	**Men**-jo	Jo	**He** men-**jat**	Jo	**Men**-gi	Jo	**Ha**-gi men-**jat**
Tu	**Men**-ges	Tu	**Has** men-**jat**	Tu	**Men**-gis	Tu	**Ha**-gis men-**jat**
Ell	**Men**-ja	Ell	**Ha** men-**jat**	Ell	**Men**-gi	Ell	**Ha**-gi men-**jat**
No.	Men-**gem**	Nos.	**Hem** men-**jat**	Nos.	Men-**gem**	Nos.	**Hà**-gim men-**jat**
Vos.	Men-**geu**	Vos.	**Heu** men-**jat**	Vos.	Men-**geu**	Vos.	**Hà**-giu men-**jat**
Ells	**Men**-gen	Ells	**Han** men-**jat**	Ells	**Men**-gin	Ells	**Ha**-gin men-**jat**
Imperfet		*Past Plusquamperfet*		*Imperfet past*		*Plusquamperfet past*	
Jo	Men-**ja**-va	Jo	**Ha**-**vi**-a men-**jat**	Jo	Men-**gés**	Jo	**Ha**-**gués** men-**jat**
Tu	Men-**ja**-ves	Tu	**Ha**-**vi**-es men-**jat**	Tu	Men-**ges**-sis	Tu	**Ha**-**gues**-sis men-**jat**
Ell	Men-**ja**-va	Ell	**Ha**-**vi**-a men-**jat**	Ell	Men-**gés**	Ell	**Ha**-**gués** men-**jat**
No.	Men-**jà**-vem	Nos.	**Ha**-**ví**-em men-**jat**	Nos	Men-**gés**-sim	Nos.	**Ha**-**gués**-sim men-**jat**
Vos.	Men-**jà**-veu	Vos.	**Ha**-**ví**-eu men-**jat**	Vos.	Men-**gés**-siu	Vos.	**Ha**-**gués**-siu men-**jat**
Ells	Men-**ja**-ven	Ells	**Ha**-**vi**-en men-**jat**	Ells	Men-**ges**-sin	Ells	**Ha**-**gues**-sin men-**jat**

Past Simple		*Past Perifrastic*		*Past Anterior perifrastic*
Jo	Men-**gí**	Jo	**Vaig** men-**jar**	**Vaig** ha-**ver** men-**jat**
Tu	Men-**ja**-res	Tu	**Vas** men-**jar**	**Vas** ha-**ver** men-**jat**
Ell	Men-**jà**	Ell	**Va** men-**jar**	**Va** ha-**ver** men-**jat**
Nos	Men-**jà**-rem	Nos.	**Vam** men-**jar**	**Vam** ha-**ver** men-**jat**
Vos.	Men-**jà**-reu	Vos.	**Vau** men-**jar**	**Vau** ha-**ver** men-**jat**
Ells	Men-**ja**-ren	Ells	**Van** men-**jar**	**Van** ha-**ver** men-**jat**

Future Simple		*Future Compound*	
Jo	Men-ja-**ré**	Jo	**Hau**-**ré** men-**jat**
Tu	Men-ja-**ràs**	Tu	**Hau**-**ràs** men-**jat**
Ell	Men-ja-**rà**	Ell	**Hau**-**rà** men-**jat**
Nos.	Men-ja-**rem**	Nos.	**Hau**-**rem** men-**jat**
Vos.	Men-ja-**reu**	Vos.	**Hau**-**reu** men-**jat**
Ells	Men-ja-**ran**	Ells	**Hau**-**ran** men-**jat**

Conditional Simple		*Conditional Compound*		IMPERATIVE	
Jo	Men-ja-**ri**-a	Jo	**Hau**-**ri**-a men-**jat**		
Tu	Men-ja-**ri**-es	Tu	**Hau**-**ri**-es men-**jat**	**Men**-ja	*(Tu)*
Ell	Men-ja-**ri**-a	Ell	**Hau**-**ri**-a men-**jat**	**Men**-gi	*(Ell)*
Nos	Men-ja-**rí**-em	Nos.	**Hau**-**rí**-em men-**jat**	Men-**gem**	*(Nos.)*
Vos.	Men-ja-**rí**-eu	Vos.	**Hau**-**rí**-eu men-**jat**	Men-**geu**	*(Vos.)*
Ells	Men-ja-**ri**-en	Ells	**Hau**-**ri**-en men-**jat**	**Men**-gin	*(Ells)*

IMPERSONAL		
	SIMPLE	COMPOUND
Infinitive	Men-**jar**	**Ha**-**ver** men-**jat**
Participle	Men-**jat**	-
Gerund	Men-j**ant**	**Ha**-**vent** men-**jat**

TO ENTER - ENTRAR

PERSONAL							
INDICATIVE				**SUBJUNCTIVE**			
SIMPLE		**COMPOUND**		**SIMPLE**		**COMPOUND**	
Present		*Past Indefinite*		*Present*		*Past Perfet*	
Jo	**En**-tro	Jo	**He** en-**trat**	Jo	**En**-tri	Jo	**Ha**-gi en-**trat**
Tu	**En**-tres	Tu	**Has** en-**trat**	Tu	**En**-tris	Tu	**Ha**-gis en-**trat**
Ell	**En**-tra	Ell	**Ha** en-**trat**	Ell	**En**-tri	Ell	**Ha**-gi en-**trat**
No.	En-**trem**	Nos.	**Hem** en-**trat**	Nos.	En-**trem**	Nos.	**Hà**-gim en-**trat**
Vos.	En-**treu**	Vos.	**Heu** en-**trat**	Vos.	En-**treu**	Vos.	**Hà**-giu en-**trat**
Ells	**En**-tren	Ells	**Han** en-**trat**	Ells	**En**-trin	Ells	**Ha**-gin en-**trat**
Imperfet		*Past Plusquamperfet*		*Imperfet past*		*Plusquamperfet past*	
Jo	En-**tra**-va	Jo	Ha-**vi**-a en-**trat**	Jo	**En**-trés	Jo	**Ha**-gués en-**trat**
Tu	En-**tra**-ves	Tu	Ha-**vi**-es en-**trat**	Tu	En-**tres**-sis	Tu	**Ha**-gues-sis en-**trat**
Ell	En-**tra**-va	Ell	Ha-**vi**-a en-**trat**	Ell	En-**trés**	Ell	**Ha**-gués en-**trat**
No.	En-**trà**-vem	Nos.	Ha-**ví**-em en-**trat**	Nos	En-**trés**-sim	Nos.	**Ha**-gués-sim en-**trat**
Vos.	En-**trà**-veu	Vos.	Ha-**ví**-eu en-**trat**	Vos.	En-**trés**-siu	Vos.	**Ha**-gués-siu en-**trat**
Ells	En-**tra**-ven	Ells	Ha-**vi**-en en-**trat**	Ells	En-**tres**-sin	Ells	**Ha**-gues-sin en-**trat**

Past Simple		*Past Perifrastic*		*Past Anterior perifrastic*			
Jo	En-**trí**	Jo	**Vaig** en-**trar**	**Vaig** ha-**ver** en-**trat**			
Tu	En-**tra**-res	Tu	**Vas** en-**trar**	**Vas** ha-**ver** en-**trat**			
Ell	En-**trà**	Ell	**Va** en-**trar**	**Va** ha-**ver** en-**trat**			
Nos	En-**trà**-rem	Nos.	**Vam** en-**trar**	**Vam** ha-**ver** en-**trat**			
Vos.	En-**trà**-reu	Vos.	**Vau** en-**trar**	**Vau** ha-**ver** en-**trat**			
Ells	En-**tra**-ren	Ells	**Van** en-**trar**	**Van** ha-**ver** en-**trat**			

Future Simple		*Future Compound*					
Jo	En-tra-**ré**	Jo	Hau-**ré** en-**trat**				
Tu	En-tra-**ràs**	Tu	Hau-**ràs** en-**trat**				
Ell	En-tra-**rà**	Ell	Hau-**rà** en-**trat**				
Nos.	En-tra-**rem**	Nos.	Hau-**rem** en-**trat**				
Vos.	En-tra-**reu**	Vos.	Hau-**reu** en-**trat**				
Ells	En-tra-**ran**	Ells	Hau-**ran** en-**trat**				

Conditional Simple		*Conditional Compound*		**IMPERATIVE**			
Jo	En-tra-**ri**-a	Jo	Hau-**ri**-a en-**trat**				
Tu	En-tra-**ri**-es	Tu	Hau-**ri**-es en-**trat**	**En**-tra		(Tu)	
Ell	En-tra-**ri**-a	Ell	Hau-**ri**-a en-**trat**	**En**-tri		(Ell)	
Nos	En-tra-**rí**-em	Nos.	Hau-**rí**-em en-**trat**	En-**trem**		(Nos.)	
Vos.	En-tra-**rí**-eu	Vos.	Hau-**rí**-eu en-**trat**	En-**treu**		(Vos.)	
Ells	En-tra-**ri**-en	Ells	Hau-**ri**-en en-**trat**	**En**-trin		(Ells)	

IMPERSONAL		
	SIMPLE	**COMPOUND**
Infinitive	En-**trar**	Ha-**ver** en-**trat**
Participle	En-**trat**	-
Gerund	En-**trant**	Ha-**vent** en-**trat**

TO EXIT - SORTIR

PERSONAL						
INDICATIVE				**SUBJUNCTIVE**		
SIMPLE		**COMPOUND**		**SIMPLE**		**COMPOUND**
Present		*Past Indefinite*		*Present*		*Past Perfet*
Jo	**Sur**-to	Jo	**He** sor-**tit**	Jo	**Sur**-ti	Jo	**Ha**-gi sor-**tit**
Tu	**Surts**	Tu	**Has** sor-**tit**	Tu	**Sur**-tis	Tu	**Ha**-gis sor-**tit**
Ell	**Surt**	Ell	**Ha** sor-**tit**	Ell	**Sur**-ti	Ell	**Ha**-gi sor-**tit**
No.	Sor-**tim**	Nos.	**Hem** sor-**tit**	Nos.	Sor-**tim**	Nos.	**Hà**-gim sor-**tit**
Vos.	Sor-**tiu**	Vos.	**Heu** sor-**tit**	Vos.	Sor-**tiu**	Vos.	**Hà**-giu sor-**tit**
Ells	**Sur**-ten	Ells	**Han** sor-**tit**	Ells	**Sur**-tin	Ells	**Ha**-gin sor-**tit**
Imperfet		*Past Plusquamperfet*		*Imperfet past*		*Plusquamperfet past*
Jo	Sor-**ti**-a	Jo	Ha-**vi**-a sor-**tit**	Jo	Sor-**tís**	Jo	Ha-**gués** sor-**tit**
Tu	Sor-**ti**-es	Tu	Ha-**vi**-es sor-**tit**	Tu	Sor-**tis**-sis	Tu	Ha-**gues**-sis sor-**tit**
Ell	Sor-**ti**-a	Ell	Ha-**vi**-a sor-**tit**	Ell	Sor-**tís**	Ell	Ha-**gués** sor-**tit**
No.	Sor-**tí**-em	Nos.	Ha-**ví**-em sor-**tit**	Nos	Sor-**tís**-sim	Nos.	Ha-**gués**-sim sor-**tit**
Vos.	Sor-**tí**-eu	Vos.	Ha-**ví**-eu sor-**tit**	Vos.	Sor-**tís**-siu	Vos.	Ha-**gués**-siu sor-**tit**
Ells	Sor-**ti**-en	Ells	Ha-**vi**-en sor-**tit**	Ells	Sor-**tis**-sin	Ells	Ha-**gues**-sin sor-**tit**

Past Simple		*Past Perifrastic*		*Past Anterior perifrastic*
Jo	Sor-**tí**	Jo	**Vaig** sor-**tir**	**Vaig** ha-**ver** sor-**tit**
Tu	Sor-**ti**-res	Tu	**Vas** sor-**tir**	**Vas** ha-**ver** sor-**tit**
Ell	Sor-**tí**	Ell	**Va** sor-**tir**	**Va** ha-**ver** sor-**tit**
Nos	Sor-**tí**-rem	Nos.	**Vam** sor-**tir**	**Vam** ha-**ver** sor-**tit**
Vos.	Sor-**tí**-reu	Vos.	**Vau** sor-**tir**	**Vau** ha-**ver** sor-**tit**
Ells	Sor-**ti**-ren	Ells	**Van** sor-**tir**	**Van** ha-**ver** sor-**tit**

Future Simple		*Future Compound*	
Jo	Sor-ti-**ré**	Jo	Hau-**ré** sor-**tit**
Tu	Sor-ti-**ràs**	Tu	Hau-**ràs** sor-**tit**
Ell	Sor-ti-**rà**	Ell	Hau-**rà** sor-**tit**
Nos.	Sor-ti-**rem**	Nos.	Hau-**rem** sor-**tit**
Vos.	Sor-ti-**reu**	Vos.	Hau-**reu** sor-**tit**
Ells	Sor-ti-**ran**	Ells	Hau-**ran** sor-**tit**

Conditional Simple		*Conditional Compound*		**IMPERATIVE**	
Jo	Sor-ti-**ri**-a	Jo	Hau-**ri**-a sor-**tit**		
Tu	Sor-ti-**ri**-es	Tu	Hau-**ri**-es sor-**tit**	**Surt**	*(Tu)*
Ell	Sor-ti-**ri**-a	Ell	Hau-**ri**-a sor-**tit**	**Sur**-ti	*(Ell)*
Nos	Sor-ti-**rí**-em	Nos.	Hau-**rí**-em sor-**tit**	Sor-**tim**	*(Nos.)*
Vos.	Sor-ti-**rí**-eu	Vos.	Hau-**rí**-eu sor-**tit**	Sor-**tiu**	*(Vos.)*
Ells	Sor-ti-**ri**-en	Ells	Hau-**ri**-en sor-**tit**	**Sur**-tin	*(Ells)*

IMPERSONAL		
	SIMPLE	**COMPOUND**
Infinitive	Sor **tir**	Ha-**ver** sor-**tit**
Participle	Sor-**tit**	-
Gerund	Sor-**tint**	Ha-**vent** sor-**tit**

TO EXPLAIN - EXPLICAR

PERSONAL				
INDICATIVE			**SUBJUNCTIVE**	
SIMPLE	**COMPOUND**		**SIMPLE**	**COMPOUND**
Present	*Past Indefinite*		*Present*	*Past Perfet*
Jo Ex-**pli**-co	Jo **He** ex-pli-**cat**		Jo Ex-**pli**-qui	Jo **Ha**-gi ex-pli-**cat**
Tu Ex-**pli**-ques	Tu **Has** ex-pli-**cat**		Tu Ex-**pli**-quis	Tu **Ha**-gis ex-pli-**cat**
Ell Ex-**pli**-ca	Ell **Ha** ex-pli-**cat**		Ell Ex-**pli**-qui	Ell **Ha**-gi ex-pli-**cat**
No. Ex-pli-**quem**	Nos. **Hem** ex-pli-**cat**		Nos. Ex-pli-**quem**	Nos. **Hà**-gim ex-pli-**cat**
Vos. Ex-pli-**queu**	Vos. **Heu** ex-pli-**cat**		Vos. Ex-pli-**queu**	Vos. **Hà**-giu ex-pli-**cat**
Ells Ex-**pli**-quen	Ells **Han** ex-pli-**cat**		Ells Ex-**pli**-quin	Ells **Ha**-gin ex-pli-**cat**
Imperfet	*Past Plusquamperfet*		*Imperfet past*	*Plusquamperfet past*
Jo Ex-pli-**ca**-va	Jo Ha-**vi**-a ex-pli-**cat**		Jo Ex-pli-**qués**	Jo Ha-**gués** ex-pli-**cat**
Tu Ex-pli-**ca**-ves	Tu Ha-**vi**-es ex-pli-**cat**		Tu Ex-pli-**ques**-sis	Tu Ha-**gues**-sis ex-pli-**cat**
Ell Ex-pli-**ca**-va	Ell Ha-**vi**-a ex-pli-**cat**		Ell Ex-pli-**qués**	Ell Ha-**gués** ex-pli-**cat**
No. Ex-pli-**cà**-vem	Nos. Ha-**ví**-em ex-pli-**cat**		Nos Ex-pli-**qués**-sim	Nos. Ha-**gués**-sim ex-pli-**cat**
Vos. Ex-pli-**cà**-veu	Vos. Ha-**ví**-eu ex-pli-**cat**		Vos. Ex-pli-**qués**-siu	Vos. Ha-**gués**-siu ex-pli-**cat**
Ells Ex-pli-**ca**-ven	Ells Ha-**vi**-en ex-pli-**cat**		Ells Ex-pli-**ques**-sin	Ells Ha-**gues**-sin ex-pli-**cat**

Past Simple	*Past Perifrastic*	*Past Anterior perifrastic*
Jo Ex-pli-**quí**	Jo **Vaig** ex-pli-**car**	**Vaig** ha-**ver** ex-pli-**cat**
Tu Ex-pli-**ca**-res	Tu **Vas** ex-pli-**car**	**Vas** ha-**ver** ex-pli-**cat**
Ell Ex-pli-**cà**	Ell **Va** ex-pli-**car**	**Va** ha-**ver** ex-pli-**cat**
Nos Ex-pli-**cà**-rem	Nos. **Vam** ex-pli-**car**	**Vam** ha-**ver** ex-pli-**cat**
Vos. Ex-pli-**cà**-reu	Vos. **Vau** ex-pli-**car**	**Vau** ha-**ver** ex-pli-**cat**
Ells Ex-pli-**ca**-ren	Ells **Van** ex-pli-**car**	**Van** ha-**ver** ex-pli-**cat**

Future Simple	*Future Compound*
Jo Ex-pli-ca-**ré**	Jo Hau-**ré** ex-pli-**cat**
Tu Ex-pli-ca-**ràs**	Tu Hau-**ràs** ex-pli-**cat**
Ell Ex-pli-ca-**rà**	Ell Hau-**rà** ex-pli-**cat**
Nos. Ex-pli-ca-**rem**	Nos. Hau-**rem** ex-pli-**cat**
Vos. Ex-pli-ca-**reu**	Vos. Hau-**reu** ex-pli-**cat**
Ells Ex-pli-ca-**ran**	Ells Hau-**ran** ex-pli-**cat**

Conditional Simple	*Conditional Compound*	**IMPERATIVE**	
Jo Ex-pli-ca-**ri**-a	Jo Hau-**ri**-a ex-pli-**cat**		
Tu Ex-pli-ca-**ri**-es	Tu Hau-**ri**-es ex-pli-**cat**	Ex-**pli**-ca	*(Tu)*
Ell Ex-pli-ca-**ri**-a	Ell Hau-**ri**-a ex-pli-**cat**	Ex-**pli**-qui	*(Ell)*
Nos. Ex-pli-ca-**rí**-em	Nos. Hau-**rí**-em ex-pli-**cat**	Ex-pli-**quem**	*(Nos.)*
Vos. Ex-pli-ca-**rí**-eu	Vos. Hau-**rí**-eu ex-pli-**cat**	Ex-pli-**queu**	*(Vos.)*
Ells Ex-pli-ca-**ri**-en	Ells Hau-**ri**-en ex-pli-**cat**	Ex-**pli**-quin	*(Ells)*

IMPERSONAL		
	SIMPLE	**COMPOUND**
Infinitive	Ex-pli-**car**	Ha-**ver** ex-pli-**cat**
Participle	Ex-pli-**cat**	-
Gerund	Ex-pli-c**ant**	Ha-**vent** ex-pli-**cat**

TO FALL - CAURE

PERSONAL				
INDICATIVE			**SUBJUNCTIVE**	
SIMPLE	**COMPOUND**		**SIMPLE**	**COMPOUND**
Present	*Past Indefinite*		*Present*	*Past Perfet*
Jo **Caic**	Jo **He** cai-**gut**		Jo **Cai**-gui	Jo **Ha**-gi cai-**gut**
Tu **Caus**	Tu **Has** cai-**gut**		Tu **Cai**-guis	Tu **Ha**-gis cai-**gut**
Ell **Cau**	Ell **Ha** cai-**gut**		Ell **Cai**-gui	Ell **Ha**-gi cai-**gut**
No. Ca-**iem**	Nos. **Hem** cai-**gut**		Nos. Cai-**guem**	Nos. **Hà**-gim cai-**gut**
Vos. Ca-**ieu**	Vos. **Heu** cai-**gut**		Vos. Cai-**gueu**	Vos. **Hà**-giu cai-**gut**
Ells **Ca**-uen	Ells **Han** cai-**gut**		Ells **Cai**-guin	Ells **Ha**-gin cai-**gut**
Imperfet	*Past Plusquamperfet*		*Imperfet past*	*Plusquamperfet past*
Jo **Que**-ia	Jo Ha-**vi**-a cai-**gut**		Jo Cai-**gués**	Jo Ha-**gués** cai-**gut**
Tu **Que**-ies	Tu Ha-**vi**-es cai-**gut**		Tu Cai-**gues**-sis	Tu Ha-**gues**-sis cai-**gut**
Ell **Que**-ia	Ell Ha-**vi**-a cai-**gut**		Ell Cai-**gués**	Ell Ha-**gués** cai-**gut**
No. **Què**-iem	Nos. Ha-**ví**-em cai-**gut**		Nos Cai-**gués**-sim	Nos. Ha-**gués**-sim cai-**gut**
Vos. **Què**-ieu	Vos. Ha-**ví**-eu cai-**gut**		Vos. Cai-**gués**-siu	Vos. Ha-**gués**-siu cai-**gut**
Ells **Que**-ien	Ells Ha-**vi**-en cai-**gut**		Ells Cai-**gues**-sin	Ells Ha-**gues**-sin cai-**gut**

Past Simple	*Past Perifrastic*	*Past Anterior perifrastic*
Jo Cai-**guí**	Jo **Vaig cau**-re	**Vaig** ha-**ver** cai-**gut**
Tu Cai-**gue**-res	Tu **Vas cau**-re	**Vas** ha-**ver** cai-**gut**
Ell Cai-**gué**	Ell **Va cau**-re	**Va** ha-**ver** cai-**gut**
Nos Cai-**gué**-rem	Nos. **Vam cau**-re	**Vam** ha-**ver** cai-**gut**
Vos. Cai-**gué**-reu	Vos. **Vau cau**-re	**Vau** ha-**ver** cai-**gut**
Ells Cai-**gue**-ren	Ells **Van cau**-re	**Van** ha-**ver** cai-**gut**

Future Simple	*Future Compound*
Jo Cau-**ré**	Jo Hau-**ré** cai-**gut**
Tu Cau-**ràs**	Tu Hau-**ràs** cai-**gut**
Ell Cau-**rà**	Ell Hau-**rà** cai-**gut**
Nos. Cau-**rem**	Nos. Hau-**rem** cai-**gut**
Vos. Cau-**reu**	Vos. Hau-**reu** cai-**gut**
Ells Cau-**ran**	Ells Hau-**ran** cai-**gut**

Conditional Simple	*Conditional Compound*	**IMPERATIVE**	
Jo Cau-**ri**-a	Jo Hau-**ri**-a cai-**gut**		
Tu Cau-**ri**-es	Tu Hau-**ri**-es cai-**gut**	**Cau**	*(Tu)*
Ell Cau-**ri**-a	Ell Hau-**ri**-a cai-**gut**	**Cai**-gui	*(Ell)*
Nos Cau-**rí**-em	Nos. Hau-**rí**-em cai-**gut**	Cai-**guem**	*(Nos.)*
Vos. Cau-**rí**-eu	Vos. Hau-**rí**-eu cai-**gut**	Ca-**ieu**	*(Vos.)*
Ells Cau-**ri**-en	Ells Hau-**ri**-en cai-**gut**	**Cai**-guin	*(Ells)*

IMPERSONAL		
	SIMPLE	**COMPOUND**
Infinitive	**Cau**-re	Ha-**ver** cai-**gut**
Participle	Cai-**gut**	-
Gerund	Ca-**ient**	Ha-**vent** cai-**gut**

TO FEEL - SENTIR

PERSONAL						
INDICATIVE				**SUBJUNCTIVE**		
SIMPLE		**COMPOUND**		**SIMPLE**		**COMPOUND**
Present		*Past Indefinite*		*Present*		*Past Perfet*
Jo	**Sen**-to	Jo	**He** sen-**tit**	Jo	**Sen**-ti	Jo	**Ha**-gi sen-**tit**
Tu	**Sents**	Tu	**Has** sen-**tit**	Tu	**Sen**-tis	Tu	**Ha**-gis sen-**tit**
Ell	**Sent**	Ell	**Ha** sen-**tit**	Ell	**Sen**-ti	Ell	**Ha**-gi sen-**tit**
No.	Sen-**tim**	Nos.	**Hem** sen-**tit**	Nos.	Sen-**tim**	Nos.	**Hà**-gim sen-**tit**
Vos.	Sen-**tiu**	Vos.	**Heu** sen-**tit**	Vos.	Sen-**tiu**	Vos.	**Hà**-giu sen-**tit**
Ells	**Sen**-ten	Ells	**Han** sen-**tit**	Ells	**Sen**-tin	Ells	**Ha**-gin sen-**tit**
Imperfet		*Past Plusquamperfet*		*Imperfet past*		*Plusquamperfet past*
Jo	Sen-**ti**-a	Jo	Ha-**vi**-a sen-**tit**	Jo	Sen-**tís**	Jo	Ha-**gués** sen-**tit**
Tu	Sen-**ti**-es	Tu	Ha-**vi**-es sen-**tit**	Tu	Sen-**tis**-sis	Tu	Ha-**gues**-sis sen-**tit**
Ell	Sen-**ti**-a	Ell	Ha-**vi**-a sen-**tit**	Ell	Sen-**tís**	Ell	Ha-**gués** sen-**tit**
No.	Sen-**tí**-em	Nos.	Ha-**ví**-em sen-**tit**	Nos	Sen-**tís**-sim	Nos.	Ha-**gués**-sim sen-**tit**
Vos.	Sen-**tí**-eu	Vos.	Ha-**ví**-eu sen-**tit**	Vos.	Sen-**tís**-siu	Vos.	Ha-**gués**-siu sen-**tit**
Ells	Sen-**ti**-en	Ells	Ha-**vi**-en sen-**tit**	Ells	Sen-**tis**-sin	Ells	Ha-**gues**-sin sen-**tit**

Past Simple		*Past Perifrastic*		*Past Anterior perifrastic*		
Jo	Sen-**tí**	Jo	**Vaig** sen-**tir**	**Vaig** ha-**ver** sen-**tit**		
Tu	Sen-**ti**-res	Tu	**Vas** sen-**tir**	**Vas** ha-**ver** sen-**tit**		
Ell	Sen-**tí**	Ell	**Va** sen-**tir**	**Va** ha-**ver** sen-**tit**		
Nos	Sen-**tí**-rem	Nos.	**Vam** sen-**tir**	**Vam** ha-**ver** sen-**tit**		
Vos.	Sen-**tí**-reu	Vos.	**Vau** sen-**tir**	**Vau** ha-**ver** sen-**tit**		
Ells	Sen-**ti**-ren	Ells	**Van** sen-**tir**	**Van** ha-**ver** sen-**tit**		

Future Simple		*Future Compound*				
Jo	Sen-ti-**ré**	Jo	Hau-**ré** sen-**tit**			
Tu	Sen-ti-**ràs**	Tu	Hau-**ràs** sen-**tit**			
Ell	Sen-ti-**rà**	Ell	Hau-**rà** sen-**tit**			
Nos.	Sen-ti-**rem**	Nos.	Hau-**rem** sen-**tit**			
Vos.	Sen-ti-**reu**	Vos.	Hau-**reu** sen-**tit**			
Ells	Sen-ti-**ran**	Ells	Hau-**ran** sen-**tit**			

Conditional Simple		*Conditional Compound*		**IMPERATIVE**		
Jo	Sen-ti-**ri**-a	Jo	Hau-**ri**-a sen-**tit**			
Tu	Sen-ti-**ri**-es	Tu	Hau-**ri**-es sen-**tit**	**Sent**		*(Tu)*
Ell	Sen-ti-**ri**-a	Ell	Hau-**ri**-a sen-**tit**	**Sen**-ti		*(Ell)*
Nos	Sen-ti-**rí**-em	Nos.	Hau-**rí**-em sen-**tit**	Sen-**tim**		*(Nos.)*
Vos.	Sen-ti-**rí**-eu	Vos.	Hau-**rí**-eu sen-**tit**	Sen-**tiu**		*(Vos.)*
Ells	Sen-ti-**ri**-en	Ells	Hau-**ri**-en sen-**tit**	**Sen**-tin		*(Ells)*

IMPERSONAL		
	SIMPLE	**COMPOUND**
Infinitive	Sen-**tir**	Ha-**ver** sen-**tit**
Participle	Sen-**tit**	-
Gerund	Sen-**tint**	Ha-**vent** sen-**tit**

TO FIGHT - LLUITAR

PERSONAL				
INDICATIVE		**SUBJUNCTIVE**		
SIMPLE	**COMPOUND**	**SIMPLE**	**COMPOUND**	
Present	*Past Indefinite*	*Present*	*Past Perfet*	

INDICATIVE

	SIMPLE		COMPOUND		SUBJUNCTIVE SIMPLE		COMPOUND	
Present		**Past Indefinite**		**Present**		**Past Perfet**		
Jo	**Llui**-to	Jo	**He** llui-tat	Jo	**Llui**-ti	Jo	**Ha**-gi llui-tat
Tu	**Llui**-tes	Tu	**Has** llui-tat	Tu	**Llui**-tis	Tu	**Ha**-gis llui-tat
Ell	**Llui**-ta	Ell	**Ha** llui-tat	Ell	**Llui**-ti	Ell	**Ha**-gi llui-tat
No.	Llui-**tem**	Nos.	**Hem** llui-tat	Nos.	Llui-**tem**	Nos.	**Hà**-gim llui-tat
Vos.	Llui-**teu**	Vos.	**Heu** llui-tat	Vos.	Llui-**teu**	Vos.	**Hà**-giu llui-tat
Ells	**Llui**-ten	Ells	**Han** llui-tat	Ells	**Llui**-tin	Ells	**Ha**-gin llui-tat
Imperfet		**Past Plusquamperfet**		**Imperfet past**		**Plusquamperfet past**		
Jo	Llui-**ta**-va	Jo	Ha-**vi**-a llui-tat	Jo	Llui-**tés**	Jo	Ha-**gués** llui-tat
Tu	Llui-**ta**-ves	Tu	Ha-**vi**-es llui-**tat**	Tu	Llui-**tes**-sis	Tu	Ha-**gues**-sis llui-**tat**
Ell	Llui-**ta**-va	Ell	Ha-**vi**-a llui-tat	Ell	Llui-**tés**	Ell	Ha-**gués** llui-tat
No.	Llui-**tà**-vem	Nos.	Ha-**ví**-em llui-tat	Nos	Llui-**tés**-sim	Nos.	Ha-**gués**-sim llui-tat
Vos.	Llui-**tà**-veu	Vos.	Ha-**ví**-eu llui-tat	Vos.	Llui-**tés**-siu	Vos.	Ha-**gués**-siu llui-tat
Ells	Llui-**ta**-ven	Ells	Ha-**vi**-en llui-tat	Ells	Llui-**tes**-sin	Ells	Ha-**gues**-sin llui-tat

Past Simple		**Past Perifrastic**		**Past Anterior perifrastic**
Jo	Llui-**tí**	Jo	**Vaig** llui-tar	**Vaig** ha-**ver** llui-tat
Tu	Llui-**ta**-res	Tu	**Vas** llui-tar	**Vas** ha-**ver** llui-tat
Ell	Llui-**tà**	Ell	**Va** llui-tar	**Va** ha-**ver** llui-tat
Nos	Llui-**tà**-rem	Nos.	**Vam** llui-tar	**Vam** ha-**ver** llui-tat
Vos.	Llui-**tà**-reu	Vos.	**Vau** llui-tar	**Vau** ha-**ver** llui-tat
Ells	Llui-**tà**-ren	Ells	**Van** llui-tar	**Van** ha-**ver** llui-tat

Future Simple		**Future Compound**	
Jo	Llui-ta-**ré**	Jo	Hau-**ré** llui-tat
Tu	Llui-ta-**ràs**	Tu	Hau-**ràs** llui-tat
Ell	Llui-ta-**rà**	Ell	Hau-**rà** llui-tat
Nos.	Llui-ta-**rem**	Nos.	Hau-**rem** llui-tat
Vos.	Llui-ta-**reu**	Vos.	Hau-**reu** llui-tat
Ells	Llui-ta-**ran**	Ells	Hau-**ran** llui-tat

Conditional Simple		**Conditional Compound**		**IMPERATIVE**	
Jo	Llui-ta-**ri**-a	Jo	Hau-**ri**-a llui-tat		
Tu	Llui-ta-**ri**-es	Tu	Hau-**ri**-es llui-tat	**Llui**-ta	*(Tu)*
Ell	Llui-ta-**ri**-a	Ell	Hau-**ri**-a llui-tat	**Llui**-ti	*(Ell)*
Nos	Llui-ta-**rí**-em	Nos.	Hau-**rí**-em llui-tat	Llui-**tem**	*(Nos.)*
Vos.	Llui-ta-**rí**-eu	Vos.	Hau-**rí**-eu llui-tat	Llui-**teu**	*(Vos.)*
Ells	Llui-ta-**ri**-en	Ells	Hau-**ri**-en llui-tat	**Llui**-tin	*(Ells)*

IMPERSONAL		
	SIMPLE	**COMPOUND**
Infinitive	Llui-**tar**	Ha-**ver** llui-tat
Participle	Llui-**tat**	-
Gerund	Llui-**tant**	Ha-**vent** llui-tat

TO FIND - TROBAR

PERSONAL							
INDICATIVE				**SUBJUNCTIVE**			
SIMPLE		**COMPOUND**		**SIMPLE**		**COMPOUND**	
Present		*Past Indefinite*		*Present*		*Past Perfet*	
Jo	**Tro**-bo	Jo	**He** tro-bat	Jo	**Tro**-bi	Jo	**Ha**-gi tro-bat
Tu	**Tro**-bes	Tu	**Has** tro-bat	Tu	**Tro**-bis	Tu	**Ha**-gis tro-bat
Ell	**Tro**-ba	Ell	**Ha** tro-bat	Ell	**Tro**-bi	Ell	**Ha**-gi tro-bat
No.	Tro-**bem**	Nos.	**Hem** tro-bat	Nos.	Tro-**bem**	Nos.	**Hà**-gim tro-bat
Vos.	Tro-**beu**	Vos.	**Heu** tro-bat	Vos.	Tro-**beu**	Vos.	**Hà**-giu tro-bat
Ells	**Tro**-ben	Ells	**Han** tro-bat	Ells	**Tro**-bin	Ells	**Ha**-gin tro-bat
Imperfet		*Past Plusquamperfet*		*Imperfet past*		*Plusquamperfet past*	
Jo	Tro-**ba**-va	Jo	Ha-**vi**-a tro-bat	Jo	Tro-**bés**	Jo	Ha-**gués** tro-bat
Tu	Tro-**ba**-ves	Tu	Ha-**vi**-es tro-bat	Tu	Tro-**bes**-sis	Tu	Ha-**gues**-sis tro-**b**at
Ell	Tro-**ba**-va	Ell	Ha-**vi**-a tro-bat	Ell	Tro-**bés**	Ell	Ha-**gués** tro-bat
No.	Tro-**bà**-vem	Nos.	Ha-**ví**-em tro-**b**at	Nos	Tro-**bés**-sim	Nos.	Ha-**gués**-sim tro-**b**at
Vos.	Tro-**bà**-veu	Vos.	Ha-**ví**-eu tro-bat	Vos.	Tro-**bés**-siu	Vos.	Ha-**gués**-siu tro-bat
Ells	Tro-**ba**-ven	Ells	Ha-**vi**-en tro-**b**at	Ells	Tro-**bes**-sin	Ells	Ha-**gues**-sin tro-bat

Past Simple		*Past Perifrastic*		*Past Anterior perifrastic*
Jo	Tro-**bí**	Jo	**Vaig** tro-bar	**Vaig** ha-**ver** tro-bat
Tu	Tro-**ba**-res	Tu	**Vas** tro-bar	**Vas** ha-**ver** tro-bat
Ell	Tro-**bà**	Ell	**Va** tro-bar	**Va** ha-**ver** tro-bat
Nos	Tro-**bà**-rem	Nos.	**Vam** tro-bar	**Vam** ha-**ver** tro-bat
Vos.	Tro-**bà**-reu	Vos.	**Vau** tro-bar	**Vau** ha-**ver** tro-bat
Ells	Tro-**ba**-ren	Ells	**Van** tro-bar	**Van** ha-**ver** tro-bat

Future Simple		*Future Compound*	
Jo	Tro-ba-**ré**	Jo	Hau-**ré** tro-bat
Tu	Tro-ba-**ràs**	Tu	Hau-**ràs** tro-bat
Ell	Tro-ba-**rà**	Ell	Hau-**rà** tro-**b**at
Nos.	Tro-ba-**rem**	Nos.	Hau-**rem** tro-bat
Vos.	Tro-ba-**reu**	Vos.	Hau-**reu** tro-bat
Ells	Tro-ba-**ran**	Ells	Hau-**ran** tro-bat

Conditional Simple		*Conditional Compound*		**IMPERATIVE**	
Jo	Tro-ba-**ri**-a	Jo	Hau-**ri**-a tro-bat		
Tu	Tro-ba-**ri**-es	Tu	Hau-**ri**-es tro-bat	**Tro**-ba	*(Tu)*
Ell	Tro-ba-**ri**-a	Ell	Hau-**ri**-a tro-bat	**Tro**-bi	*(Ell)*
Nos	Tro-ba-**rí**-em	Nos.	Hau-**rí**-em tro-bat	Tro-**bem**	*(Nos.)*
Vos.	Tro-ba-**rí**-eu	Vos.	Hau-**rí**-eu tro-bat	Tro-**beu**	*(Vos.)*
Ells	Tro-ba-**ri**-en	Ells	Hau-**ri**-en tro-bat	**Tro**-bin	*(Ells)*

IMPERSONAL		
	SIMPLE	**COMPOUND**
Infinitive	Tro-**bar**	Ha-**ver** tro-**b**at
Participle	Tro-**bat**	-
Gerund	Tro-**bant**	Ha-**vent** tro-**b**at

TO FINISH - ACABAR

PERSONAL							
INDICATIVE				**SUBJUNCTIVE**			
SIMPLE		**COMPOUND**		**SIMPLE**		**COMPOUND**	
Present		*Past Indefinite*		*Present*		*Past Perfet*	
Jo	A-**ca**-bo	Jo	**He** a-ca-b**at**	Jo	A-**ca**-bi	Jo	**Ha**-gi a-ca-b**at**
Tu	A-**ca**-bes	Tu	**Has** a-ca-b**at**	Tu	A-**ca**-bis	Tu	**Ha**-gis a-ca-b**at**
Ell	A-**ca**-ba	Ell	**Ha** a-ca-b**at**	Ell	A-**ca**-bi	Ell	**Ha**-gi a-ca-b**at**
No.	A-ca-**bem**	Nos.	**Hem** a-ca-b**at**	Nos.	A-ca-**bem**	Nos.	**Hà**-gim a-ca-b**at**
Vos.	A-ca-**beu**	Vos.	**Heu** a-ca-b**at**	Vos.	A-ca-**beu**	Vos.	**Hà**-giu a-ca-b**at**
Ells	A-**ca**-ben	Ells	**Han** a-ca-b**at**	Ells	A-**ca**-bin	Ells	**Ha**-gin a-ca-b**at**
Imperfet		*Past Plusquamperfet*		*Imperfet past*		*Plusquamperfet past*	
Jo	A-ca-**ba**-va	Jo	Ha-**vi**-a a-ca-b**at**	Jo	A-ca-**bés**	Jo	Ha-**gués** a-ca-b**at**
Tu	A-ca-**ba**-ves	Tu	Ha-**vi**-es a-ca-b**at**	Tu	A-ca-**bes**-sis	Tu	Ha-**gues**-sis a-ca-b**at**
Ell	A-ca-**ba**-va	Ell	Ha-**vi**-a a-ca-b**at**	Ell	A-ca-**bés**	Ell	Ha-**gués** a-ca-b**at**
No.	A-ca-**bà**-vem	Nos.	Ha-**ví**-em a-ca-b**at**	Nos	A-ca-**bés**-sim	Nos.	Ha-**gués**-sim a-ca-b**at**
Vos.	A-ca-**bà**-veu	Vos.	Ha-**ví**-eu a-ca-b**at**	Vos.	A-ca-**bés**-siu	Vos.	Ha-**gués**-siu a-ca-b**at**
Ells	A-ca-**ba**-ven	Ells	Ha-**vi**-en a-ca-b**at**	Ells	A-ca-**bes**-sin	Ells	Ha-**gues**-sin a-ca-b**at**

Past Simple		*Past Perifrastic*		*Past Anterior perifrastic*
Jo	A-ca-**bí**	Jo	**Vaig** a-ca-bar	**Vaig** ha-**ver** a-ca-b**at**
Tu	A-ca-**ba**-res	Tu	**Vas** a-ca-bar	**Vas** ha-**ver** a-ca-b**at**
Ell	A-ca-**bà**	Ell	**Va** a-ca-bar	**Va** ha-**ver** a-ca-b**at**
Nos	A-ca-**bà**-rem	Nos.	**Vam** a-ca-bar	**Vam** ha-**ver** a-ca-b**at**
Vos.	A-ca-**bà**-reu	Vos.	**Vau** a-ca-bar	**Vau** ha-**ver** a-ca-b**at**
Ells	A-ca-**ba**-ren	Ells	**Van** a-ca-bar	**Van** ha-**ver** a-ca-b**at**

Future Simple		*Future Compound*	
Jo	A-ca-ba-**ré**	Jo	Hau-**ré** a-ca-b**at**
Tu	A-ca-ba-**ràs**	Tu	Hau-**ràs** a-ca-b**at**
Ell	A-ca-ba-**rà**	Ell	Hau-**rà** a-ca-b**at**
Nos.	A-ca-ba-**rem**	Nos.	Hau-**rem** a-ca-b**at**
Vos.	A-ca-ba-**reu**	Vos.	Hau-**reu** a-ca-b**at**
Ells	A-ca-ba-**ran**	Ells	Hau-**ran** a-ca-b**at**

Conditional Simple		*Conditional Compound*		IMPERATIVE	
Jo	A-ca-ba-**ri**-a	Jo	Hau-**ri**-a a-ca-b**at**		
Tu	A-ca-ba-**ri**-es	Tu	Hau-**ri**-es a-ca-b**at**	A-**ca**-ba	(Tu)
Ell	A-ca-ba-**ri**-a	Ell	Hau-**ri**-a a-ca-b**at**	A-**ca**-bi	(Ell)
Nos	A-ca-ba-**rí**-em	Nos.	Hau-**rí**-em a-ca-b**at**	A-ca-**bem**	(Nos.)
Vos.	A-ca-ba-**rí**-eu	Vos.	Hau-**rí**-eu a-ca-b**at**	A-ca-**beu**	(Vos.)
Ells	A-ca-ba-**ri**-en	Ells	Hau-**ri**-en a-ca-b**at**	A-**ca**-bin	(Ells)

IMPERSONAL		
	SIMPLE	**COMPOUND**
Infinitive	A-ca-**bar**	Ha-**ver** a-ca-b**at**
Participle	A-ca-**bat**	-
Gerund	A-ca-**bant**	Ha-**vent** a-ca-b**at**

TO FLY - VOLAR

PERSONAL				
INDICATIVE			**SUBJUNCTIVE**	
SIMPLE	**COMPOUND**		**SIMPLE**	**COMPOUND**

INDICATIVE / SUBJUNCTIVE

Present		Past Indefinite		Present		Past Perfet	
Jo	**Vo**-lo	Jo	**He** vo-**lat**	Jo	**Vo**-li	Jo	**Ha**-gi vo-**lat**
Tu	**Vo**-les	Tu	**Has** vo-**lat**	Tu	**Vo**-lis	Tu	**Ha**-gis vo-**lat**
Ell	**Vo**-la	Ell	**Ha** vo-**lat**	Ell	**Vo**-li	Ell	**Ha**-gi vo-**lat**
No.	**Vo**-**lem**	Nos.	**Hem** vo-**lat**	Nos.	**Vo**-**lem**	Nos.	**Hà**-gim vo-**lat**
Vos.	**Vo**-**leu**	Vos.	**Heu** vo-**lat**	Vos.	**Vo**-**leu**	Vos.	**Hà**-giu vo-**lat**
Ells	**Vo**-len	Ells	**Han** vo-**lat**	Ells	**Vo**-lin	Ells	**Ha**-gin vo-**lat**

Imperfet		Past Plusquamperfet		Imperfet past		Plusquamperfet past	
Jo	Vo-**la**-va	Jo	Ha-**vi**-a vo-**lat**	Jo	Vo-**lés**	Jo	Ha-**gués** vo-**lat**
Tu	Vo-**la**-ves	Tu	Ha-**vi**-es vo-**lat**	Tu	Vo-**les**-sis	Tu	Ha-**gues**-sis vo-**lat**
Ell	Vo-**la**-va	Ell	Ha-**vi**-a vo-**lat**	Ell	Vo-**lés**	Ell	Ha-**gués** vo-**lat**
No.	Vo-**là**-vem	Nos.	Ha-**ví**-em vo-**lat**	Nos	Vo-**lés**-sim	Nos.	Ha-**gués**-sim vo-**lat**
Vos.	Vo-**là**-veu	Vos.	Ha-**ví**-eu vo-**lat**	Vos.	Vo-**lés**-siu	Vos.	Ha-**gués**-siu vo-**lat**
Ells	Vo-**la**-ven	Ells	Ha-**vi**-en vo-**lat**	Ells	Vo-**les**-sin	Ells	Ha-**gues**-sin vo-**lat**

Past Simple		Past Perifrastic		Past Anterior perifrastic
Jo	Vo-**lí**	Jo	**Vaig** vo-**lar**	**Vaig** ha-**ver** vo-**lat**
Tu	Vo-**la**-res	Tu	**Vas** vo-lar	**Vas** ha-**ver** vo-**lat**
Ell	Vo-**là**	Ell	**Va** vo-lar	**Va** ha-**ver** vo-**lat**
Nos	Vo-**là**-rem	Nos.	**Vam** vo-lar	**Vam** ha-**ver** vo-**lat**
Vos.	Vo-**là**-reu	Vos.	**Vau** vo-lar	**Vau** ha-**ver** vo-**lat**
Ells	Vo-**la**-ren	Ells	**Van** vo-lar	**Van** ha-**ver** vo-**lat**

Future Simple		Future Compound	
Jo	Vo-la-**ré**	Jo	Hau-**ré** vo-**lat**
Tu	Vo-la-**ràs**	Tu	Hau-**ràs** vo-**lat**
Ell	Vo-la-**rà**	Ell	Hau-**rà** vo-**lat**
Nos.	Vo-la-**rem**	Nos.	Hau-**rem** vo-**lat**
Vos.	Vo-la-**reu**	Vos.	Hau-**reu** vo-**lat**
Ells	Vo-la-**ran**	Ells	Hau-**ran** vo-**lat**

Conditional Simple		Conditional Compound		IMPERATIVE	
Jo	Vo-la-**ri**-a	Jo	Hau-**ri**-a vo-**lat**		
Tu	Vo-la-**ri**-es	Tu	Hau-**ri**-es vo-**lat**	**Vo**-la	(Tu)
Ell	Vo-la-**ri**-a	Ell	Hau-**ri**-a vo-**lat**	**Vo**-li	(Ell)
Nos	Vo-la-**rí**-em	Nos.	Hau-**rí**-em vo-**lat**	**Vo**-lem	(Nos.)
Vos.	Vo-la-**rí**-eu	Vos.	Hau-**rí**-eu vo-**lat**	**Vo**-leu	(Vos.)
Ells	Vo-la-**ri**-en	Ells	Hau-**ri**-en vo-**lat**	**Vo**-lin	(Ells)

IMPERSONAL		
	SIMPLE	**COMPOUND**
Infinitive	Vo-**lar**	Ha-**ver** vo-**lat**
Participle	Vo-**lat**	-
Gerund	Vo-la**nt**	Ha-**vent** vo-**lat**

TO FORGET - OBLIDAR

PERSONAL				
INDICATIVE			**SUBJUNCTIVE**	
SIMPLE	**COMPOUND**		**SIMPLE**	**COMPOUND**

Present		*Past Indefinite*		*Present*		*Past Perfet*	
Jo	O-**bli**-do	Jo	**He** o-bli-da**t**	Jo	O-**bli**-di	Jo	**Ha**-gi o-bli-da**t**
Tu	O-**bli**-des	Tu	**Has** o-bli-da**t**	Tu	O-**bli**-dis	Tu	**Ha**-gis o-bli-da**t**
Ell	O-**bli**-da	Ell	**Ha** o-bli-da**t**	Ell	O-**bli**-di	Ell	**Ha**-gi o-bli-da**t**
No.	O-bli-**dem**	Nos.	**Hem** o-bli-da**t**	Nos.	O-bli-**dem**	Nos.	**Hà**-gim o-bli-da**t**
Vos.	O-bli-**deu**	Vos.	**Heu** o-bli-da**t**	Vos.	O-bli-**deu**	Vos.	**Hà**-giu o-bli-da**t**
Ells	O-**bli**-den	Ells	**Han** o-bli-da**t**	Ells	O-**bli**-din	Ells	**Ha**-gin o-bli-da**t**

Imperfet		*Past Plusquamperfet*		*Imperfet past*		*Plusquamperfet past*	
Jo	O-bli-**da**-va	Jo	Ha-**vi**-a o-bli-da**t**	Jo	O-bli-**dés**	Jo	Ha-**gués** o-bli-da**t**
Tu	O-bli-**da**-ves	Tu	Ha-**vi**-es o-bli-da**t**	Tu	O-bli-**des**-sis	Tu	Ha-**gues**-sis o-bli-da**t**
Ell	O-bli-**da**-va	Ell	Ha-**vi**-a o-bli-da**t**	Ell	O-bli-**dés**	Ell	Ha-**gués** o-bli-da**t**
No.	O-bli-**dà**-vem	Nos.	Ha-**ví**-em o-bli-da**t**	Nos	O-bli-**dés**-sim	Nos.	Ha-**gués**-sim o-bli-da**t**
Vos.	O-bli-**dà**-veu	Vos.	Ha-**ví**-eu o-bli-da**t**	Vos.	O-bli-**dés**-siu	Vos.	Ha-**gués**-siu o-bli-da**t**
Ells	O-bli-**da**-ven	Ells	Ha-**vi**-en o-bli-da**t**	Ells	O-bli-**des**-sin	Ells	Ha-**gues**-sin o-bli-da**t**

Past Simple		*Past Perifrastic*		*Past Anterior perifrastic*
Jo	O-bli-**dí**	Jo	**Vaig** o-bli-dar	**Vaig** ha-**ver** o-bli-da**t**
Tu	O-bli-**da**-res	Tu	**Vas** o-bli-dar	**Vas** ha-**ver** o-bli-da**t**
Ell	O-bli-**dà**	Ell	**Va** o-bli-dar	**Va** ha-**ver** o-bli-da**t**
Nos	O-bli-**dà**-rem	Nos.	**Vam** o-bli-dar	**Vam** ha-**ver** o-bli-da**t**
Vos.	O-bli-**dà**-reu	Vos.	**Vau** o-bli-dar	**Vau** ha-**ver** o-bli-da**t**
Ells	O-bli-**da**-ren	Ells	**Van** o-bli-dar	**Van** ha-**ver** o-bli-da**t**

Future Simple		*Future Compound*	
Jo	O-bli-da-**ré**	Jo	Hau-**ré** o-bli-da**t**
Tu	O-bli-da-**ràs**	Tu	Hau-**ràs** o-bli-da**t**
Ell	O-bli-da-**rà**	Ell	Hau-**rà** o-bli-da**t**
Nos.	O-bli-da-**rem**	Nos.	Hau-**rem** o-bli-da**t**
Vos.	O-bli-da-**reu**	Vos.	Hau-**reu** o-bli-da**t**
Ells	O-bli-da-**ran**	Ells	Hau-**ran** o-bli-da**t**

Conditional Simple		*Conditional Compound*		**IMPERATIVE**	
Jo	O-bli-da-**ri**-a	Jo	Hau-**ri**-a o-bli-da**t**		
Tu	O-bli-da-**ri**-es	Tu	Hau-**ri**-es o-bli-da**t**	O-**bli**-da	(Tu)
Ell	O-bli-da-**ri**-a	Ell	Hau-**ri**-a o-bli-da**t**	O-**bli**-di	(Ell)
Nos	O-bli-da-**rí**-em	Nos.	Hau-**rí**-em o-bli-da**t**	O-bli-**dem**	(Nos.)
Vos.	O-bli-da-**rí**-eu	Vos.	Hau-**rí**-eu o-bli-da**t**	O-bli-**deu**	(Vos.)
Ells	O-bli-da-**ri**-en	Ells	Hau-**ri**-en o-bli-da**t**	O-**bli**-din	(Ells)

IMPERSONAL		
	SIMPLE	**COMPOUND**
Infinitive	O-bli-**dar**	Ha-**ver** o-bli-da**t**
Participle	O-bli-**dat**	-
Gerund	O-bli-**dant**	Ha-**vent** o-bli-da**t**

TO GET UP – AIXECAR-SE*

PERSONAL							

INDICATIVE			SUBJUNCTIVE		
SIMPLE	**COMPOUND**		**SIMPLE**	**COMPOUND**	

SIMPLE — INDICATIVE

Present		*Past Indefinite*		*Present*		*Past Perfet*	
Jo	M'ai-**xe**-co	Jo	**M'he** ai-xe-cat	Jo	M'ai-**xe**-qui	Jo	**M'ha**-gi ai-xe-cat
Tu	T'ai-**xe**-ques	Tu	**T'has** ai-xe-cat	Tu	T'ai-**xe**-quis	Tu	**T'ha**-gis ai-xe-cat
Ell	S'ai-**xe**-ca	Ell	**S'ha** ai-xe-cat	Ell	S'ai-**xe**-qui	Ell	**S'ha**-gi ai-xe-cat
No.	Ens ai-xe-**quem**	Nos.	**Ens hem** ai-xe-cat	Nos.	Ens ai-xe-**quem**	Nos.	**Ens hà**-gim ai-xe-cat
Vos.	Us ai-xe-**queu**	Vos.	**Us heu** ai-xe-cat	Vos.	Us ai-xe-**queu**	Vos.	**Us hà**-giu ai-xe-cat
Ells	S'ai-**xe**-quen	Ells	**S'han** ai-xe-cat	Ells	S'ai-**xe**-quin	Ells	**S'ha**-gin ai-xe-cat

Imperfet		*Past Plusquamperfet*		*Imperfet past*		*Plusquamperfet past*	
Jo	M'ai-xe-**ca**-va	Jo	M'ha-**vi**-a ai-xe-cat	Jo	M'ai-**xe**-**qués**	Jo	M'ha-**gués** ai-xe-cat
Tu	T'ai-xe-**ca**-ves	Tu	T'ha-**vi**-es ai-xe-cat	Tu	T'ai-xe-**ques**-sis	Tu	T'ha-**gues**-sis ai-xe-cat
Ell	S'ai-xe-**ca**-va	Ell	S'ha-**vi**-a ai-xe-cat	Ell	S'ai-xe-**qués**	Ell	S'ha **gués** ai-xe-cat
No.	Ens ai-xe-**cà**-vem	Nos.	**Ens** ha-**ví**-em ai-xe-cat	Nos	Ens ai-xe-**qués**-sim	Nos.	Ens ha-**gués**-sim ai-xe-cat
Vos.	Us ai-xe-**cà**-veu	Vos.	**Us** ha-**ví**-eu ai-xe-cat	Vos.	Us ai-xe-**qués**-siu	Vos.	Us ha-**gués**-siu ai-xe-cat
Ells	S'ai-xe-**ca**-ven	Ells	S'ha-**vi**-en ai-xe-cat	Ells	S'ai-xe-**ques**-sin	Ells	S'ha-**gues**-sin ai-xe-cat

Past Simple		*Past Perifrastic***		*Past Anterior periphrastic***	
Jo	M'ai-xe-**quí**	Jo	**Vaig** ai.xe.car-me	**Vaig** ha.**ver**-me ai.xe.cat	
Tu	T'ai-xe-**ca**-res	Tu	**Vas** ai.xe.car-te	**Vas** ha.**ver**-te ai.xe.cat	
Ell	S'ai-xe-**cà**	Ell	**Va** ai.xe.car-se	**Va** ha.**ver**-se ai.xe.cat	
Nos	Ens ai-xe-**cà**-rem	Nos	**Vam** ai.xe.car-nos	**Vam** ha.**ver**-nos ai.xe.cat	
Vos.	Us ai-xe-**cà**-reu	Vos.	**Vau** ai.xe.car-vos	**Vau** ha.**ver**-vos ai.xe.cat	
Ells	S'ai-xe-**ca**-ren	Ells	**Van** ai.xe.car-se	**Van** ha.**ver**-se ai.xe.cat	

Future Simple		*Future Compound*	
Jo	M'ai-xe-ca-**ré**	Jo	M'hau-**ré** ai-xe-cat
Tu	M'ai-xe-ca-**ràs**	Tu	T'hau-**ràs** ai-xe-cat
Ell	S'ai-xe-ca-**rà**	Ell	S'hau-**rà** ai-xe-cat
Nos.	Ens ai-xe-ca-**rem**	Nos.	**Ens** hau-**rem** ai-xe-cat
Vos.	Us ai-xe-ca-**reu**	Vos.	**Us** hau-**reu** ai-xe-cat
Ells	S'ai-xe-ca-**ran**	Ells	S'hau-**ran** ai-xe-cat

Conditional Simple		*Conditional Compound*		IMPERATIVE**	
Jo	M'ai-xe-ca-**ri**-a	Jo	M'hau-**ri**-a ai-xe-cat		
Tu	T'ai-xe-ca-**ri**-es	Tu	T'hau-**ri**-es ai-xe-cat	Ai-**xe**-ca't	*(Tu)*
Ell	S'ai-xe-ca-**ri**-a	Ell	S'hau-**ri**-a ai-xe-cat	S'ai-**xe**-qui	*(Ell)*
Nos	Ens ai-xe-ca-**rí**-em	Nos.	**Ens** hau-**rí**-em ai-xe-cat	Ai-xe-**quem**-nos	*(Nos.)*
Vos.	Us ai-xe-ca-**rí**-eu	Vos.	**Us** hau-**rí**-eu ai-xe-cat	Ai-xe-**queu**-vos	*(Vos.)*
Ells	S'ai-xe-ca-**ri**-en	Ells	S'hau-**ri**-en ai-xe-cat	S'ai-**xe**-quin	*(Ells)*

IMPERSONAL		
	SIMPLE	**COMPOUND**
Infinitive	Ai.xe.**car**-se	Ha.**ver**-se ai.xe.**cat**
Participle	Ai.xe.**cat**	-
Gerund	Ai.xe.**cant**-se	Ha.**vent**-se ai.xe.**cat**

*Aixecar-se is a reflexive verb, which means that the action takes places on the subject. It is build with the weak pronouns, EM, ET, ES, ENS, US, ES and their variations depending on the place they are written.
** When the pronoun goes behind the word it is attached to it by a hyphen. In this case the syllables are separated with dots, to appreciate the difference.

TO GO - ANAR

PERSONAL							
INDICATIVE				**SUBJUNCTIVE**			
SIMPLE		**COMPOUND**		**SIMPLE**		**COMPOUND**	
Present		*Past Indefinite*		*Present*		*Past Perfet*	
Jo	**Vaig**	Jo	**He** a-**nat**	Jo	**Va**-gi	Jo	**Ha**-gi a-**nat**
Tu	**Vas**	Tu	**Has** a-**nat**	Tu	**Va**-gis	Tu	**Ha**-gis a-**nat**
Ell	**Va**	Ell	**Ha** a-**nat**	Ell	**Va**-gi	Ell	**Ha**-gi a-**nat**
No.	A-**nem**	Nos.	**Hem** a-**nat**	Nos.	A-**nem**	Nos.	**Hà**-gim a-**nat**
Vos.	A-**neu**	Vos.	**Heu** a-**nat**	Vos.	A-**neu**	Vos.	**Hà**-giu a-**nat**
Ells	**Van**	Ells	**Han** a-**nat**	Ells	**Va**-gin	Ells	**Ha**-gin a-**nat**
Imperfet		*Past Plusquamperfet*		*Imperfet past*		*Plusquamperfet past*	
Jo	A-**na**-va	Jo	Ha-**vi**-a a-**nat**	Jo	A-**nés**	Jo	Ha-**gués** a-**nat**
Tu	A-**na**-ves	Tu	Ha-**vi**-es a-**nat**	Tu	A-**nes**-sis	Tu	Ha-**gues**-sis a-**nat**
Ell	A-**na**-va	Ell	Ha-**vi**-a a-**nat**	Ell	A-**nés**	Ell	Ha-**gués** a-**nat**
No.	A-**nà**-vem	Nos.	Ha-**ví**-em a-**nat**	Nos	A-**nés**-sim	Nos.	Ha-**gués**-sim a-**nat**
Vos.	A-**nà**-veu	Vos.	Ha-**ví**-eu a-**nat**	Vos.	A-**nés**-siu	Vos.	Ha-**gués**-siu a-**nat**
Ells	A-**na**-ven	Ells	Ha-**vi**-en a-**nat**	Ells	A-**nes**-sin	Ells	Ha-**gues**-sin a-**nat**

Past Simple		*Past Perifrastic*		*Past Anterior perifrastic*			
Jo	A-**ní**	Jo	**Vaig** a-**nar**	**Vaig** ha-**ver** a-**nat**			
Tu	A-**na**-res	Tu	**Vas** a-**nar**	**Vas** ha-**ver** a-**nat**			
Ell	A-**nà**	Ell	**Va** a-**nar**	**Va** ha-**ver** a-**nat**			
Nos	A-**nà**-rem	Nos.	**Vam** a-**nar**	**Vam** ha-**ver** a-**nat**			
Vos.	A-**nà**-reu	Vos.	**Vau** a-**nar**	**Vau** ha-**ver** a-**nat**			
Ells	A-**na**-ren	Ells	**Van** a-**nar**	**Van** ha-**ver** a-**nat**			

Future Simple		*Future Compound*					
Jo	A-ni-**ré**	Jo	Hau-**ré** a-**nat**				
Tu	A-ni-**ràs**	Tu	Hau-**ràs** a-**nat**				
Ell	A-ni-**rà**	Ell	Hau-**rà** a-**nat**				
Nos.	A-ni-**rem**	Nos.	Hau-**rem** a-**nat**				
Vos.	A-ni-**reu**	Vos.	Hau-**reu** a-**nat**				
Ells	A-ni-**ran**	Ells	Hau-**ran** a-**nat**				

Conditional Simple		*Conditional Compound*		**IMPERATIVE**			
Jo	A-ni-**ri**-a	Jo	Hau-**ri**-a a-**nat**				
Tu	A-ni-**ri**-es	Tu	Hau-**ri**-es a-**nat**	**Vés**		(Tu)	
Ell	A-ni-**ri**-a	Ell	Hau-**ri**-a a-**nat**	**Va**-gi		(Ell)	
Nos	A-ni-**rí**-em	Nos.	Hau-**rí**-em a-**nat**	A-**nem**		(Nos.)	
Vos.	A-ni-**rí**-eu	Vos.	Hau-**rí**-eu a-**nat**	A-**neu**		(Vos.)	
Ells	A-ni-**ri**-en	Ells	Hau-**ri**-en a-**nat**	**Va**-gin		(Ells)	

IMPERSONAL		
	SIMPLE	**COMPOUND**
Infinitive	A-**nar**	Ha-**ver** a-**nat**
Participle	A-**nat**	-
Gerund	A-**nant**	Ha-**vent** a-**nat**

TO HAPPEN – SUCCEIR

PERSONAL					
INDICATIVE			**SUBJUNCTIVE**		
SIMPLE	**COMPOUND**		**SIMPLE**	**COMPOUND**	
Present	*Past Indefinite*		*Present*	*Past Perfet*	
Jo Suc-ce-**ei**-xo	Jo **He** suc-ce-**ï**t		Jo Suc-ce-**ei**-xi	Jo **Ha**-gi suc-ce-**ï**t	
Tu Suc-ce-**ei**-xes	Tu **Has** suc-ce-**ï**t		Tu Suc-ce-**ei**-xis	Tu **Ha**-gis suc-ce-**ï**t	
Ell Suc-ce-**eix**	Ell **Ha** suc-ce-**ï**t		Ell Suc-ce-**ei**-xi	Ell **Ha**-gi suc-ce-**ï**t	
No. Suc-ce-**ïm**	Nos **Hem** suc-ce-**ï**t		Nos Suc-ce-**ïm**	Nos **Hà**-gim suc-ce-**ï**t	
Vos. Suc-ce-**ïu**	Vos. **Heu** suc-ce-**ï**t		Vos. Suc-ce-**ïu**	Vos. **Hà**-giu suc-ce-**ï**t	
Ells Suc-ce-**ei**-xen	Ells **Han** suc-ce-**ï**t		Ells Suc-ce-**ei**-xin	Ells **Ha**-gin suc-ce-**ï**t	
Imperfet	*Past Plusquamperfet*		*Imperfet past*	*Plusquamperfet past*	
Jo Suc-ce-**i**-a	Jo Ha-**vi**-a suc-ce-**ï**t		Jo Suc-ce-**ís**	Jo Ha-**gués** suc-ce-**ï**t	
Tu Suc-ce-**i**-es	Tu Ha-**vi**-es suc-ce-**ï**t		Tu Suc-ce-**ïs**-sis	Tu Ha-**gues**-sis suc-ce-**ï**t	
Ell Suc-ce-**i**-a	Ell Ha-**vi**-a suc-ce-**ï**t		Ell Suc-ce-**ís**	Ell Ha-**gués** suc-ce-**ï**t	
No. Suc-ce-**í**-em	Nos Ha-**ví**-em suc-ce-**ï**t		Nos Suc-ce-**ís**-sim	Nos Ha-**gués**-sim suc-ce-**ï**t	
Vos. Suc-ce-**í**-eu	Vos. Ha-**ví**-eu suc-ce-**ï**t		Vos. Suc-ce-**ís**-siu	Vos. Ha-**gués**-siu suc-ce-**ï**t	
Ells Suc-ce-**i**-en	Ells Ha-**vi**-en suc-ce-**ï**t		Ells Suc-ce-**ïs**-sin	Ells Ha-**gues**-sin suc-ce-**ï**t	

Past Simple	*Past Perifrastic*	*Past Anterior perifrastic*
Jo Suc-ce-**í**	Jo **Vaig** suc-ce-**ir**	**Vaig** ha-**ver** suc-ce-**ï**t
Tu Suc-ce-**í**-res	Tu **Vas** suc-ce-**ir**	**Vas** ha-**ver** suc-ce-**ï**t
Ell Suc-ce-**í**	Ell **Va** suc-ce-**ir**	**Va** ha-**ver** suc-ce-**ï**t
Nos Suc-ce-**í**-rem	Nos. **Vam** suc-ce-**ir**	**Vam** ha-**ver** suc-ce-**ï**t
Vos. Suc-ce-**í**-reu	Vos. **Vau** suc-ce-**ir**	**Vau** ha-**ver** suc-ce-**ï**t
Ells Suc-ce-**í**-ren	Ells **Van** suc-ce-**ir**	**Van** ha-**ver** suc-ce-**ï**t

Future Simple	*Future Compound*
Jo Suc-ce-i-**ré**	Jo Hau-**ré** suc-ce-**ï**t
Tu Suc-ce-i-**ràs**	Tu Hau-**ràs** suc-ce-**ï**t
Ell Suc-ce-i-**rà**	Ell Hau-**rà** suc-ce-**ï**t
Nos. Suc-ce-i-**rem**	Nos. Hau-**rem** suc-ce-**ï**t
Vos. Suc-ce-i-**reu**	Vos. Hau-**reu** suc-ce-**ï**t
Ells Suc-ce-i-**ran**	Ells Hau-**ran** suc-ce-**ï**t

Conditional Simple	*Conditional Compound*	**IMPERATIVE**	
Jo Suc-ce-i-**ri**-a	Jo Hau-**ri**-a suc-ce-**ï**t		
Tu Suc-ce-i-**ri**-es	Tu Hau-**ri**-es suc-ce-**ï**t	Suc-ce-**eix**	(Tu)
Ell Suc-ce-i-**ri**-a	Ell Hau-**ri**-a suc-ce-**ï**t	Suc-ce-**ei**-xi	(Ell)
Nos Suc-ce-i-**rí**-em	Nos. Hau-**rí**-em suc-ce-**ï**t	Suc-ce-**ïm**	(Nos.)
Vos. Suc-ce-i-**rí**-eu	Vos. Hau-**rí**-eu suc-ce-**ï**t	Suc-ce-**ïu**	(Vos.)
Ells Suc-ce-i-**ri**-en	Ells Hau-**ri**-en suc-ce-**ï**t	Suc-ce-**ei**-xin	(Ells)

IMPERSONAL		
	SIMPLE	**COMPOUND**
Infinitive	Suc-ce-**ir**	Ha-**ver** suc-ce-**ï**t
Participle	Suc-ce-**ï**t	-
Gerund	Suc-ce-**int**	Ha-**vent** suc-ce-**ï**t

TO HAVE – HAVER (Auxiliary Verb)

PERSONAL							
INDICATIVE				SUBJUNCTIVE			
SIMPLE		COMPOUND		SIMPLE		COMPOUND	
Present		*Past Indefinite*		*Present*		*Past Perfet*	
Jo	**Haig / he**	Jo	**He** ha-**gut**	Jo	**Ha**-gi	Jo	**Ha**-gi ha-**gut**
Tu	**Has**	Tu	**Has** ha-**gut**	Tu	**Ha**-gis	Tu	**Ha**-gis ha-**gut**
Ell	**Ha**	Ell	**Ha** ha-**gut**	Ell	**Ha**-gi	Ell	**Ha**-gi ha-**gut**
No.	**Hem**	Nos	**Hem** ha-**gut**	Nos	**Hà**-gim	Nos	**Hà**-gim ha-**gut**
Vos.	**Heu**	Vos.	**Heu** ha-**gut**	Vos.	**Hà**-giu	Vos.	**Hà**-giu ha-**gut**
Ells	**Han**	Ells	**Han** ha-**gut**	Ells	**Ha**-gin	Ells	**Ha**-gin ha-**gut**
Imperfet		*Past Plusquamperfet*		*Imperfet past*		*Plusquamperfet past*	
Jo	Ha-**vi**-a	Jo	Ha-**vi**-a ha-**gut**	Jo	Ha-**gués**	Jo	Ha-**gués** ha-**gut**
Tu	Ha-**vi**-es	Tu	Ha-**vi**-es ha-**gut**	Tu	Ha-**gues**-sis	Tu	Ha-**gues**-sis ha-**gut**
Ell	Ha-**vi**-a	Ell	Ha-**vi**-a ha-**gut**	Ell	Ha-**gués**	Ell	Ha-**gués** ha-**gut**
No.	Ha-**ví**-em	Nos	Ha-**ví**-em ha-**gut**	Nos	Ha-**gués**-sim	Nos	Ha-**gués**-sim ha-**gut**
Vos.	Ha-**ví**-eu	Vos.	Ha-**ví**-eu ha-**gut**	Vos.	Ha-**gués**-siu	Vos.	Ha-**gués**-siu ha-**gut**
Ells	Ha-**vi**-en	Ells	Ha-**vi**-en ha-**gut**	Ells	Ha-**gues**-sin	Ells	Ha-**gues**-sin ha-**gut**

Past Simple		*Past Perifrastic*		*Past Anterior perifrastic*
Jo	Ha-**guí**	Jo	**Vaig** suc-ce-**ir**	**Vaig** ha-**ver** ha-**gut**
Tu	Ha-**gue**-res	Tu	**Vas** suc-ce-**ir**	**Vas** ha-**ver** ha-**gut**
Ell	Ha-**gué**	Ell	**Va** suc-ce-**ir**	**Va** ha-**ver** ha-**gut**
Nos	Ha-**gué**-rem	Nos.	**Vam** suc-ce-**ir**	**Vam** ha-**ver** ha-**gut**
Vos.	Ha-**gué**-reu	Vos.	**Vau** suc-ce-**ir**	**Vau** ha-**ver** ha-**gut**
Ells	Ha-**gue**-ren	Ells	**Van** suc-ce-**ir**	**Van** ha-**ver** ha-**gut**

Future Simple		*Future Compound*	
Jo	Hau-**ré**	Jo	Hau-**ré** ha-**gut**
Tu	Hau-**ràs**	Tu	Hau-**ràs** ha-**gut**
Ell	Hau-**rà**	Ell	Hau-**rà** ha-**gut**
Nos.	Hau-**rem**	Nos.	Hau-**rem** ha-**gut**
Vos.	Hau-**reu**	Vos.	Hau-**reu** ha-**gut**
Ells	Hau-**ran**	Ells	Hau-**ran** ha-**gut**

Conditional Simple		*Conditional Compound*		IMPERATIVE
Jo	Hau-**ri**-a	Jo	Hau-**ri**-a ha-**gut**	
Tu	Hau-**ri**-es	Tu	Hau-**ri**-es ha-**gut**	*(Tu)*
Ell	Hau-**ri**-a	Ell	Hau-**ri**-a ha-**gut**	*(Ell)*
Nos	Hau-**rí**-em	Nos.	Hau-**rí**-em ha-**gut**	*(Nos.)*
Vos.	Hau-**rí**-eu	Vos.	Hau-**rí**-eu ha-**gut**	*(Vos.)*
Ells	Hau-**ri**-en	Ells	Hau-**ri**-en ha-**gut**	*(Ells)*

IMPERSONAL		
	SIMPLE	COMPOUND
Infinitive	Ha-**ver**	Ha-**ver** ha-**gut**
Participle	Ha-**gut**	-
Gerund	Ha-**vent**	Ha-**vent** ha-**gut**

TO HAVE – TENIR (To have something/To Possess)

PERSONAL						
INDICATITE				**SUBJUNCTITE**		
SIMPLE		**COMPOUND**		**SIMPLE**		**COMPOUND**
Present		*Past Indefinite*		*Present*		*Past Perfet*
Jo	**Tinc**	Jo	**He** tin-**gut**	Jo	**Tin**-gui	Jo	**Ha**-gi tin-**gut**
Tu	**Tens**	Tu	**Has** tin-**gut**	Tu	**Tin**-guis	Tu	**Ha**-gis tin-**gut**
Ell	**Té**	Ell	**Ha** tin-**gut**	Ell	**Tin**-gui	Ell	**Ha**-gi tin-**gut**
No.	Te-**nim**	Nos.	**Hem** tin-**gut**	Nos.	**Tin**-guem	Nos.	**Hà**-gim tin-**gut**
Vos.	Te-**niu**	Vos.	**Heu** tin-**gut**	Vos.	**Tin**-gueu	Vos.	**Hà**-giu tin-**gut**
Ells	**Té**-nen	Ells	**Han** tin-**gut**	Ells	**Tin**-guin	Ells	**Ha**-gin tin-**gut**

Imperfet		*Past Plusquamperfet*		*Imperfet past*		*Plusquamperfet past*
Jo	Te-**ni**-a	Jo	Ha-**vi**-a tin-**gut**	Jo	**Tin**-gués	Jo	Ha-**gués** tin-**gut**
Tu	Te-**ni**-es	Tu	Ha-**vi**-es tin-**gut**	Tu	**Tin**-gues-sis	Tu	Ha-**gues**-sis tin-**gut**
Ell	Te-**ni**-a	Ell	Ha-**vi**-a tin-**gut**	Ell	**Tin**-gués	Ell	Ha-**gués** tin-**gut**
No.	Te-**ní**-em	Nos.	Ha-**ví**-em tin-**gut**	Nos	**Tin**-gués-sim	Nos.	Ha-**gués**-sim tin-**gut**
Vos.	Te-**ní**-eu	Vos.	Ha-**ví**-eu tin-**gut**	Vos.	**Tin**-gués-siu	Vos.	Ha-**gués**-siu tin-**gut**
Ells	Te-**ni**-en	Ells	Ha-**vi**-en tin-**gut**	Ells	**Tin**-gues-sin	Ells	Ha-**gues**-sin tin-**gut**

Past Simple		*Past Perifrastic*		*Past Anterior perifrastic*
Jo	Tin-**guí**	Jo	**Vaig** te-**nir**	**Vaig** ha-**ter** tin-**gut**
Tu	Tin-**gue**-res	Tu	**Vas** te-**nir**	**Vas** ha-**ter** tin-**gut**
Ell	Tin-**gué**	Ell	**Va** te-**nir**	**Va** ha-**ter** tin-**gut**
Nos	Tin-**gué**-rem	Nos.	**Vam** te-**nir**	**Vam** ha-**ter** tin-**gut**
Vos.	Tin-**gué**-reu	Vos.	**Vau** te-**nir**	**Vau** ha-**ter** tin-**gut**
Ells	Tin-**gue**-ren	Ells	**Van** te-**nir**	**Van** ha-**ter** tin-**gut**

Future Simple		*Future Compound*	
Jo	Tin-**dré**	Jo	Hau-**ré** tin-**gut**
Tu	Tin-**dràs**	Tu	Hau-**ràs** tin-**gut**
Ell	Tin-**drà**	Ell	Hau-**rà** tin-**gut**
Nos.	Tin-**drem**	Nos.	Hau-**rem** tin-**gut**
Vos.	Tin-**dreu**	Vos.	Hau-**reu** tin-**gut**
Ells	Tin-**dran**	Ells	Hau-**ran** tin-**gut**

Conditional Simple		*Conditional Compound*		**IMPERATITE**	
Jo	Tin-**dri**-a	Jo	Hau-**ri**-a tin-**gut**		
Tu	Tin-**dri**-es	Tu	Hau-**ri**-es tin-**gut**	**Tin**-guis (té)	(Tu)
Ell	Tin-**dri**-a	Ell	Hau-**ri**-a tin-**gut**	**Tin**-gui	(Ell)
Nos	Tin-**drí**-em	Nos.	Hau-**rí**-em tin-**gut**	Tin-**guem**	(Nos.)
Vos.	Tin-**drí**-eu	Vos.	Hau-**rí**-eu tin-**gut**	Te-**niu**	(Vos.)
Ells	Tin-**dri**-en	Ells	Hau-**ri**-en tin-**gut**	**Tin**-guin	(Ells)

IMPERSONAL		
	SIMPLE	**COMPOUND**
Infinitite	Te-**nir**	Ha-**ter** tin-**gut**
Participle	Tin-**gut**	-
Gerund	Te-**nint**	Ha-**tent** tin-**gut**

TO HEAR - SENTIR

PERSONAL							
INDICATIVE				SUBJUNCTIVE			
SIMPLE		COMPOUND		SIMPLE		COMPOUND	
Present		*Past Indefinite*		*Present*		*Past Perfet*	
Jo	**Sen**-to	Jo	**He** sen-**tit**	Jo	**Sen**-ti	Jo	**Ha**-gi sen-**tit**
Tu	**Sents**	Tu	**Has** sen-**tit**	Tu	**Sen**-tis	Tu	**Ha**-gis sen-**tit**
Ell	**Sent**	Ell	**Ha** sen-**tit**	Ell	**Sen**-ti	Ell	**Ha**-gi sen-**tit**
No.	Sen-**tim**	Nos.	**Hem** sen-**tit**	Nos.	Sen-**tim**	Nos.	**Hà**-gim sen-**tit**
Vos.	Sen-**tiu**	Vos.	**Heu** sen-**tit**	Vos.	Sen-**tiu**	Vos.	**Hà**-giu sen-**tit**
Ells	**Sen**-ten	Ells	**Han** sen-**tit**	Ells	**Sen**-tin	Ells	**Ha**-gin sen-**tit**
Imperfet		*Past Plusquamperfet*		*Imperfet past*		*Plusquamperfet past*	
Jo	Sen-**ti**-a	Jo	**Ha**-**vi**-a sen-**tit**	Jo	Sen-**tís**	Jo	**Ha**-**gués** sen-**tit**
Tu	Sen-**ti**-es	Tu	**Ha**-**vi**-es sen-**tit**	Tu	Sen-**tis**-sis	Tu	**Ha**-**gues**-sis sen-**tit**
Ell	Sen-**ti**-a	Ell	**Ha**-**vi**-a sen-**tit**	Ell	Sen-**tís**	Ell	**Ha**-**gués** sen-**tit**
No.	Sen-**tí**-em	Nos.	**Ha**-**ví**-em sen-**tit**	Nos	Sen-**tís**-sim	Nos.	**Ha**-**gués**-sim sen-**tit**
Vos.	Sen-**tí**-eu	Vos.	**Ha**-**ví**-eu sen-**tit**	Vos.	Sen-**tís**-siu	Vos.	**Ha**-**gués**-siu sen-**tit**
Ells	Sen-**ti**-en	Ells	**Ha**-**vi**-en sen-**tit**	Ells	Sen-**tis**-sin	Ells	**Ha**-**gues**-sin sen-**tit**

Past Simple		*Past Perifrastic*		*Past Anterior perifrastic*			
Jo	Sen-**tí**	Jo	**Vaig** sen-**tir**	**Vaig** ha-**ver** sen-**tit**			
Tu	Sen-**ti**-res	Tu	**Vas** sen-**tir**	**Vas** ha-**ver** sen-**tit**			
Ell	Sen-**tí**	Ell	**Va** sen-**tir**	**Va** ha-**ver** sen-**tit**			
Nos	Sen-**tí**-rem	Nos.	**Vam** sen-**tir**	**Vam** ha-**ver** sen-**tit**			
Vos.	Sen-**tí**-reu	Vos.	**Vau** sen-**tir**	**Vau** ha-**ver** sen-**tit**			
Ells	Sen-**ti**-ren	Ells	**Van** sen-**tir**	**Van** ha-**ver** sen-**tit**			

Future Simple		*Future Compound*					
Jo	Sen-ti-**ré**	Jo	Hau-**ré** sen-**tit**				
Tu	Sen-ti-**ràs**	Tu	Hau-**ràs** sen-**tit**				
Ell	Sen-ti-**rà**	Ell	Hau-**rà** sen-**tit**				
Nos.	Sen-ti-**rem**	Nos.	Hau-**rem** sen-**tit**				
Vos.	Sen-ti-**reu**	Vos.	Hau-**reu** sen-**tit**				
Ells	Sen-ti-**ran**	Ells	Hau-**ran** sen-**tit**				

Conditional Simple		*Conditional Compound*		IMPERATIVE			
Jo	Sen-ti-**ri**-a	Jo	Hau-**ri**-a sen-**tit**				
Tu	Sen-ti-**ri**-es	Tu	Hau-**ri**-es sen-**tit**	**Sent**		(Tu)	
Ell	Sen-ti-**ri**-a	Ell	Hau-**ri**-a sen-**tit**	**Sen**-ti		(Ell)	
Nos	Sen-ti-**rí**-em	Nos.	Hau-**rí**-em sen-**tit**	Sen-**tim**		(Nos.)	
Vos.	Sen-ti-**rí**-eu	Vos.	Hau-**rí**-eu sen-**tit**	Sen-**tiu**		(Vos.)	
Ells	Sen-ti-**ri**-en	Ells	Hau-**ri**-en sen-**tit**	**Sen**-tin		(Ells)	

IMPERSONAL		
	SIMPLE	COMPOUND
Infinitive	Sen-**tir**	Ha-**ver** sen-**tit**
Participle	Sen-**tit**	-
Gerund	Sen-**tint**	Ha-**vent** sen-**tit**

TO HELP - AJUDAR

PERSONAL				
INDICATIVE			**SUBJUNCTIVE**	
SIMPLE	**COMPOUND**		**SIMPLE**	**COMPOUND**

Present		Past Indefinite		Present		Past Perfet	
Jo	A-**ju**-do	Jo	**He** a-ju-d**at**	Jo	A-**ju**-di	Jo	**Ha**-gi a-ju-d**at**
Tu	A-**ju**-des	Tu	**Has** a-ju-d**at**	Tu	A-**ju**-dis	Tu	**Ha**-gis a-ju-d**at**
Ell	A-**ju**-da	Ell	**Ha** a-ju-d**at**	Ell	A-**ju**-di	Ell	**Ha**-gi a-ju-d**at**
No.	A-ju-**dem**	Nos.	**Hem** a-ju-d**at**	Nos.	A-ju-**dem**	Nos.	**Hà**-gim a-ju-d**at**
Vos.	A-ju-**deu**	Vos.	**Heu** a-ju-d**at**	Vos.	A-ju-**deu**	Vos.	**Hà**-giu a-ju-d**at**
Ells	A-**ju**-den	Ells	**Han** a-ju-d**at**	Ells	A-**ju**-din	Ells	**Ha**-gin a-ju-d**at**

Imperfet		Past Plusquamperfet		Imperfet past		Plusquamperfet past	
Jo	A-ju-**da**-va	Jo	Ha-**vi**-a a-ju-d**at**	Jo	A-ju-**dés**	Jo	Ha-**gués** a-ju-d**at**
Tu	A-ju-**da**-ves	Tu	Ha-**vi**-es a-ju-d**at**	Tu	A-ju-**des**-sis	Tu	Ha-**gues**-sis a-ju-d**at**
Ell	A-ju-**da**-va	Ell	Ha-**vi**-a a-ju-d**at**	Ell	A-ju-**dés**	Ell	Ha-**gués** a-ju-d**at**
No.	A-ju-**dà**-vem	Nos.	Ha-**ví**-em a-ju-d**at**	Nos	A-ju-**dés**-sim	Nos.	Ha-**gués**-sim a-ju-d**at**
Vos.	A-ju-**dà**-veu	Vos.	Ha-**ví**-eu a-ju-d**at**	Vos.	A-ju-**dés**-siu	Vos.	Ha-**gués**-siu a-ju-d**at**
Ells	A-ju-**da**-ven	Ells	Ha-**vi**-en a-ju-d**at**	Ells	A-ju-**des**-sin	Ells	Ha-**gués**-sin a-ju-d**at**

Past Simple		Past Perifrastic		Past Anterior perifrastic
Jo	A-ju-**dí**	Jo	**Vaig** a-ju-dar	**Vaig** ha-**ver** a-ju-d**at**
Tu	A-ju-**da**-res	Tu	**Vas** a-ju-dar	**Vas** ha-**ver** a-ju-d**at**
Ell	A-ju-**dà**	Ell	**Va** a-ju-dar	**Va** ha-**ver** a-ju-d**at**
Nos	A-ju-**dà**-rem	Nos.	**Vam** a-ju-dar	**Vam** ha-**ver** a-ju-d**at**
Vos.	A-ju-**dà**-reu	Vos.	**Vau** a-ju-dar	**Vau** ha-**ver** a-ju-d**at**
Ells	A-ju-**da**-ren	Ells	**Van** a-ju-dar	**Van** ha-**ver** a-ju-d**at**

Future Simple		Future Compound	
Jo	A-ju-da-**ré**	Jo	Hau-**ré** a-ju-d**at**
Tu	A-ju-da-**ràs**	Tu	Hau-**ràs** a-ju-d**at**
Ell	A-ju-da-**rà**	Ell	Hau-**rà** a-ju-d**at**
Nos.	A-ju-da-**rem**	Nos.	Hau-**rem** a-ju-d**at**
Vos.	A-ju-da-**reu**	Vos.	Hau-**reu** a-ju-d**at**
Ells	A-ju-da-**ran**	Ells	Hau-**ran** a-ju-d**at**

Conditional Simple		Conditional Compound		IMPERATIVE	
Jo	A-ju-da-**ri**-a	Jo	Hau-**ri**-a a-ju-d**at**		
Tu	A-ju-da-**ri**-es	Tu	Hau-**ri**-es a-ju-d**at**	A-**ju**-da	(Tu)
Ell	A-ju-da-**ri**-a	Ell	Hau-**ri**-a a-ju-d**at**	A-**ju**-di	(Ell)
Nos	A-ju-da-**rí**-em	Nos.	Hau-**rí**-em a-ju-d**at**	A-**ju**-dem	(Nos.)
Vos.	A-ju-da-**rí**-eu	Vos.	Hau-**rí**-eu a-ju-d**at**	A-**ju**-deu	(Vos.)
Ells	A-ju-da-**ri**-en	Ells	Hau-**ri**-en a-ju-d**at**	A-**ju**-din	(Ells)

IMPERSONAL		
	SIMPLE	**COMPOUND**
Infinitive	A-ju-**dar**	Ha-**ver** a-ju-d**at**
Participle	A-ju-d**at**	-
Gerund	A-ju-**dant**	Ha-**vent** a-ju-d**at**

TO HOLD - AGUANTAR

PERSONAL							
INDICATIVE				**SUBJUNCTIVE**			
SIMPLE		**COMPOUND**		**SIMPLE**		**COMPOUND**	
Present		*Past Indefinite*		*Present*		*Past Perfet*	
Jo	A-**guan**-to	Jo	**He** a-guan-**tat**	Jo	A-**guan**-ti	Jo	**Ha**-gi a-guan-**tat**
Tu	A-**guan**-tes	Tu	**Has** a-guan-**tat**	Tu	A-**guan**-tis	Tu	**Ha**-gis a-guan-**tat**
Ell	A-**guan**-ta	Ell	**Ha** a-guan-**tat**	Ell	A-**guan**-ti	Ell	**Ha**-gi a-guan-**tat**
No.	A-guan-**tem**	Nos.	**Hem** a-guan-**tat**	Nos.	A-guan-**tem**	Nos.	**Hà**-gim a-guan-**tat**
Vos.	A-guan-**teu**	Vos.	**Heu** a-guan-**tat**	Vos.	A-guan-**teu**	Vos.	**Hà**-giu a-guan-**tat**
Ells	A-**guan**-ten	Ells	**Han** a-guan-**tat**	Ells	A-**guan**-tin	Ells	**Ha**-gin a-guan-**tat**
Imperfet		*Past Plusquamperfet*		*Imperfet past*		*Plusquamperfet past*	
Jo	A-guan-**ta**-va	Jo	Ha-**vi**-a a-guan-**tat**	Jo	A-guan-**tés**	Jo	Ha-**gués** a-guan-**tat**
Tu	A-guan-**ta**-ves	Tu	Ha-**vi**-es a-guan-**tat**	Tu	A-guan-**tes**-sis	Tu	Ha-**gues**-sis a-guan-**tat**
Ell	A-guan-**ta**-va	Ell	Ha-**vi**-a a-guan-**tat**	Ell	A-guan-**tés**	Ell	Ha-**gués** a-guan-**tat**
No.	A-guan-**tà**-vem	Nos.	Ha-**ví**-em a-guan-**tat**	Nos	A-guan-**tés**-sim	Nos.	Ha-**gués**-sim a-guan-**tat**
Vos.	A-guan-**tà**-veu	Vos.	Ha-**ví**-eu a-guan-**tat**	Vos.	A-guan-**tés**-siu	Vos.	Ha-**gués**-siu a-guan-**tat**
Ells	A-guan-**ta**-ven	Ells	Ha-**vi**-en a-guan-**tat**	Ells	A-guan-**tes**-sin	Ells	Ha-**gues**-sin a-guan-**tat**

Past Simple		*Past Perifrastic*		*Past Anterior perifrastic*
Jo	A-guan-**tí**	Jo	**Vaig** a-guan-**tar**	**Vaig** ha-**ver** a-guan-**tat**
Tu	A-guan-**ta**-res	Tu	**Vas** a-guan-**tar**	**Vas** ha-**ver** a-guan-**tat**
Ell	A-guan-**tà**	Ell	**Va** a-guan-**tar**	**Va** ha-**ver** a-guan-**tat**
Nos	A-guan-**tà**-rem	Nos.	**Vam** a-guan-**tar**	**Vam** ha-**ver** a-guan-**tat**
Vos.	A-guan-**tà**-reu	Vos.	**Vau** a-guan-**tar**	**Vau** ha-**ver** a-guan-**tat**
Ells	A-guan-**ta**-ren	Ells	**Van** a-guan-**tar**	**Van** ha-**ver** a-guan-**tat**

Future Simple		*Future Compound*	
Jo	A-guan-ta-**ré**	Jo	Hau-**ré** a-guan-**tat**
Tu	A-guan-ta-**ràs**	Tu	Hau-**ràs** a-guan-**tat**
Ell	A-guan-ta-**rà**	Ell	Hau-**rà** a-guan-**tat**
Nos.	A-guan-ta-**rem**	Nos.	Hau-**rem** a-guan-**tat**
Vos.	A-guan-ta-**reu**	Vos.	Hau-**reu** a-guan-**tat**
Ells	A-guan-ta-**ran**	Ells	Hau-**ran** a-guan-**tat**

Conditional Simple		*Conditional Compound*		**IMPERATIVE**	
Jo	A-guan-ta-**ri**-a	Jo	Hau-**ri**-a a-guan-**tat**		
Tu	A-guan-ta-**ri**-es	Tu	Hau-**ri**-es a-guan-**tat**	A-**guan**-ta	(Tu)
Ell	A-guan-ta-**ri**-a	Ell	Hau-**ri**-a a-guan-**tat**	A-**guan**-ti	(Ell)
Nos	A-guan-ta-**rí**-em	Nos.	Hau-**rí**-em a-guan-**tat**	A-guan-**tem**	(Nos.)
Vos.	A-guan-ta-**rí**-eu	Vos.	Hau-**rí**-eu a-guan-**tat**	A-guan-**teu**	(Vos.)
Ells	A-guan-ta-**ri**-en	Ells	Hau-**ri**-en a-guan-**tat**	A-**guan**-tin	(Ells)

IMPERSONAL		
	SIMPLE	**COMPOUND**
Infinitive	A-guan-**tar**	Ha-**ver** a-guan-**tat**
Participle	A-guan-**tat**	-
Gerund	A-guan-t**ant**	Ha-**vent** a-guan-**tat**

TO INCREASE - AUGMENTAR

PERSONAL							
INDICATIVE				**SUBJUNCTIVE**			
SIMPLE		**COMPOUND**		**SIMPLE**		**COMPOUND**	
Present		*Past Indefinite*		*Present*		*Past Perfet*	
Jo	Aug-**men**-to	Jo	**He** aug-men-**tat**	Jo	Aug-**men**-ti	Jo	**Ha**-gi aug-men-**tat**
Tu	Aug-**men**-tes	Tu	**Has** aug-men-**tat**	Tu	Aug-**men**-tis	Tu	**Ha**-gis aug-men-**tat**
Ell	Aug-**men**-ta	Ell	**Ha** aug-men-**tat**	Ell	Aug-**men**-ti	Ell	**Ha**-gi aug-men-**tat**
No.	Aug-men-**tem**	Nos.	**Hem** aug-men-**tat**	Nos.	Aug-men-**tem**	Nos	**Hà**-gim aug-men-**tat**
Vos.	Aug-men-**teu**	Vos.	**Heu** aug-men-**tat**	Vos.	Aug-men-**teu**	Vos.	**Hà**-giu aug-men-**tat**
Ells	Aug-**men**-ten	Ells	**Han** aug-men-**tat**	Ells	Aug-**men**-tin	Ells	**Ha**-gin aug-men-**tat**
Imperfet		*Past Plusquamperfet*		*Imperfet past*		*Plusquamperfet past*	
Jo	Aug-men-**ta**-va	Jo	Ha-**vi**-a aug-men-**tat**	Jo	Aug-men-**tés**	Jo	Ha-**gués** aug-men-**tat**
Tu	Aug-men-**ta**-ves	Tu	Ha-**vi**-es aug-men-**tat**	Tu	Aug-men-**tes**-sis	Tu	Ha-**gues**-sis aug-men-**tat**
Ell	Aug-men-**ta**-va	Ell	Ha-**vi**-a aug-men-**tat**	Ell	Aug-men-**tés**	Ell	Ha-**gués** aug-men-**tat**
Nos	Aug-men-**tà**-vem	Nos.	Ha-**ví**-em aug-men-**tat**	Nos	Aug-men-**tés**-sim	Nos	Ha-**gués**-sim aug-men-**tat**
Vos.	Aug-men-**tà**-veu	Vos.	Ha-**ví**-eu aug-men-**tat**	Vos.	Aug-men-**tés**-siu	Vos.	Ha-**gués**-siu aug-men-**tat**
Ells	Aug-men-**ta**-ven	Ells	Ha-**vi**-en aug-men-**tat**	Ells	Aug-men-**tes**-sin	Ells	Ha-**gués**-sin aug-men-**tat**

Past Simple		*Past Perifrastic*		*Past Anterior perifrastic*
Jo	Aug-men-**tí**	Jo	**Vaig** aug-men-**tar**	**Vaig** ha-**ver** aug-men-**tat**
Tu	Aug-men-**ta**-res	Tu	**Vas** aug-men-**tar**	**Vas** ha-**ver** aug-men-**tat**
Ell	Aug-men-**tà**	Ell	**Va** aug-men-**tar**	**Va** ha-**ver** aug-men-**tat**
Nos	Aug-men-**tà**-rem	No	**Vam** aug-men-**tar**	**Vam** ha-**ver** aug-men-**tat**
Vos.	Aug-men-**tà**-reu	Vo	**Vau** aug-men-**tar**	**Vau** ha-**ver** aug-men-**tat**
Ells	Aug-men-**ta**-ren	Ells	**Van** aug-men-**tar**	**Van** ha-**ver** aug-men-**tat**

Future Simple		*Future Compound*	
Jo	Aug-men-ta-**ré**	Jo	Hau-**ré** aug-men-**tat**
Tu	Aug-men-ta-**ràs**	Tu	Hau-**ràs** aug-men-**tat**
Ell	Aug-men-ta-**rà**	Ell	Hau-**rà** aug-men-**tat**
Nos	Aug-men-ta-**rem**	Nos.	Hau-**rem** aug-men-**tat**
Vos.	Aug-men-ta-**reu**	Vos.	Hau-**reu** aug-men-**tat**
Ells	Aug-men-ta-**ran**	Ells	Hau-**ran** aug-men-**tat**

Conditional Simple		*Conditional Compound*		**IMPERATIVE**	
Jo	Aug-men-ta-**ri**-a	Jo	Hau-**ri**-a aug-men-**tat**		
Tu	Aug-men-ta-**ri**-es	Tu	Hau-**ri**-es aug-men-**tat**	Aug-**men**-ta	(Tu)
Ell	Aug-men-ta-**ri**-a	Ell	Hau-**ri**-a aug-men-**tat**	Aug-**men**-ti	(Ell)
Nos	Aug-men-ta-**rí**-em	Nos.	Hau-**rí**-em aug-men-**tat**	Aug-men-**tem**	(Nos.)
Vos.	Aug-men-ta-**rí**-eu	Vos.	Hau-**rí**-eu aug-men-**tat**	Aug-men-**teu**	(Vos.)
Ells	Aug-men-ta-**ri**-en	Ells	Hau-**ri**-en aug-men-**tat**	Aug-**men**-tin	(Ells)

IMPERSONAL		
	SIMPLE	**COMPOUND**
Infinitive	Aug-men-**tar**	Ha-**ver** aug-men-**tat**
Participle	Aug-men-**tat**	-
Gerund	Aug-men-t**ant**	Ha-**vent** aug-men-**tat**

TO INTRODUCE (Something) - INTRODUIR

PERSONAL					
INDICATIVE			**SUBJUNCTIVE**		
SIMPLE	**COMPOUND**		**SIMPLE**	**COMPOUND**	
Present	*Past Indefinite*		*Present*	*Past Perfet*	
Jo Intro-du-**ei**-xo	Jo **He** intro-du-**ït**		Jo Intro-du-**ei**-xi	Jo **Ha**-gi intro-du-**ït**	
Tu Intro-du-**ei**-xes	Tu **Has** intro-du-**ït**		Tu Intro-du-**ei**-xis	Tu **Ha**-gis intro-du-**ït**	
Ell Intro-du-**eix**	Ell **Ha** intro-du-**ït**		Ell Intro-du-**ei**-xi	Ell **Ha**-gi intro-du-**ït**	
No. Intro-du-**ïm**	Nos **Hem** intro-du-**ït**		Nos Intro-du-**ïm**	Nos **Hà**-gim intro-du-**ït**	
Vos. Intro-du-**ïu**	Vos. **Heu** intro-du-**ït**		Vos. Intro-du-**ïu**	Vos. **Hà**-giu intro-du-**ït**	
Ells Intro-du-**ei**-xen	Ells **Han** intro-du-**ït**		Ells Intro-du-**ei**-xin	Ells **Ha**-gin intro-du-**ït**	
Imperfet	*Past Plusquamperfet*		*Imperfet past*	*Plusquamperfet past*	
Jo Intro-du-**ï**-a	Jo Ha-**vi**-a intro-du-**ït**		Jo Intro-du-**ís**	Jo Ha-**gués** intro-du-**ït**	
Tu Intro-du-**ï**-es	Tu Ha-**vi**-es intro-du-**ït**		Tu Intro-du-**ïs**-sis	Tu Ha-**gues**-sis intro-du-**ït**	
Ell Intro-du-**ï**-a	Ell Ha-**vi**-a intro-du-**ït**		Ell Intro-du-**ís**	Ell Ha-**gués** intro-du-**ït**	
No. Intro-du-**í**-em	Nos Ha-**ví**-em intro-du-**ït**		Nos Intro-du-**ís**-sim	Nos Ha-**gués**-sim intro-du-**ït**	
Vos. Intro-du-**í**-eu	Vos. Ha-**ví**-eu intro-du-**ït**		Vos. Intro-du-**ís**-siu	Vos. Ha-**gués**-siu intro-du-**ït**	
Ells Intro-du-**ï**-en	Ells Ha-**vi**-en intro-du-**ït**		Ells Intro-du-**ïs**-sin	Ells Ha-**gues**-sin intro-du-**ït**	

Past Simple	*Past Perifrastic*	*Past Anterior perifrastic*
Jo Intro-du-**í**	Jo **Vaig** intro-du-**ir**	**Vaig** ha-**ver** intro-du-**ït**
Tu Intro-du-**ï**-res	Tu **Vas** intro-du-**ir**	**Vas** ha-**ver** intro-du-**ït**
Ell Intro-du-**í**	Ell **Va** intro-du-**ir**	**Va** ha-**ver** intro-du-**ït**
Nos Intro-du-**í**-rem	Nos. **Vam** intro-du-**ir**	**Vam** ha-**ver** intro-du-**ït**
Vos. Intro-du-**í**-reu	Vos. **Vau** intro-du-**ir**	**Vau** ha-**ver** intro-du-**ït**
Ells Intro-du-**í**-ren	Ells **Van** intro-du-**ir**	**Van** ha-**ver** intro-du-**ït**

Future Simple	*Future Compound*
Jo Intro-du-i-**ré**	Jo Hau-**ré** intro-du-**ït**
Tu Intro-du-i-**ràs**	Tu Hau-**ràs** intro-du-**ït**
Ell Intro-du-i-**rà**	Ell Hau-**rà** intro-du-**ït**
Nos. Intro-du-i-**rem**	Nos. Hau-**rem** intro-du-**ït**
Vos. Intro-du-i-**reu**	Vos. Hau-**reu** intro-du-**ït**
Ells Intro-du-i-**ran**	Ells Hau-**ran** intro-du-**ït**

Conditional Simple	*Conditional Compound*	**IMPERATIVE**	
Jo Intro-du-i-**ri**-a	Jo Hau-**ri**-a intro-du-**ït**		
Tu Intro-du-i-**ri**-es	Tu Hau-**ri**-es intro-du-**ït**	Intro-du-**eix**	*(Tu)*
Ell Intro-du-i-**ri**-a	Ell Hau-**ri**-a intro-du-**ït**	Intro-du-**ei**-xi	*(Ell)*
Nos Intro-du-i-**rí**-em	Nos. Hau-**rí**-em intro-du-**ït**	Intro-du-**ïm**	*(Nos.)*
Vos. Intro-du-i-**rí**-eu	Vos. Hau-**rí**-eu intro-du-**ït**	Intro-du-**ïu**	*(Vos.)*
Ells Intro-du-i-**ri**-en	Ells Hau-**ri**-en intro-du-**ït**	Intro-du-**ei**-xin	*(Ells)*

IMPERSONAL		
	SIMPLE	**COMPOUND**
Infinitive	Intro-du-**ir**	Ha-**ver** intro-du-**ir**
Participle	Intro-du-**ït**	-
Gerund	Intro-du-**int**	Ha-**vent** intro-du-**ir**

TO INTRODUCE (Someone) - PRESENTAR

PERSONAL				
INDICATIVE			**SUBJUNCTIVE**	
SIMPLE	**COMPOUND**		**SIMPLE**	**COMPOUND**
Present	*Past Indefinite*		*Present*	*Past Perfet*
Jo Pre-**sen**-to	Jo **He** pre-sen-**tat**		Jo Pre-**sen**-ti	Jo **Ha**-gi pre-sen-**tat**
Tu Pre-**sen**-tes	Tu **Has** pre-sen-**tat**		Tu Pre-**sen**-tis	Tu **Ha**-gis pre-sen-**tat**
Ell Pre-**sen**-ta	Ell **Ha** pre-sen-**tat**		Ell Pre-**sen**-ti	Ell **Ha**-gi pre-sen-**tat**
No. Pre-sen-**tem**	Nos. **Hem** pre-sen-**tat**		Nos. Pre-sen-**tem**	Nos **Hà**-gim pre-sen-**tat**
Vos. Pre-sen-**teu**	Vos. **Heu** pre-sen-**tat**		Vos. Pre-sen-**teu**	Vos. **Hà**-giu pre-sen-**tat**
Ells Pre-**sen**-ten	Ells **Han** pre-sen-**tat**		Ells Pre-**sen**-tin	Ells **Ha**-gin pre-sen-**tat**
Imperfet	*Past Plusquamperfet*		*Imperfet past*	*Plusquamperfet past*
Jo Pre-sen-**ta**-va	Jo Ha-**vi**-a pre-sen-**tat**		Jo Pre-sen-**tés**	Jo Ha-**gués** pre-sen-**tat**
Tu Pre-sen-**ta**-ves	Tu Ha-**vi**-es pre-sen-**tat**		Tu Pre-sen-**tes**-sis	Tu Ha-**gues**-sis pre-sen-**tat**
Ell Pre-sen-**ta**-va	Ell Ha-**vi**-a pre-sen-**tat**		Ell Pre-sen-**tés**	Ell Ha-**gués** pre-sen-**tat**
Nos Pre-sen-**tà**-vem	Nos. Ha-**ví**-em pre-sen-**tat**		Nos Pre-sen-**tés**-sim	Nos Ha-**gués**-sim pre-sen-**tat**
Vos. Pre-sen-**tà**-veu	Vos. Ha-**ví**-eu pre-sen-**tat**		Vos. Pre-sen-**tés**-siu	Vos. Ha-**gués**-siu pre-sen-**tat**
Ells Pre-sen-**ta**-ven	Ells Ha-**vi**-en pre-sen-**tat**		Ells Pre-sen-**tes**-sin	Ells Ha-**gues**-sin pre-sen-**tat**

Past Simple	Past Perifrastic	Past Anterior perifrastic
Jo Pre-sen-**tí**	Jo **Vaig** pre-sen-**tar**	**Vaig** ha-**ver** pre-sen-**tat**
Tu Pre-sen-**ta**-res	Tu **Vas** pre-sen-**tar**	**Vas** ha-**ver** pre-sen-**tat**
Ell Pre-sen-**tà**	Ell **Va** pre-sen-**tar**	**Va** ha-**ver** pre-sen-**tat**
Nos Pre-sen-**tà**-rem	No **Vam** pre-sen-**tar**	**Vam** ha-**ver** pre-sen-**tat**
Vos. Pre-sen-**tà**-reu	Vo **Vau** pre-sen-**tar**	**Vau** ha-**ver** pre-sen-**tat**
Ells Pre-sen-**ta**-ren	Ells **Van** pre-sen-**tar**	**Van** ha-**ver** pre-sen-**tat**

Future Simple	Future Compound
Jo Pre-sen-ta-**ré**	Jo Hau-**ré** pre-sen-**tat**
Tu Pre-sen-ta-**ràs**	Tu Hau-**ràs** pre-sen-**tat**
Ell Pre-sen-ta-**rà**	Ell Hau-**rà** pre-sen-**tat**
Nos Pre-sen-ta-**rem**	Nos. Hau-**rem** pre-sen-**tat**
Vos. Pre-sen-ta-**reu**	Vos. Hau-**reu** pre-sen-**tat**
Ells Pre-sen-ta-**ran**	Ells Hau-**ran** pre-sen-**tat**

Conditional Simple	Conditional Compound	IMPERATIVE	
Jo Pre-sen-ta-**ri**-a	Jo Hau-**ri**-a pre-sen-**tat**		
Tu Pre-sen-ta-**ri**-es	Tu Hau-**ri**-es pre-sen-**tat**	Pre-**sen**-ta	*(Tu)*
Ell Pre-sen-ta-**ri**-a	Ell Hau-**ri**-a pre-sen-**tat**	Pre-**sen**-ti	*(Ell)*
Nos Pre-sen-ta-**rí**-em	Nos. Hau-**rí**-em pre-sen-**tat**	Pre-sen-**tem**	*(Nos.)*
Vos. Pre-sen-ta-**rí**-eu	Vos. Hau-**rí**-eu pre-sen-**tat**	Pre-sen-**teu**	*(Vos.)*
Ells Pre-sen-ta-**ri**-en	Ells Hau-**ri**-en pre-sen-**tat**	Pre-**sen**-tin	*(Ells)*

IMPERSONAL		
	SIMPLE	**COMPOUND**
Infinitive	Pre-sen-**tar**	Ha-**ver** pre-sen-**tat**
Participle	Pre-sen-**tat**	-
Gerund	Pre-sen-t**ant**	Ha-**vent** pre-sen-**tat**

TO INVITE - CONVIDAR

PERSONAL							
INDICATIVE				**SUBJUNCTIVE**			
SIMPLE		**COMPOUND**		**SIMPLE**		**COMPOUND**	
Present		*Past Indefinite*		*Present*		*Past Perfet*	
Jo	Con-**vi**-do	Jo	**He** con-vi-dat	Jo	Con-**vi**-di	Jo	**Ha**-gi con-vi-dat
Tu	Con-**vi**-des	Tu	**Has** con-vi-dat	Tu	Con-**vi**-dis	Tu	**Ha**-gis con-vi-dat
Ell	Con-**vi**-da	Ell	**Ha** con-vi-dat	Ell	Con-**vi**-di	Ell	**Ha**-gi con-vi-dat
No.	Con-vi-**dem**	Nos.	**Hem** con-vi-dat	Nos.	Con-vi-**dem**	Nos	**Hà**-gim con-vi-dat
Vos.	Con-vi-**deu**	Vos.	**Heu** con-vi-dat	Vos.	Con-vi-**deu**	Vos.	**Hà**-giu con-vi-dat
Ells	Con-**vi**-den	Ells	**Han** con-vi-dat	Ells	Con-**vi**-din	Ells	**Ha**-gin con-vi-dat
Imperfet		*Past Plusquamperfet*		*Imperfet past*		*Plusquamperfet past*	
Jo	Con-vi-da-va	Jo	Ha-**vi**-a con-vi-dat	Jo	Con-vi-**dés**	Jo	Ha-**gués** con-vi-dat
Tu	Con-vi-da-ves	Tu	Ha-**vi**-es con-vi-dat	Tu	Con-vi-**des**-sis	Tu	Ha-**gues**-sis con-vi-dat
Ell	Con-vi-da-va	Ell	Ha-**vi**-a con-vi-dat	Ell	Con-vi-**dés**	Ell	Ha-**gués** con-vi-dat
Nos	Con-vi-**dà**-vem	Nos.	Ha-**ví**-em con-vi-dat	Nos	Con-vi-**dés**-sim	Nos	Ha-**gués**-sim con-vi-dat
Vos.	Con-vi-**dà**-veu	Vos.	Ha-**ví**-eu con-vi-dat	Vos.	Con-vi-**dés**-siu	Vos.	Ha-**gués**-siu con-vi-dat
Ells	Con-vi-da-ven	Ells	Ha-**vi**-en con-vi-dat	Ells	Con-vi-**des**-sin	Ells	Ha-**gues**-sin con-vi-dat

Past Simple		*Past Perifrastic*		*Past Anterior perifrastic*
Jo	Con-vi-**dí**	Jo	**Vaig** con-vi-dar	**Vaig** ha-**ver** con-vi-dat
Tu	Con-vi-**da**-res	Tu	**Vas** con-vi-dar	**Vas** ha-**ver** con-vi-dat
Ell	Con-vi-**dà**	Ell	**Va** con-vi-dar	**Va** ha-**ver** con-vi-dat
Nos	Con-vi-**dà**-rem	No	**Vam** con-vi-dar	**Vam** ha-**ver** con-vi-dat
Vos.	Con-vi-**dà**-reu	Vo	**Vau** con-vi-dar	**Vau** ha-**ver** con-vi-dat
Ells	Con-vi-**da**-ren	Ells	**Van** con-vi-dar	**Van** ha-**ver** con-vi-dat

Future Simple		*Future Compound*	
Jo	Con-vi-da-**ré**	Jo	Hau-**ré** con-vi-dat
Tu	Con-vi-da-**ràs**	Tu	Hau-**ràs** con-vi-dat
Ell	Con-vi-da-**rà**	Ell	Hau-**rà** con-vi-dat
Nos	Con-vi-da-**rem**	Nos.	Hau-**rem** con-vi-dat
Vos.	Con-vi-da-**reu**	Vos.	Hau-**reu** con-vi-dat
Ells	Con-vi-da-**ran**	Ells	Hau-**ran** con-vi-dat

Conditional Simple		*Conditional Compound*		**IMPERATIVE**	
Jo	Con-vi-da-**ri**-a	Jo	Hau-**ri**-a con-vi-dat		
Tu	Con-vi-da-**ri**-es	Tu	Hau-**ri**-es con-vi-dat	Con-**vi**-da	(Tu)
Ell	Con-vi-da-**ri**-a	Ell	Hau-**ri**-a con-vi-dat	Con-**vi**-di	(Ell)
Nos	Con-vi-da-**rí**-em	Nos.	Hau-**rí**-em con-vi-dat	Con-vi-**dem**	(Nos.)
Vos.	Con-vi-da-**rí**-eu	Vos.	Hau-**rí**-eu con-vi-dat	Con-vi-**deu**	(Vos.)
Ells	Con-vi-da-**ri**-en	Ells	Hau-**ri**-en con-vi-dat	Con-**vi**-din	(Ells)

IMPERSONAL		
	SIMPLE	**COMPOUND**
Infinitive	Con-vi-**dar**	Ha-**ver** con-vi-**dat**
Participle	Con-vi-**dat**	-
Gerund	Con-vi-**dant**	Ha-**vent** con-vi-**dat**

TO KILL - MATAR

PERSONAL							
INDICATIVE				**SUBJUNCTIVE**			
SIMPLE		**COMPOUND**		**SIMPLE**		**COMPOUND**	
Present		*Past Indefinite*		*Present*		*Past Perfet*	
Jo	**Ma**-to	Jo	**He** ma-**tat**	Jo	**Ma**-ti	Jo	**Ha**-gi ma-**tat**
Tu	**Ma**-tes	Tu	**Has** ma-**tat**	Tu	**Ma**-tis	Tu	**Ha**-gis ma-**tat**
Ell	**Ma**-ta	Ell	**Ha** ma-**tat**	Ell	**Ma**-ti	Ell	**Ha**-gi ma-**tat**
No.	Ma-**tem**	Nos.	**Hem** ma-**tat**	Nos.	Ma-**tem**	Nos	**Hà**-gim ma-**tat**
Vos.	Ma-**teu**	Vos.	**Heu** ma-**tat**	Vos.	Ma-**teu**	Vos.	**Hà**-giu ma-**tat**
Ells	**Ma**-ten	Ells	**Han** ma-**tat**	Ells	**Ma**-tin	Ells	**Ha**-gin ma-**tat**
Imperfet		*Past Plusquamperfet*		*Imperfet past*		*Plusquamperfet past*	
Jo	Ma-**ta**-va	Jo	Ha-**vi**-a ma-**tat**	Jo	Ma-**tés**	Jo	Ha-**gués** ma-**tat**
Tu	Ma-**ta**-ves	Tu	Ha-**vi**-es ma-**tat**	Tu	Ma-**tes**-sis	Tu	Ha-**gues**-sis ma-**tat**
Ell	Ma-**ta**-va	Ell	Ha-**vi**-a ma-**tat**	Ell	Ma-**tés**	Ell	Ha-**gués** ma-**tat**
Nos	Ma-**tà**-vem	Nos.	Ha-**ví**-em ma-**tat**	Nos	Ma-**tés**-sim	Nos	Ha-**gués**-sim ma-**tat**
Vos.	Ma-**tà**-veu	Vos.	Ha-**ví**-eu ma-**tat**	Vos.	Ma-**tés**-siu	Vos.	Ha-**gués**-siu ma-**tat**
Ells	Ma-**ta**-ven	Ells	Ha-**vi**-en ma-**tat**	Ells	Ma-**tes**-sin	Ells	Ha-**gues**-sin ma-**tat**

Past Simple		*Past Perifrastic*		*Past Anterior perifrastic*
Jo	Ma-**tí**	Jo	**Vaig** ma-**tar**	**Vaig** ha-**ver** ma-**tat**
Tu	Ma-**ta**-res	Tu	**Vas** ma-**tar**	**Vas** ha-**ver** ma-**tat**
Ell	Ma-**tà**	Ell	**Va** ma-**tar**	**Va** ha-**ver** ma-**tat**
Nos	Ma-**tà**-rem	No	**Vam** ma-**tar**	**Vam** ha-**ver** ma-**tat**
Vos.	Ma-**tà**-reu	Vo	**Vau** ma-**tar**	**Vau** ha-**ver** ma-**tat**
Ells	Ma-**ta**-ren	Ells	**Van** ma-**tar**	**Van** ha-**ver** ma-**tat**

Future Simple		*Future Compound*	
Jo	Ma-ta-**ré**	Jo	Hau-**ré** ma-**tat**
Tu	Ma-ta-**ràs**	Tu	Hau-**ràs** ma-**tat**
Ell	Ma-ta-**rà**	Ell	Hau-**rà** ma-**tat**
Nos	Ma-ta-**rem**	Nos.	Hau-**rem** ma-**tat**
Vos.	Ma-ta-**reu**	Vos.	Hau-**reu** ma-**tat**
Ells	Ma-ta-**ran**	Ells	Hau-**ran** ma-**tat**

Conditional Simple		*Conditional Compound*		**IMPERATIVE**	
Jo	Ma-ta-**ri**-a	Jo	Hau-**ri**-a ma-**tat**		
Tu	Ma-ta-**ri**-es	Tu	Hau-**ri**-es ma-**tat**	**Ma**-ta	*(Tu)*
Ell	Ma-ta-**ri**-a	Ell	Hau-**ri**-a ma-**tat**	**Ma**-ti	*(Ell)*
Nos	Ma-ta-**rí**-em	Nos.	Hau-**rí**-em ma-**tat**	Ma-**tem**	*(Nos.)*
Vos.	Ma-ta-**rí**-eu	Vos.	Hau-**rí**-eu ma-**tat**	Ma-**teu**	*(Vos.)*
Ells	Ma-ta-**ri**-en	Ells	Hau-**ri**-en ma-**tat**	**Ma**-tin	*(Ells)*

IMPERSONAL		
	SIMPLE	**COMPOUND**
Infinitive	Ma-**tar**	Ha-**ver** ma-**tat**
Participle	Ma-**tat**	-
Gerund	Ma-**tant**	Ha-**vent** ma-**tat**

TO KISS – BESAR

Only used in literature. In Catalan is more common to say "donar un petó", to give a kiss, although the verb besar is grammatically right.

PERSONAL			
INDICATIVE		**SUBJUNCTIVE**	
SIMPLE	**COMPOUND**	**SIMPLE**	**COMPOUND**

INDICATIVE — SIMPLE / COMPOUND & SUBJUNCTIVE — SIMPLE / COMPOUND

Present / *Past Indefinite* / *Present* / *Past Perfet*

	Present		Past Indefinite		Present		Past Perfet
Jo	**Be**-so	Jo	**He** be-sat	Jo	**Be**-si	Jo	**Ha**-gi be-**sat**
Tu	**Be**-ses	Tu	**Has** be-sat	Tu	**Be**-sis	Tu	**Ha**-gis be-**sat**
Ell	**Be**-sa	Ell	**Ha** be-**sat**	Ell	**Be**-si	Ell	**Ha**-gi be-**sat**
No.	Be-**sem**	Nos.	**Hem** be-sat	Nos.	Be-**sem**	Nos	**Hà**-gim be-**sat**
Vos.	Be-**seu**	Vos.	**Heu** be-sat	Vos.	Be-**seu**	Vos.	**Hà**-giu be-**sat**
Ells	**Be**-sen	Ells	**Han** be-sat	Ells	**Be**-sin	Ells	**Ha**-gin be-**sat**

Imperfet / *Past Plusquamperfet* / *Imperfet past* / *Plusquamperfet past*

	Imperfet		Past Plusquamperfet		Imperfet past		Plusquamperfet past
Jo	Be-**sa**-va	Jo	Ha-**vi**-a be-**sat**	Jo	Be-**sés**	Jo	Ha-**gués** be-**sat**
Tu	Be-**sa**-ves	Tu	Ha-**vi**-es be-**sat**	Tu	Be-**ses**-sis	Tu	Ha-**gues**-sis be-**sat**
Ell	Be-**sa**-va	Ell	Ha-**vi**-a be-**sat**	Ell	Be-**sés**	Ell	Ha-**gués** be-**sat**
Nos	Be-**sà**-vem	Nos.	Ha-**ví**-em be-**sat**	Nos	Be-**sés**-sim	Nos	Ha-**gués**-sim be-**sat**
Vos.	Be-**sà**-veu	Vos.	Ha-**ví**-eu be-**sat**	Vos.	Be-**sés**-siu	Vos.	Ha-**gués**-siu be-**sat**
Ells	Be-**sa**-ven	Ells	Ha-**vi**-en be-**sat**	Ells	Be-**ses**-sin	Ells	Ha-**gues**-sin be-**sat**

Past Simple / *Past Perifrastic* / *Past Anterior perifrastic*

	Past Simple		Past Perifrastic	Past Anterior perifrastic
Jo	Be-**sí**	Jo	**Vaig** be-sar	**Vaig** ha-**ver** be-sat
Tu	Be-**sa**-res	Tu	**Vas** be-sar	**Vas** ha-ver be-sat
Ell	Be-**sà**	Ell	**Va** be-sar	**Va** ha-ver be-sat
Nos	Be-**sà**-rem	No	**Vam** be-sar	**Vam** ha-ver be-sat
Vos.	Be-**sà**-reu	Vo	**Vau** be-sar	**Vau** ha-ver be-sat
Ells	Be-**sa**-ren	Ells	**Van** be-sar	**Van** ha-ver be-sat

Future Simple / *Future Compound*

	Future Simple		Future Compound
Jo	Be-sa-**ré**	Jo	Hau-**ré** be-**sat**
Tu	Be-sa-**ràs**	Tu	Hau-**ràs** be-**sat**
Ell	Be-sa-**rà**	Ell	Hau-**rà** be-**sat**
Nos	Be-sa-**rem**	Nos.	Hau-**rem** be-**sat**
Vos.	Be-sa-**reu**	Vos.	Hau-**reu** be-**sat**
Ells	Be-sa-**ran**	Ells	Hau-**ran** be-**sat**

Conditional Simple / *Conditional Compound* / **IMPERATIVE**

	Conditional Simple		Conditional Compound	IMPERATIVE	
Jo	Be-sa-**ri**-a	Jo	Hau-**ri**-a be-**sat**		
Tu	Be-sa-**ri**-es	Tu	Hau-**ri**-es be-**sat**	**Be**-sa	*(Tu)*
Ell	Be-sa-**ri**-a	Ell	Hau-**ri**-a be-**sat**	**Be**-si	*(Ell)*
Nos	Be-sa-**rí**-em	Nos.	Hau-**rí**-em be-**sat**	Be-**sem**	*(Nos.)*
Vos.	Be-sa-**rí**-eu	Vos.	Hau-**rí**-eu be-**sat**	Be-**seu**	*(Vos.)*
Ells	Be-sa-**ri**-en	Ells	Hau-**ri**-en be-**sat**	**Be**-sin	*(Ells)*

IMPERSONAL		
	SIMPLE	**COMPOUND**
Infinitive	Be-sar	Ha-**ver** be-**sat**
Participle	Be-sat	-
Gerund	Be-sant	Ha-**vent** be-**sat**

TO KNOW - SABER

PERSONAL				
INDICATIVE			**SUBJUNCTIVE**	
SIMPLE	**COMPOUND**		**SIMPLE**	**COMPOUND**

Present		*Past Indefinite*			*Present*		*Past Perfet*		
Jo	**Sé**	Jo	**He** sa-**but**		Jo	**Sà**-pi-ga	Jo	**Ha**-gi sa-**but**	
Tu	**Saps**	Tu	**Has** sa-**but**		Tu	**Sà**-pi-gues	Tu	**Ha**-gis sa-**but**	
Ell	**Sap**	Ell	**Ha** sa-**but**		Ell	**Sà**-pi-ga	Ell	**Ha**-gi sa-**but**	
No.	Sa-**bem**	Nos.	**Hem** sa-**but**		Nos.	Sa-pi-**guem**	Nos	**Hà**-gim sa-**but**	
Vos.	Sa-**beu**	Vos.	**Heu** sa-**but**		Vos.	Sa-pi-**gueu**	Vos.	**Hà**-giu sa-**but**	
Ells	**Sa**-ben	Ells	**Han** sa-**but**		Ells	**Sà**-pi-guen	Ells	**Ha**-gin sa-**but**	
Imperfet		*Past Plusquamperfet*			*Imperfet past*		*Plusquamperfet past*		
Jo	Sa-**bi**-a	Jo	Ha-**vi**-a sa-**but**		Jo	Sa-**bés**	Jo	Ha-**gués** sa-**but**	
Tu	Sa-**bi**-es	Tu	Ha-**vi**-es sa-**but**		Tu	Sa-**bes**-sis	Tu	Ha-**gues**-sis sa-**but**	
Ell	Sa-**bi**-a	Ell	Ha-**vi**-a sa-**but**		Ell	Sa-**bés**	Ell	Ha-**gués** sa-**but**	
Nos	Sa-**bí**-em	Nos.	Ha-**ví**-em sa-**but**		Nos	Sa-**bés**-sim	Nos	Ha-**gués**-sim sa-**but**	
Vos.	Sa-**bí**-eu	Vos.	Ha-**ví**-eu sa-**but**		Vos.	Sa-**bés**-siu	Vos.	Ha-**gués**-siu sa-**but**	
Ells	Sa-**bi**-en	Ells	Ha-**vi**-en sa-**but**		Ells	Sa-**bes**-sin	Ells	Ha-**gues**-sin sa-**but**	

Past Simple		*Past Perifrastic*		*Past Anterior perifrastic*
Jo	Sa-**bí**	Jo	**Vaig** sa-**ber**	**Vaig** ha-**ver** sa-**but**
Tu	Sa-**be**-res	Tu	**Vas** sa-**ber**	**Vas** ha-**ver** sa-**but**
Ell	Sa-**bé**	Ell	**Va** sa-**ber**	**Va** ha-**ver** sa-**but**
Nos	Sa-**bé**-rem	No	**Vam** sa-**ber**	**Vam** ha-**ver** sa-**but**
Vos.	Sa-**bé**-reu	Vo	**Vau** sa-**ber**	**Vau** ha-**ver** sa-**but**
Ells	Sa-**be**-ren	Ells	**Van** sa-**ber**	**Van** ha-**ver** sa-**but**

Future Simple		*Future Compound*	
Jo	Sa-**bré**	Jo	Hau-**ré** sa-**but**
Tu	Sa-**bràs**	Tu	Hau-**ràs** sa-**but**
Ell	Sa-**brà**	Ell	Hau-**rà** sa-**but**
Nos	Sa-**brem**	Nos.	Hau-**rem** sa-**but**
Vos.	Sa-**breu**	Vos.	Hau-**reu** sa-**but**
Ells	Sa-**bran**	Ells	Hau-**ran** sa-**but**

Conditional Simple		*Conditional Compound*		**IMPERATIVE**	
Jo	Sa-**bri**-a	Jo	Hau-**ri**-a sa-**but**		
Tu	Sa-**bri**-es	Tu	Hau-**ri**-es sa-**but**	**Sà**-pi-gues	*(Tu)*
Ell	Sa-**bri**-a	Ell	Hau-**ri**-a sa-**but**	**Sà**-pi-ga	*(Ell)*
Nos	Sa-**brí**-em	Nos.	Hau-**rí**-em sa-**but**	Sa-pi-**guem**	*(Nos.)*
Vos.	Sa-**brí**-eu	Vos.	Hau-**rí**-eu sa-**but**	Sa-pi-**gueu**	*(Vos.)*
Ells	Sa-**bri**-en	Ells	Hau-**ri**-en sa-**but**	**Sà**-pi-guen	*(Ells)*

IMPERSONAL		
	SIMPLE	**COMPOUND**
Infinitive	Sa-**ber**	Ha-**ver** sa-**but**
Participle	Sa-**but**	-
Gerund	Sa-**bent**	Ha-**vent** sa-**but**

TO LAUGH - RIURE

PERSONAL							
INDICATIVE				**SUBJUNCTIVE**			
SIMPLE		**COMPOUND**		**SIMPLE**		**COMPOUND**	
Present		*Past Indefinite*		*Present*		*Past Perfet*	
Jo	**Ric**	Jo	**He** ri-**gut**	Jo	**Ri**-gui	Jo	**Ha**-gi ri-**gut**
Tu	**Rius**	Tu	**Has** ri-**gut**	Tu	**Ri**-guis	Tu	**Ha**-gis ri-**gut**
Ell	**Riu**	Ell	**Ha** ri-**gut**	Ell	**Ri**-gui	Ell	**Ha**-gi ri-**gut**
No.	Ri-**em**	Nos.	**Hem** ri-**gut**	Nos.	Ri-**guem**	Nos.	**Hà**-gim ri-**gut**
Vos.	Ri-**eu**	Vos.	**Heu** ri-**gut**	Vos.	Ri-**gueu**	Vos.	**Hà**-giu ri-**gut**
Ells	**Ri**-uen	Ells	**Han** ri-**gut**	Ells	**Ri**-guin	Ells	**Ha**-gin ri-**gut**
Imperfet		*Past Plusquamperfet*		*Imperfet past*		*Plusquamperfet past*	
Jo	**Re**-ia	Jo	Ha-**vi**-a ri-**gut**	Jo	Ri-**gués**	Jo	Ha-**gués** ri-**gut**
Tu	**Re**-ies	Tu	Ha-**vi**-es ri-**gut**	Tu	Ri-**gues**-sis	Tu	Ha-**gues**-sis ri-**gut**
Ell	**Re**-ia	Ell	Ha-**vi**-a ri-**gut**	Ell	Ri-**gués**	Ell	Ha-**gués** ri-**gut**
No.	**Rè**-iem	Nos.	Ha-**ví**-em ri-**gut**	Nos.	Ri-**gués**-sim	Nos.	Ha-**gués**-sim ri-**gut**
Vos.	**Rè**-ieu	Vos.	Ha-**ví**-eu ri-**gut**	Vos.	Ri-**gués**-siu	Vos.	Ha-**gués**-siu ri-**gut**
Ells	**Re**-ien	Ells	Ha-**vi**-en ri-**gut**	Ells	Ri-**gues**-sin	Ells	Ha-**gués**-sin ri-**gut**

Past Simple		*Past Perifrastic*		*Past Anterior perifrastic*
Jo	Ri-**guí**	Jo	**Vaig** riu-**re**	**Vaig** ha-**ver** ri-**gut**
Tu	Ri-**gue**-res	Tu	**Vas** riu-**re**	**Vas** ha-**ver** ri-**gut**
Ell	Ri-**gué**	Ell	**Va** riu-**re**	**Va** ha-**ver** ri-**gut**
Nos.	Ri-**gué**-rem	Nos.	**Vam** riu-**re**	**Vam** ha-**ver** ri-**gut**
Vos.	Ri-**gué**-reu	Vos.	**Vau** riu-**re**	**Vau** ha-**ver** ri-**gut**
Ells	Ri-**gue**-ren	Ells	**Van** riu-**re**	**Van** ha-**ver** ri-**gut**

Future Simple		*Future Compound*	
Jo	Riu-**ré**	Jo	Hau-**ré** ri-**gut**
Tu	Riu-**ràs**	Tu	Hau-**ràs** ri-**gut**
Ell	Riu-**rà**	Ell	Hau-**rà** ri-**gut**
Nos.	Riu-**rem**	Nos.	Hau-**rem** ri-**gut**
Vos.	Riu-**reu**	Vos.	Hau-**reu** ri-**gut**
Ells	Riu-**ran**	Ells	Hau-**ran** ri-**gut**

Conditional Simple		*Conditional Compound*		**IMPERATIVE**	
Jo	Riu-**ri**-a	Jo	Hau-**ri**-a ri-**gut**		
Tu	Riu-**ri**-es	Tu	Hau-**ri**-es ri-**gut**	**Riu**	*(Tu)*
Ell	Riu-**ri**-a	Ell	Hau-**ri**-a ri-**gut**	**Ri**-gui	*(Ell)*
Nos.	Riu-**rí**-em	Nos.	Hau-**rí**-em ri-**gut**	Ri-**guem**	*(Nos.)*
Vos.	Riu-**rí**-eu	Vos.	Hau-**rí**-eu ri-**gut**	Ri-**veu**	*(Vos.)*
Ells	Riu-**ri**-en	Ells	Hau-**ri**-en ri-**gut**	**Ri**-guin	*(Ells)*

IMPERSONAL		
	SIMPLE	**COMPOUND**
Infinitive	**Riu**-re	Ha-**ver** ri-**gut**
Participle	Ri-**gut**	-
Gerund	Ri-**ent**	Ha-**vent** ri-**gut**

TO LEARN - APRENDRE

PERSONAL					
INDICATIVE			**SUBJUNCTIVE**		
SIMPLE		**COMPOUND**	**SIMPLE**		**COMPOUND**
Present		*Past Indefinite*	*Present*		*Past Perfet*
Jo	A-**prenc**	Jo	**He** a-**près**	Jo	A-**pren**-gui	Jo	**Ha**-gi a-**près**
Tu	A-**prens**	Tu	**Has** a-**près**	Tu	A-**pren**-guis	Tu	**Ha**-gis a-**près**
Ell	A-**prèn**	Ell	**Ha** a-**près**	Ell	A-**pren**-gui	Ell	**Ha**-gi a-**près**
No.	A-pre-**nem**	Nos.	**Hem** a-**près**	Nos.	A-pren-**guem**	Nos	**Hà**-gim a-**près**
Vos.	A-pre-**neu**	Vos.	**Heu** a-**près**	Vos.	A-pren-**gueu**	Vos.	**Hà**-giu a-**près**
Ells	A-**pre**-nen	Ells	**Han** a-**près**	Ells	A-**pren**-guin	Ells	**Ha**-gin a-**près**
Imperfet		*Past Plusquamperfet*	*Imperfet past*		*Plusquamperfet past*
Jo	A-pre-**ni**-a	Jo	Ha-**vi**-a a-**près**	Jo	A-pren-**gués**	Jo	Ha-**gués** a-**près**
Tu	A-pre-**ni**-es	Tu	Ha-**vi**-es a-**près**	Tu	A-pren-**gues**-sis	Tu	Ha-**gues**-sis a-**près**
Ell	A-pre-**ni**-a	Ell	Ha-**vi**-a a-**près**	Ell	A-pren-**gués**	Ell	Ha-**gués** a-**près**
No.	A-pre-**ní**-em	Nos.	Ha-**ví**-em a-**près**	Nos.	A-pren-**gués**-sim	Nos	Ha-**gués**-sim a-**près**
Vos.	A-pre-**ní**-eu	Vos.	Ha-**ví**-eu a-**près**	Vos.	A-pren-**gués**-siu	Vos.	Ha-**gués**-siu a-**près**
Ells	A-pre-**ni**-en	Ells	Ha-**vi**-en a-**près**	Ells	A-pren-**gues**-sin	Ells	Ha-**gues**-sin a-**près**
Past Simple		*Past Perifrastic*	*Past Anterior perifrastic*		
Jo	A-pren-**guí**	Jo	**Vaig** a-pre-**ndre**	**Vaig** ha-**ver** a-**près**		
Tu	A-pren-**gue**-res	Tu	**Vas** a-pre-**ndre**	**Vas** ha-**ver** a-**près**		
Ell	A-pren-**gué**	Ell	**Va** a-pre-**ndre**	**Va** ha-**ver** a-**près**		
Nos.	A-pren-**gué**-rem	Nos.	**Vam** a-pre-**ndre**	**Vam** ha-**ver** a-**près**		
Vos.	A-pren-**gué**-reu	Vos.	**Vau** a-pre-**ndre**	**Vau** ha-**ver** a-**près**		
Ells	A-pren-**gue**-ren	Ells	**Van** a-pre-**ndre**	**Van** ha-**ver** a-**près**		
Future Simple		*Future Compound*			
Jo	A-pren-**dré**	Jo	Hau-**ré** a-**près**		
Tu	A-pren-**dràs**	Tu	Hau-**ràs** a-**près**		
Ell	A-pren-**drà**	Ell	Hau-**rà** a-**près**		
Nos.	A-pren-**drem**	Nos.	Hau-**rem** a-**près**		
Vos.	A-pren-**dreu**	Vos.	Hau-**reu** a-**près**		
Ells	A-pren-**dran**	Ells	Hau-**ran** a-**près**		
Conditional Simple		*Conditional Compound*	**IMPERATIVE**		
Jo	A-pren-**dri**-a	Jo	Hau-**ri**-a a-**près**			
Tu	A-pren-**dri**-es	Tu	Hau-**ri**-es a-**près**	A-**prèn**	(Tu)
Ell	A-pren-**dri**-a	Ell	Hau-**ri**-a a-**près**	A-**pren**-gui	(Ell)
Nos.	A-pren-**drí**-em	Nos.	Hau-**rí**-em a-**près**	A-pren-**guem**	(Nos.)
Vos.	A-pren-**drí**-eu	Vos.	Hau-**rí**-eu a-**près**	A-pre-**neu**	(Vos.)
Ells	A-pren-**dri**-en	Ells	Hau-**ri**-en a-**près**	A-**pren**-guin	(Ells)

IMPERSONAL		
	SIMPLE	**COMPOUND**
Infinitive	A-pren-**dre**	Ha-**ver** a-**près**
Participle	A-**près**	-
Gerund	A-pre-**nent**	Ha-**vent** a-**près**

TO LIE DOWN – ESTIRAR-SE*

PERSONAL				
INDICATIVE			**SUBJUNCTIVE**	
SIMPLE	**COMPOUND**		**SIMPLE**	**COMPOUND**
Present	*Past Indefinite*		*Present*	*Past Perfet*
Jo M'es-**ti**-ro	Jo **M'he** es-ti-**rat**		Jo M'es-**ti**-ri	Jo **M'ha**-gi es-ti-**rat**
Tu T'es-**ti**-res	Tu **T'has** es-ti-**rat**		Tu T'es-**ti**-ris	Tu **T'ha**-gis es-ti-**rat**
Ell S'es-**ti**-ra	Ell **S'ha** es-ti-**rat**		Ell S'es-**ti**-ri	Ell **S'ha**-gi es-ti-**rat**
No. Ens es-ti-**rem**	Nos. **Ens hem** es-ti-**rat**		Nos. Ens es-ti-**rem**	Nos. **Ens hà**-gim es-ti-**rat**
Vos. Us es-ti-**reu**	Vos. **Us heu** es-ti-**rat**		Vos. Us es-ti-**reu**	Vos. **Us hà**-giu es-ti-**rat**
Ells S'es-**ti**-ren	Ells **S'han** es-ti-**rat**		Ells S'es-**ti**-rin	Ells **S'ha**-gin es-ti-**rat**
Imperfet	*Past Plusquamperfet*		*Imperfet past*	*Plusquamperfet past*
Jo M'es-**ti**-**ra**-va	Jo M'ha-**vi**-a es-ti-**rat**		Jo M'es-ti-**rés**	Jo M'ha-**gués** es-ti-**rat**
Tu T'es-**ti**-**ra**-ves	Tu T'ha-**vi**-es es-ti-**rat**		Tu T'es-**ti**-**res**-sis	Tu T'ha-**gues**-sis es-ti-**rat**
Ell S'es-**ti**-**ra**-va	Ell S'ha-**vi**-a es-ti-**rat**		Ell S'es-**ti**-**rés**	Ell S'ha-**gués** es-ti-**rat**
No. Ens es-ti-**rà**-vem	Nos. **Ens ha**-**ví**-em es-ti-**rat**		Nos Ens es-ti-**rés**-sim	Nos. Ens ha-**gués**-sim es-ti-**rat**
Vos. Us es-ti-**rà**-veu	Vos. **Us ha**-**ví**-eu es-ti-**rat**		Vos. Us es-ti-**rés**-siu	Vos. Us ha-**gués**-siu es-ti-**rat**
Ells S'es-**ti**-**ra**-ven	Ells **S'ha**-**vi**-en es-ti-**rat**		Ells S'es-**ti**-**res**-sin	Ells **S'ha**-**gues**-sin es-ti-**rat**

Past Simple	*Past Perifrastic***	*Past Anterior periphrastic***	
Jo M'es-ti-**rí**	Jo Vaig es.ti.**rar**-me	Vaig ha.**ver**-me es.ti.**rat**	
Tu T'es-ti-**ra**-res	Tu Vas es.ti.**rar**-te	Vas ha.**ver**-te es.ti.**rat**	
Ell S'es-ti-**rà**	Ell Va es.ti.**rar**-se	Va ha.**ver**-se es.ti.**rat**	
Nos Ens es-ti-**rà**-rem	Nos Vam es.ti.**rar**-nos	Vam ha.**ver**-nos es.ti.**rat**	
Vos. Us es-ti-**rà**-reu	Vos. Vau es.ti.**rar**-vos	Vau ha.**ver**-vos es.ti.**rat**	
Ells S'es-ti-**ra**-ren	Ells Van es.ti.**rar**-se	Van ha.**ver**-se es.ti.**rat**	

Future Simple	*Future Compound*	
Jo M'es-ti-ra-**ré**	Jo M'hau-**ré** es-ti-**rat**	
Tu M'es-ti-ra-**ràs**	Tu T'hau-**ràs** es-ti-**rat**	
Ell S'es-ti-ra-**rà**	Ell S'hau-**rà** es-ti-**rat**	
Nos. Ens es-ti-ra-**rem**	Nos. **Ens hau-rem** es-ti-**rat**	
Vos. Us es-ti-ra-**reu**	Vos. **Us hau-reu** es-ti-**rat**	
Ells S'es-ti-ra-**ran**	Ells S'hau-**ran** es-ti-**rat**	

Conditional Simple	*Conditional Compound*	**IMPERATIVE****	
Jo M'es-ti-ra-**ri**-a	Jo M'hau-**ri**-a es-ti-**rat**		
Tu T'es-ti-ra-**ri**-es	Tu T'hau-**ri**-es es-ti-**rat**	Es-**ti**-ra't	(Tu)
Ell S'es-ti-ra-**ri**-a	Ell S'hau-**ri**-a es-ti-**rat**	S'es-**ti**-ri	(Ell)
Nos Ens es-ti-ra-**rí**-em	Nos. **Ens hau-rí**-em es-ti-**rat**	Es-ti-**rem**-nos	(Nos.)
Vos. Us es-ti-ra-**rí**-eu	Vos. **Us hau-rí**-eu es-ti-**rat**	Es-ti-**reu**-vos	(Vos.)
Ells S'es-ti-ra-**ri**-en	Ells S'hau-**ri**-en es-ti-**rat**	S'es-**ti**-rin	(Ells)

IMPERSONAL		
	SIMPLE	**COMPOUND**
Infinitive	Es.ti.**rar**-se	Ha.**ver**-se es.ti.**rat**
Participle	Es.ti.**rat**	-
Gerund	Es.ti.**rant**-se	Ha.**vent**-se es.ti.**rat**

*Estirar-se is a reflexive verb, which means that the action takes places on the subject. It is build with the weak pronouns, EM, ET, ES, ENS, US, ES and their variations depending on the place they are written.
** When the pronoun goes behind the word it is attached to it by a hyphen. In this case the syllables are separated with dots, to appreciate the difference.

TO LIKE - AGRADAR

PERSONAL					
INDICATIVE			**SUBJUNCTIVE**		
SIMPLE	**COMPOUND**		**SIMPLE**	**COMPOUND**	
Present	*Past Indefinite*		*Present*	*Past Perfet*	
Jo A-**gra**-do	Jo **He** a-gra-**dat**		Jo A-**gra**-di	Jo **Ha**-gi a-gra-**dat**	
Tu A-**gra**-des	Tu **Has** a-gra-**dat**		Tu A-**gra**-dis	Tu **Ha**-gis a-gra-**dat**	
Ell A-**gra**-da	Ell **Ha** a-gra-**dat**		Ell A-**gra**-di	Ell **Ha**-gi a-gra-**dat**	
No. A-gra-**dem**	Nos. **Hem** a-gra-**dat**		Nos. A-gra-**dem**	Nos. **Hà**-gim a-gra-**dat**	
Vos. A-gra-**deu**	Vos. **Heu** a-gra-**dat**		Vos. A-gra-**deu**	Vos. **Hà**-giu a-gra-**dat**	
Ells A-**gra**-den	Ells **Han** a-gra-**dat**		Ells A-**gra**-din	Ells **Ha**-gin a-gra-**dat**	
Imperfet	*Past Plusquamperfet*		*Imperfet past*	*Plusquamperfet past*	
Jo A-gra-**da**-va	Jo Ha-**vi**-a a-gra-**dat**		Jo A-gra-**dés**	Jo Ha-**gués** a-gra-**dat**	
Tu A-gra-**da**-ves	Tu Ha-**vi**-es a-gra-**dat**		Tu A-gra-**des**-sis	Tu Ha-**gues**-sis a-gra-**dat**	
Ell A-gra-**da**-va	Ell Ha-**vi**-a a-gra-**dat**		Ell A-gra-**dés**	Ell Ha-**gués** a-gra-**dat**	
No. A-gra-**dà**-vem	Nos. Ha-**ví**-em a-gra-**dat**		Nos A-gra-**dés**-sim	Nos. Ha-**gués**-sim a-gra-**dat**	
Vos. A-gra-**dà**-veu	Vos. Ha-**ví**-eu a-gra-**dat**		Vos. A-gra-**dés**-siu	Vos. Ha-**gués**-siu a-gra-**dat**	
Ells A-gra-**da**-ven	Ells Ha-**vi**-en a-gra-**dat**		Ells A-gra-**des**-sin	Ells Ha-**gues**-sin a-gra-**dat**	
Past Simple	*Past Perifrastic*	*Past Anterior perifrastic*			
Jo A-gra-**dí**	Jo **Vaig** a-gra-**dar**	**Vaig** ha-**ver** a-gra-**dat**			
Tu A-gra-**da**-res	Tu **Vas** a-gra-**dar**	**Vas** ha-**ver** a-gra-**dat**			
Ell A-gra-**dà**	Ell **Va** a-gra-**dar**	**Va** ha-**ver** a-gra-**dat**			
Nos A-gra-**dà**-rem	Nos. **Vam** a-gra-**dar**	**Vam** ha-**ver** a-gra-**dat**			
Vos. A-gra-**dà**-reu	Vos. **Vau** a-gra-**dar**	**Vau** ha-**ver** a-gra-**dat**			
Ells A-gra-**da**-ren	Ells **Van** a-gra-**dar**	**Van** ha-**ver** a-gra-**dat**			
Future Simple	*Future Compound*				
Jo A-gra-da-**ré**	Jo Hau-**ré** a-gra-**dat**				
Tu A-gra-da-**ràs**	Tu Hau-**ràs** a-gra-**dat**				
Ell A-gra-da-**rà**	Ell Hau-**rà** a-gra-**dat**				
Nos. A-gra-da-**rem**	Nos. Hau-**rem** a-gra-**dat**				
Vos. A-gra-da-**reu**	Vos. Hau-**reu** a-gra-**dat**				
Ells A-gra-da-**ran**	Ells Hau-**ran** a-gra-**dat**				
Conditional Simple	*Conditional Compound*		**IMPERATIVE**		
Jo A-gra-da-**ri**-a	Jo Hau-**ri**-a a-gra-**dat**				
Tu A-gra-da-**ri**-es	Tu Hau-**ri**-es a-gra-**dat**		A-**gra**-da	(Tu)	
Ell A-gra-da-**ri**-a	Ell Hau-**ri**-a a-gra-**dat**		A-**gra**-di	(Ell)	
Nos A-gra-da-**rí**-em	Nos. Hau-**rí**-em a-gra-**dat**		A-gra-**dem**	(Nos.)	
Vos. A-gra-da-**rí**-eu	Vos. Hau-**rí**-eu a-gra-**dat**		A-gra-**deu**	(Vos.)	
Ells A-gra-da-**ri**-en	Ells Hau-**ri**-en a-gra-**dat**		A-**gra**-din	(Ells)	

IMPERSONAL		
	SIMPLE	**COMPOUND**
Infinitive	A-gra-**dar**	Ha-**ver** a-gra-**dat**
Participle	A-gra-**dat**	-
Gerund	A-gra-**dant**	Ha-**vent** a-gra-**dat**

TO LISTEN - ESCOLTAR

PERSONAL							
INDICATIVE				SUBJUNCTIVE			
SIMPLE		COMPOUND		SIMPLE		COMPOUND	
Present		Past Indefinite		Present		Past Perfet	
Jo	Es-**col**-to	Jo	**He** es-col-t**at**	Jo	Es-**col**-ti	Jo	**Ha**-gi es-col-t**at**
Tu	Es-**col**-tes	Tu	**Has** es-col-t**at**	Tu	Es-**col**-tis	Tu	**Ha**-gis es-col-t**at**
Ell	Es-**col**-ta	Ell	**Ha** es-col-t**at**	Ell	Es-**col**-ti	Ell	**Ha**-gi es-col-t**at**
No.	Es-col-**tem**	Nos.	**Hem** es-col-t**at**	Nos.	Es-col-**tem**	Nos.	**Hà**-gim es-col-t**at**
Vos.	Es-col-**teu**	Vos.	**Heu** es-col-t**at**	Vos.	Es-col-**teu**	Vos.	**Hà**-giu es-col-t**at**
Ells	Es-**col**-ten	Ells	**Han** es-col-t**at**	Ells	Es-**col**-tin	Ells	**Ha**-gin es-col-t**at**
Imperfet		Past Plusquamperfet		Imperfet past		Plusquamperfet past	
Jo	Es-col-**ta**-va	Jo	Ha-**vi**-a es-col-t**at**	Jo	Es-col-**tés**	Jo	Ha-**gués** es-col-t**at**
Tu	Es-col-**ta**-ves	Tu	Ha-**vi**-es es-col-t**at**	Tu	Es-col-**tes**-sis	Tu	Ha-**gues**-sis es-col-t**at**
Ell	Es-col-**ta**-va	Ell	Ha-**vi**-a es-col-t**at**	Ell	Es-col-**tés**	Ell	Ha-**gués** es-col-t**at**
No.	Es-col-**tà**-vem	Nos.	Ha-**ví**-em es-col-t**at**	Nos	Es-col-**tés**-sim	Nos.	Ha-**gués**-sim es-col-t**at**
Vos.	Es-col-**tà**-veu	Vos.	Ha-**ví**-eu es-col-t**at**	Vos.	Es-col-**tés**-siu	Vos.	Ha-**gués**-siu es-col-t**at**
Ells	Es-col-**ta**-ven	Ells	Ha-**vi**-en es-col-t**at**	Ells	Es-col-**tes**-sin	Ells	Ha-**gues**-sin es-col-t**at**

Past Simple		Past Perifrastic		Past Anterior perifrastic
Jo	Es-col-**tí**	Jo	**Vaig** es-col-tar	**Vaig** ha-**ver** es-col-tat
Tu	Es-col-**ta**-res	Tu	**Vas** es-col-tar	**Vas** ha-**ver** es-col-tat
Ell	Es-col-**tà**	Ell	**Va** es-col-tar	**Va** ha-**ver** es-col-tat
Nos	Es-col-**tà**-rem	Nos.	**Vam** es-col-tar	**Vam** ha-**ver** es-col-tat
Vos.	Es-col-**tà**-reu	Vos.	**Vau** es-col-tar	**Vau** ha-**ver** es-col-tat
Ells	Es-col-**ta**-ren	Ells	**Van** es-col-tar	**Van** ha-**ver** es-col-tat

Future Simple		Future Compound	
Jo	Es-col-ta-**ré**	Jo	Hau-**ré** es-col-t**at**
Tu	Es-col-ta-**ràs**	Tu	Hau-**ràs** es-col-t**at**
Ell	Es-col-ta-**rà**	Ell	Hau-**rà** es-col-t**at**
Nos.	Es-col-ta-**rem**	Nos.	Hau-**rem** es-col-t**at**
Vos.	Es-col-ta-**reu**	Vos.	Hau-**reu** es-col-t**at**
Ells	Es-col-ta-**ran**	Ells	Hau-**ran** es-col-t**at**

Conditional Simple		Conditional Compound		IMPERATIVE	
Jo	Es-col-ta-**ri**-a	Jo	Hau-**ri**-a es-col-t**at**		
Tu	Es-col-ta-**ri**-es	Tu	Hau-**ri**-es es-col-t**at**	Es-**col**-ta	(Tu)
Ell	Es-col-ta-**ri**-a	Ell	Hau-**ri**-a es-col-t**at**	Es-**col**-ti	(Ell)
Nos	Es-col-ta-**rí**-em	Nos.	Hau-**rí**-em es-col-t**at**	Es-col-**tem**	(Nos.)
Vos.	Es-col-ta-**rí**-eu	Vos.	Hau-**rí**-eu es-col-t**at**	Es-col-**teu**	(Vos.)
Ells	Es-col-ta-**ri**-en	Ells	Hau-**ri**-en es-col-t**at**	Es-**col**-tin	(Ells)

IMPERSONAL		
	SIMPLE	COMPOUND
Infinitive	Es-col-**tar**	Ha-**ver** es-col-t**at**
Participle	Es-col-**tat**	-
Gerund	Es-col-**tant**	Ha-**vent** es-col-t**at**

TO LIVE - VIURE

PERSONAL							

INDICATIVE				SUBJUNCTIVE			
SIMPLE		COMPOUND			SIMPLE		COMPOUND
Present		*Past Indefinite*			*Present*		*Past Perfet*
Jo	**Visc**	Jo	**He** vis-**cut**		Jo	**Vis**-qui	Jo	**Ha**-gi vis-**cut**
Tu	**Vius**	Tu	**Has** vis-**cut**		Tu	**Vis**-quis	Tu	**Ha**-gis vis-**cut**
Ell	**Viu**	Ell	**Ha** vis-**cut**		Ell	**Vis**-qui	Ell	**Ha**-gi vis-**cut**
No.	Vi-**vim**	Nos.	**Hem** vis-**cut**		Nos.	Vis-**quem**	Nos.	**Hà**-gim vis-**cut**
Vos.	Vi-**viu**	Vos.	**Heu** vis-**cut**		Vos.	Vis-**queu**	Vos.	**Hà**-giu vis-**cut**
Ells	Vi-uen	Ells	**Han** vis-**cut**		Ells	**Vis**-quin	Ells	**Ha**-gin vis-**cut**
Imperfet		*Past Plusquamperfet*			*Imperfet past*		*Plusquamperfet past*
Jo	Vi-**vi**-a	Jo	Ha-**vi**-a vis-**cut**		Jo	Vis-**qués**	Jo	Ha-**gués** vis-**cut**
Tu	Vi-**vi**-es	Tu	Ha-**vi**-es vis-**cut**		Tu	Vis-**ques**-sis	Tu	Ha-**gues**-sis vis-**cut**
Ell	Vi-**vi**-a	Ell	Ha-**vi**-a vis-**cut**		Ell	Vis-**qués**	Ell	Ha-**gués** vis-**cut**
No.	Vi-**ví**-em	Nos.	Ha-**ví**-em vis-**cut**		Nos	Vis-**qués**-sim	Nos.	Ha-**gués**-sim vis-**cut**
Vos.	Vi-**ví**-eu	Vos.	Ha-**ví**-eu vis-**cut**		Vos.	Vis-**qués**-siu	Vos.	Ha-**gués**-siu vis-**cut**
Ells	Vi-**vi**-en	Ells	Ha-**vi**-en vis-**cut**		Ells	Vis-**ques**-sin	Ells	Ha-**gues**-sin vis-**cut**

Past Simple		Past Perifrastic		Past Anterior perifrastic
Jo	Vis-**quí**	Jo	**Vaig** viu-**re**	**Vaig** ha-**ver** vis-**cut**
Tu	Vis-**que**-res	Tu	**Vas** viu-**re**	**Vas** ha-**ver** vis-**cut**
Ell	Vis-**qué**	Ell	**Va** viu-**re**	**Va** ha-**ver** vis-**cut**
Nos	Vis-**qué**-rem	Nos.	**Vam** viu-**re**	**Vam** ha-**ver** vis-**cut**
Vos.	Vis-**qué**-reu	Vos.	**Vau** viu-**re**	**Vau** ha-**ver** vis-**cut**
Ells	Vis-**que**-ren	Ells	**Van** viu-**re**	**Van** ha-**ver** vis-**cut**

Future Simple		Future Compound	
Jo	Viu-**ré**	Jo	Hau-**ré** vis-**cut**
Tu	Viu-**ràs**	Tu	Hau-**ràs** vis-**cut**
Ell	Viu-**rà**	Ell	Hau-**rà** vis-**cut**
Nos.	Viu-**rem**	Nos.	Hau-**rem** vis-**cut**
Vos.	Viu-**reu**	Vos.	Hau-**reu** vis-**cut**
Ells	Viu-**ran**	Ells	Hau-**ran** vis-**cut**

Conditional Simple		Conditional Compound		IMPERATIVE	
Jo	Viu-**ri**-a	Jo	Hau-**ri**-a vis-**cut**		
Tu	Viu-**ri**-es	Tu	Hau-**ri**-es vis-**cut**	**Viu**	*(Tu)*
Ell	Viu-**ri**-a	Ell	Hau-**ri**-a vis-**cut**	**Vis**-qui	*(Ell)*
Nos	Viu-**rí**-em	Nos.	Hau-**rí**-em vis-**cut**	Vis-**quem**	*(Nos.)*
Vos.	Viu-**rí**-eu	Vos.	Hau-**rí**-eu vis-**cut**	Vi-**viu**	*(Vos.)*
Ells	Viu-**ri**-en	Ells	Hau-**ri**-en vis-**cut**	**Vis**-quin	*(Ells)*

IMPERSONAL		
	SIMPLE	COMPOUND
Infinitive	Viu-**re**	Ha-**ver** vis-**cut**
Participle	Vis-**cut**	-
Gerund	Vi-**vint**	Ha-**vent** vis-**cut**

TO LOSE - PERDRE

PERSONAL			
INDICATIVE		**SUBJUNCTIVE**	
SIMPLE	**COMPOUND**	**SIMPLE**	**COMPOUND**

Present		*Past Indefinite*		*Present*		*Past Perfet*	
Jo	**Per**-do	Jo	**He** per-**dut**	Jo	**Per**-di	Jo	**Ha**-gi per-**dut**
Tu	**Perds**	Tu	**Has** per-**dut**	Tu	**Per**-dis	Tu	**Ha**-gis per-**dut**
Ell	**Perd**	Ell	**Ha** per-**dut**	Ell	**Per**-di	Ell	**Ha**-gi per-**dut**
No.	Per-**dem**	Nos.	**Hem** per-**dut**	Nos.	Per-**dem**	Nos.	**Hà** gim per-**dut**
Vos.	Per-**deu**	Vos.	**Heu** per-**dut**	Vos.	Per-**deu**	Vos.	**Hà**-giu per-**dut**
Ells	**Per**-den	Ells	**Han** per-**dut**	Ells	**Per**-din	Ells	**Ha**-gin per-**dut**

Imperfet		*Past Plusquamperfet*		*Imperfet past*		*Plusquamperfet past*	
Jo	Per-**di**-a	Jo	Ha-**vi**-a per-**dut**	Jo	Per-**dés**	Jo	Ha-**gués** per-**dut**
Tu	Per-**di**-es	Tu	Ha-**vi**-es per-**dut**	Tu	Per-**des**-sis	Tu	Ha-**gues**-sis per-**dut**
Ell	Per-**di**-a	Ell	Ha-**vi**-a per-**dut**	Ell	Per-**dés**	Ell	Ha-**gués** per-**dut**
No.	Per-**dí**-em	Nos.	Ha-**ví**-em per-**dut**	Nos	Per-**dés**-sim	Nos.	Ha-**gués**-sim per-**dut**
Vos.	Per-**dí**-eu	Vos.	Ha-**ví**-eu per-**dut**	Vos.	Per-**dés**-siu	Vos.	Ha-**gués**-siu per-**dut**
Ells	Per-**di**-en	Ells	Ha-**vi**-en per-**dut**	Ells	Per-**des**-sin	Ells	Ha-**gues**-sin per-**dut**

Past Simple		*Past Perifrastic*		*Past Anterior perifrastic*
Jo	Per-**dí**	Jo	**Vaig** per-**dre**	**Vaig** ha-**ver** per-**dut**
Tu	Per-**de**-res	Tu	**Vas** per-**dre**	**Vas** ha-**ver** per-**dut**
Ell	Per-**dé**	Ell	**Va** per-**dre**	**Va** ha-**ver** per-**dut**
Nos	Per-**dé**-rem	Nos.	**Vam** per-**dre**	**Vam** ha-**ver** per-**dut**
Vos	Per-**dé**-reu	Vos.	**Vau** per-**dre**	**Vau** ha-**ver** per-**dut**
Ells	Per-**de**-ren	Ells	**Van** per-**dre**	**Van** ha-**ver** per-**dut**

Future Simple		*Future Compound*	
Jo	Per-**dré**	Jo	Hau-**ré** per-**dut**
Tu	Per-**dràs**	Tu	Hau-**ràs** per-**dut**
Ell	Per-**drà**	Ell	Hau-**rà** per-**dut**
Nos.	Per-**drem**	Nos.	Hau-**rem** per-**dut**
Vos.	Per-**dreu**	Vos.	Hau-**reu** per-**dut**
Ells	Per-**dran**	Ells	Hau-**ran** per-**dut**

Conditional Simple		*Conditional Compound*		**IMPERATIVE**	
Jo	Per-**dri**-a	Jo	Hau-**ri**-a per-**dut**		*(Tu)*
Tu	Per-**dri**-es	Tu	Hau-**ri**-es per-**dut**	**Perd**	*(Ell)*
Ell	Per-**dri**-a	Ell	Hau-**ri**-a per-**dut**	**Per**-di	*(Nos.)*
Nos	Per-**drí**-em	Nos.	Hau-**rí**-em per-**dut**	Per-**dem**	*(Vos.)*
Vos	Per-**drí**-eu	Vos.	Hau-**rí**-eu per-**dut**	Per-**deu**	*(Ells)*
Ells	Per-**dri**-en	Ells	Hau-**ri**-en per-**dut**	**Per**-din	

IMPERSONAL		
	SIMPLE	**COMPOUND**
Infinitive	Per-**dre**	Ha-**ver** per-**dut**
Participle	Per-**dut**	-
Gerund	Per-**dent**	Ha-**vent** per-**dut**

TO LOVE - ESTIMAR

PERSONAL				
INDICATIVE			**SUBJUNCTIVE**	
SIMPLE	**COMPOUND**		**SIMPLE**	**COMPOUND**
Present	*Past Indefinite*		*Present*	*Past Perfet*
Jo Es-**ti**-mo	Jo **He** es-ti-**mat**		Jo Es-**ti**-mi	Jo **Ha**-gi es-ti-**mat**
Tu Es-**ti**-mes	Tu **Has** es-ti-**mat**		Tu Es-**ti**-mis	Tu **Ha**-gis es-ti-**mat**
Ell Es-**ti**-ma	Ell **Ha** es-ti-**mat**		Ell Es-**ti**-mi	Ell **Ha**-gi es-ti-**mat**
No. Es-ti-**mem**	Nos. **Hem** es-ti-**mat**		Nos. Es-ti-**mem**	Nos. **Hà**-gim es-ti-**mat**
Vos. Es-ti-**meu**	Vos. **Heu** es-ti-**mat**		Vos. Es-ti-**meu**	Vos. **Hà**-giu es-ti-**mat**
Ells Es-**ti**-men	Ells **Han** es-ti-**mat**		Ells Es-**ti**-min	Ells **Ha**-gin es-ti-**mat**
Imperfet	*Past Plusquamperfet*		*Imperfet past*	*Plusquamperfet past*
Jo Es-ti-**ma**-va	Jo Ha-**vi**-a es-ti-**mat**		Jo Es-ti-**més**	Jo Ha-**gués** es-ti-**mat**
Tu Es-ti-**ma**-ves	Tu Ha-**vi**-es es-ti-**mat**		Tu Es-ti-**mes**-sis	Tu Ha-**gues**-sis es-ti-**mat**
Ell Es-ti-**ma**-va	Ell Ha-**vi**-a es-ti-**mat**		Ell Es-ti-**més**	Ell Ha-**gués** es-ti-**mat**
No. Es-ti-**mà**-vem	Nos. Ha-**ví**-em es-ti-**mat**		Nos Es-ti-**més**-sim	Nos. Ha-**gués**-sim es-ti-**mat**
Vos. Es-ti-**mà**-veu	Vos. Ha-**ví**-eu es-ti-**mat**		Vos. Es-ti-**més**-siu	Vos. Ha-**gués**-siu es-ti-**mat**
Ells Es-ti-**ma**-ven	Ells Ha-**vi**-en es-ti-**mat**		Ells Es-ti-**mes**-sin	Ells Ha-**gues**-sin es-ti-**mat**

Past Simple	*Past Perifrastic*	*Past Anterior perifrastic*
Jo Es-ti-**mí**	Jo **Vaig** es-ti-**mar**	**Vaig** ha-**ver** es-ti-**mat**
Tu Es-ti-**ma**-res	Tu **Vas** es-ti-**mar**	**Vas** ha-**ver** es-ti-**mat**
Ell Es-ti-**mà**	Ell **Va** es-ti-**mar**	**Va** ha-**ver** es-ti-**mat**
Nos Es-ti-**mà**-rem	Nos. **Vam** es-ti-**mar**	**Vam** ha-**ver** es-ti-**mat**
Vos. Es-ti-**mà**-reu	Vos. **Vau** es-ti-**mar**	**Vau** ha-**ver** es-ti-**mat**
Ells Es-ti-**ma**-ren	Ells **Van** es-ti-**mar**	**Van** ha-**ver** es-ti-**mat**

Future Simple	*Future Compound*
Jo Es-ti-ma-**ré**	Jo Hau-**ré** es-ti-**mat**
Tu Es-ti-ma-**ràs**	Tu Hau-**ràs** es-ti-**mat**
Ell Es-ti-ma-**rà**	Ell Hau-**rà** es-ti-**mat**
Nos. Es-ti-ma-**rem**	Nos. Hau-**rem** es-ti-**mat**
Vos. Es-ti-ma-**reu**	Vos. Hau-**reu** es-ti-**mat**
Ells Es-ti-ma-**ran**	Ells Hau-**ran** es-ti-**mat**

Conditional Simple	*Conditional Compound*	**IMPERATIVE**	
Jo Es-ti-ma-**ri**-a	Jo Hau-**ri**-a es-ti-**mat**		
Tu Es-ti-ma-**ri**-es	Tu Hau-**ri**-es es-ti-**mat**	Es-**ti**-ma	*(Tu)*
Ell Es-ti-ma-**ri**-a	Ell Hau-**ri**-a es-ti-**mat**	Es-**ti**-mi	*(Ell)*
Nos Es-ti-ma-**rí**-em	Nos. Hau-**rí**-em es-ti-**mat**	Es-ti-**mem**	*(Nos.)*
Vos. Es-ti-ma-**rí**-eu	Vos. Hau-**rí**-eu es-ti-**mat**	Es-ti-**meu**	*(Vos.)*
Ells Es-ti-ma-**ri**-en	Ells Hau-**ri**-en es-ti-**mat**	Es-**ti**-min	*(Ells)*

IMPERSONAL		
	SIMPLE	**COMPOUND**
Infinitive	Es-ti-**mar**	Ha-**ver** es-ti-**mat**
Participle	Es-ti-**mat**	-
Gerund	Es-ti-**mant**	Ha-**vent** es-ti-**mat**

TO MEET – CONÈIXER

PERSONAL			
INDICATIVE		**SUBJUNCTIVE**	
SIMPLE	**COMPOUND**	**SIMPLE**	**COMPOUND**

Present		*Past Indefinite*		*Present*		*Past Perfet*	
Jo	Co-**nec**	Jo	**He** co-ne-**gut**	Jo	Co-**ne**-gui	Jo	**Ha**-gi co-ne-**gut**
Tu	Co-**nei**-xes	Tu	**Has** co-ne-**gut**	Tu	Co-**ne**-guis	Tu	**Ha**-gis co-ne-**gut**
Ell	Co-**neix**	Ell	**Ha** co-ne-**gut**	Ell	Co-**ne**-gui	Ell	**Ha**-gi co-ne-**gut**
No.	Co-nei-**xem**	Nos.	**Hem** co-ne-**gut**	Nos	Co-ne-**guem**	Nos	**Hà**-gim co-ne-**gut**
Vos.	Co-nei-**xeu**	Vos.	**Heu** co-ne-**gut**	Vos.	Co-ne-**gueu**	Vos.	**Hà**-giu co-ne-**gut**
Ells	Co-**nei**-xen	Ells	**Han** co-ne-**gut**	Ells	Co-**ne**-guin	Ells	**Ha**-gin co-ne-**gut**

Imperfet		*Past Plusquamperfet*		*Imperfet past*		*Plusquamperfet past*	
Jo	Co-nei-**xi**-a	Jo	Ha-**vi**-a co-ne-**gut**	Jo	Co-ne-**gués**	Jo	Ha-**gués** co-ne-**gut**
Tu	Co-nei-**xi**-es	Tu	Ha-**vi**-es co-ne-**gut**	Tu	Co-ne-**gues**-sis	Tu	Ha-**gues**-sis co-ne-**gut**
Ell	Co-nei-**xi**-a	Ell	Ha-**vi**-a co-ne-**gut**	Ell	Co-ne-**gués**	Ell	Ha-**gués** co-ne-**gut**
No.	Co-nei-**xí**-em	Nos.	Ha-**ví**-em co-ne-**gut**	Nos	Co-ne-**gués**-sim	Nos	Ha-**gués**-sim co-ne-**gut**
Vos.	Co-nei-**xí**-eu	Vos.	Ha-**ví**-eu co-ne-**gut**	Vos.	Co-ne-**gués**-siu	Vos.	Ha-**gués**-siu co-ne-**gut**
Ells	Co-nei-**xi**-en	Ells	Ha-**vi**-en co-ne-**gut**	Ells	Co-ne-**gues**-sin	Ells	Ha-**gues**-sin co-ne-**gut**

Past Simple		*Past Perifrastic*		*Past Anterior perifrastic*
Jo	Co-ne-**guí**	Jo	**Vaig** co-**nèi**-xer	**Vaig** ha-**ver** co-ne-**gut**
Tu	Co-ne-**gue**-res	Tu	**Vas** co-**nèi**-xer	**Vas** ha-**ver** co-ne-**gut**
Ell	Co-ne-**gué**	Ell	**Va** co-**nèi**-xer	**Va** ha-**ver** co-ne-**gut**
Nos	Co-ne-**gué**-rem	Nos.	**Vam** co-**nèi**-xer	**Vam** ha-**ver** co-ne-**gut**
Vos.	Co-ne-**gué**-reu	Vos.	**Vau** co-**nèi**-xer	**Vau** ha-**ver** co-ne-**gut**
Ells	Co-ne-**gue**-ren	Ells	**Van** co-**nèi**-xer	**Van** ha-**ver** co-ne-**gut**

Future Simple		*Future Compound*	
Jo	Co-nei-xe-**ré**	Jo	Hau-**ré** co-ne-**gut**
Tu	Co-nei-xe-**ràs**	Tu	Hau-**ràs** co-ne-**gut**
Ell	Co-nei-xe-**rà**	Ell	Hau-**rà** co-ne-**gut**
Nos.	Co-nei-xe-**rem**	Nos.	Hau-**rem** co-ne-**gut**
Vos.	Co-nei-xe-**reu**	Vos.	Hau-**reu** co-ne-**gut**
Ells	Co-nei-xe-**ran**	Ells	Hau-**ran** co-ne-**gut**

Conditional Simple		*Conditional Compound*		**IMPERATIVE**	
Jo	Co-nei-xe-**ri**-a	Jo	Hau-**ri**-a co-ne-**gut**		
Tu	Co-nei-xe-**ri**-es	Tu	Hau-**ri**-es co-ne-**gut**	Co-**neix**	(Tu)
Ell	Co-nei-xe-**ri**-a	Ell	Hau-**ri**-a co-ne-**gut**	Co-**ne**-gui	(Ell)
Nos	Co-nei-xe-**rí**-em	Nos.	Hau-**rí**-em co-ne-**gut**	Co-ne-**guem**	(Nos.)
Vos.	Co-nei-xe-**rí**-eu	Vos.	Hau-**rí**-eu co-ne-**gut**	Co-nei-**xeu**	(Vos.)
Ells	Co-nei-xe-**ri**-en	Ells	Hau-**ri**-en co-ne-**gut**	Co-**ne**-guin	(Ells)

IMPERSONAL		
	SIMPLE	**COMPOUND**
Infinitive	Co-**nèi**-xer	Ha-**ver** co-ne-**gut**
Participle	Co-ne-**gut**	-
Gerund	Co-nei-**xent**	Ha-**vent** co-ne-**gut**

TO NEED - NECESSITAR

PERSONAL							
INDICATIVE				**SUBJUNCTIVE**			
SIMPLE		**COMPOUND**		**SIMPLE**		**COMPOUND**	
Present		*Past Indefinite*		*Present*		*Past Perfet*	
Jo	Ne-ces-**si**-to	Jo	**He** ne-ces-si-**tat**	Jo	Ne-ces-**si**-ti	Jo	**Ha**-gi ne-ces-si-**tat**
Tu	Ne-ces-**si**-tes	Tu	**Has** ne-ces-si-**tat**	Tu	Ne-ces-**si**-tis	Tu	**Ha**-gis ne-ces-si-**tat**
Ell	Ne-ces-**si**-ta	Ell	**Ha** ne-ces-si-**tat**	Ell	Ne-ces-**si**-ti	Ell	**Ha**-gi ne-ces-si-**tat**
No.	Ne-ces-si-**tem**	Nos.	**Hem** ne-ces-si-**tat**	Nos.	Ne-ces-si-**tem**	Nos	**Hà**-gim ne-ces-si-**tat**
Vos.	Ne-ces-si-**teu**	Vos.	**Heu** ne-ces-si-**tat**	Vos.	Ne-ces-si-**teu**	Vos.	**Hà**-giu ne-ces-si-**tat**
Ells	Ne-ces-**si**-ten	Ells	**Han** ne-ces-si-**tat**	Ells	Ne-ces-**si**-tin	Ells	**Ha**-gin ne-ces-si-**tat**
Imperfet		*Past Plusquamperfet*		*Imperfet past*		*Plusquamperfet past*	
Jo	Ne-ces-si-**ta**-va	Jo	Ha-**vi**-a ne-ces-si-**tat**	Jo	Ne-ces-si-**tés**	Jo	Ha-**gués** ne-ces-si-**tat**
Tu	Ne-ces-si-**ta**-ves	Tu	Ha-**vi**-es ne-ces-si-**tat**	Tu	Ne-ces-si-**tes**-sis	Tu	Ha-**gues**-sis ne-ces-si-**tat**
Ell	Ne-ces-si-**ta**-va	Ell	Ha-**vi**-a ne-ces-si-**tat**	Ell	Ne-ces-si-**tés**	Ell	Ha-**gués** ne-ces-si-**tat**
Nos	Ne-ces-si-**tà**-vem	Nos.	Ha-**ví**-em ne-ces-si-**tat**	Nos	Ne-ces-si-**tés**-sim	Nos	Ha-**gués**-sim ne-ces-si-**tat**
Vos.	Ne-ces-si-**tà**-veu	Vos.	Ha-**ví**-eu ne-ces-si-**tat**	Vos.	Ne-ces-si-**tés**-siu	Vos.	Ha-**gués**-siu ne-ces-si-**tat**
Ells	Ne-ces-si-**ta**-ven	Ells	Ha-**vi**-en ne-ces-si-**tat**	Ells	Ne-ces-si-**tes**-sin	Ells	Ha-**gues**-sin ne-ces-si-**tat**

Past Simple		*Past Perifrastic*		*Past Anterior perifrastic*
Jo	Ne-ces-si-**tí**	Jo	**Vaig** ne-ces-si-tar	**Vaig** ha-**ver** ne-ces-si-**tat**
Tu	Ne-ces-si-**ta**-res	Tu	**Vas** ne-ces-si-tar	**Vas** ha-**ver** ne-ces-si-**tat**
Ell	Ne-ces-si-**tà**	Ell	**Va** ne-ces-si-tar	**Va** ha-**ver** ne-ces-si-**tat**
Nos	Ne-ces-si-**tà**-rem	Nos / Vos. / Ells	**Vam** ne-ces-si-tar	**Vam** ha-**ver** ne-ces-si-**tat**
Vos.	Ne-ces-si-**tà**-reu		**Vau** ne-ces-si-tar	**Vau** ha-**ver** ne-ces-si-**tat**
Ells	Ne-ces-si-**ta**-ren		**Van** ne-ces-si-tar	**Van** ha-**ver** ne-ces-si-**tat**

Future Simple		*Future Compound*	
Jo	Ne-ces-si-ta-**ré**	Jo	Hau-**ré** ne-ces-si-**tat**
Tu	Ne-ces-si-ta-**ràs**	Tu	Hau-**ràs** ne-ces-si-**tat**
Ell	Ne-ces-si-ta-**rà**	Ell	Hau-**rà** ne-ces-si-**tat**
Nos	Ne-ces-si-ta-**rem**	Nos.	Hau-**rem** ne-ces-si-**tat**
Vos.	Ne-ces-si-ta-**reu**	Vos.	Hau-**reu** ne-ces-si-**tat**
Ells	Ne-ces-si-ta-**ran**	Ells	Hau-**ran** ne-ces-si-**tat**

Conditional Simple		*Conditional Compound*		**IMPERATIVE**		
Jo	Ne-ces-si-ta-**ri**-a	Jo	Hau-**ri**-a ne-ces-si-**tat**			
Tu	Ne-ces-si-ta-**ri**-es	Tu	Hau-**ri**-es ne-ces-si-**tat**	Ne-ces-**si**-ta	*(Tu)*	
Ell	Ne-ces-si-ta-**ri**-a	Ell	Hau-**ri**-a ne-ces-si-**tat**	Ne-ces-**si**-ti	*(Ell)*	
Nos	Ne-ces-si-ta-**rí**-em	Nos.	Hau-**rí**-em ne-ces-si-**tat**	Ne-ces-si-**tem**	*(Nos.)*	
Vos.	Ne-ces-si-ta-**rí**-eu	Vos.	Hau-**rí**-eu ne-ces-si-**tat**	Ne-ces-si-**teu**	*(Vos.)*	
Ells	Ne-ces-si-ta-**ri**-en	Ells	Hau-**ri**-en ne-ces-si-**tat**	Ne-ces-**si**-tin	*(Ells)*	

IMPERSONAL		
	SIMPLE	**COMPOUND**
Infinitive	Ne-ces-si-**tar**	Ha-**ver** ne-ces-si-**tat**
Participle	Ne-ces-si-**tat**	-
Gerund	Ne-ces-si-**tant**	Ha-**vent** ne-ces-si-**tat**

TO NOTICE - NOTAR

PERSONAL							
INDICATIVE				**SUBJUNCTIVE**			
SIMPLE		**COMPOUND**		**SIMPLE**		**COMPOUND**	
Present		*Past Indefinite*		*Present*		*Past Perfet*	
Jo	**No**-to	Jo	**He** no-**tat**	Jo	**No**-ti	Jo	**Ha**-gi no-**tat**
Tu	**No**-tes	Tu	**Has** no-**tat**	Tu	**No**-tis	Tu	**Ha**-gis no-**tat**
Ell	**No**-ta	Ell	**Ha** no-**tat**	Ell	**No**-ti	Ell	**Ha**-gi no-**tat**
No.	**No**-**tem**	Nos.	**Hem** no-**tat**	Nos.	**No**-**tem**	Nos.	**Hà**-gim no-**tat**
Vos.	**No**-**teu**	Vos.	**Heu** no-**tat**	Vos.	**No**-**teu**	Vos.	**Hà**-giu no-**tat**
Ells	**No**-ten	Ells	**Han** no-**tat**	Ells	**No**-tin	Ells	**Ha**-gin no-**tat**
Imperfet		*Past Plusquamperfet*		*Imperfet past*		*Plusquamperfet past*	
Jo	No-**ta**-va	Jo	Ha-**vi**-a no-**tat**	Jo	No-**tés**	Jo	Ha-**gués** no-**tat**
Tu	No-**ta**-ves	Tu	Ha-**vi**-es no-**tat**	Tu	No-**tes**-sis	Tu	Ha-**gues**-sis no-**tat**
Ell	No-**ta**-va	Ell	Ha-**vi**-a no-**tat**	Ell	No-**tés**	Ell	Ha-**gués** no-**tat**
No.	No-**tà**-vem	Nos.	Ha-**ví**-em no-**tat**	Nos	No-**tés**-sim	Nos.	Ha-**gués**-sim no-**tat**
Vos.	No-**tà**-veu	Vos.	Ha-**ví**-eu no-**tat**	Vos.	No-**tés**-siu	Vos.	Ha-**gués**-siu no-**tat**
Ells	No-**ta**-ven	Ells	Ha-**vi**-en no-**tat**	Ells	No-**tes**-sin	Ells	Ha-**gues**-sin no-**tat**

Past Simple		*Past Perifrastic*		*Past Anterior perifrastic*
Jo	No-**tí**	Jo	**Vaig** no-**tar**	**Vaig** ha-**ver** no-**tat**
Tu	No-**ta**-res	Tu	**Vas** no-**tar**	**Vas** ha-**ver** no-**tat**
Ell	No-**tà**	Ell	**Va** no-**tar**	**Va** ha-**ver** no-**tat**
Nos	No-**tà**-rem	Nos.	**Vam** no-**tar**	**Vam** ha-**ver** no-**tat**
Vos.	No-**tà**-reu	Vos.	**Vau** no-**tar**	**Vau** ha-**ver** no-**tat**
Ells	No-**ta**-ren	Ells	**Van** no-**tar**	**Van** ha-**ver** no-**tat**

Future Simple		*Future Compound*	
Jo	No-ta-**ré**	Jo	Hau-**ré** no-**tat**
Tu	No-ta-**ràs**	Tu	Hau-**ràs** no-**tat**
Ell	No-ta-**rà**	Ell	Hau-**rà** no-**tat**
Nos.	No-ta-**rem**	Nos.	Hau-**rem** no-**tat**
Vos.	No-ta-**reu**	Vos.	Hau-**reu** no-**tat**
Ells	No-ta-**ran**	Ells	Hau-**ran** no-**tat**

Conditional Simple		*Conditional Compound*		**IMPERATIVE**	
Jo	No-ta-**ri**-a	Jo	Hau-**ri**-a no-**tat**		
Tu	No-ta-**ri**-es	Tu	Hau-**ri**-es no-**tat**	**No**-ta	(Tu)
Ell	No-ta-**ri**-a	Ell	Hau-**ri**-a no-**tat**	**No**-ti	(Ell)
Nos	No-ta-**rí**-em	Nos.	Hau-**rí**-em no-**tat**	No-**tem**	(Nos.)
Vos.	No-ta-**rí**-eu	Vos.	Hau-**rí**-eu no-**tat**	No-**teu**	(Vos.)
Ells	No-ta-**ri**-en	Ells	Hau-**ri**-en no-**tat**	**No**-tin	(Ells)

IMPERSONAL		
	SIMPLE	**COMPOUND**
Infinitive	No-**tar**	Ha-**ver** no-**tat**
Participle	No-**tat**	-
Gerund	No-**tant**	Ha-**vent** no-**tat**

TO OPEN - OBRIR

PERSONAL							
INDICATIVE				**SUBJUNCTIVE**			
SIMPLE		**COMPOUND**		**SIMPLE**		**COMPOUND**	
Preo-bre		*Past Indefinite*		*Preo-bre*		*Past Perfet*	
Jo	**O**-bro	Jo	**He** o-**bert**	Jo	**O**-bri	Jo	**Ha**-gi o-**bert**
Tu	**O**-bres	Tu	**Has** o-**bert**	Tu	**O**-bris	Tu	**Ha**-gis o-**bert**
Ell	**O**-bre	Ell	**Ha** o-**bert**	Ell	**O**-bri	Ell	**Ha**-gi o-**bert**
No.	**O**-**brim**	Nos.	**Hem** o-**bert**	Nos.	**O**-**brim**	Nos.	**Hà**-gim o-**bert**
Vos.	**O**-**briu**	Vos.	**Heu** o-**bert**	Vos.	**O**-**briu**	Vos.	**Hà**-giu o-**bert**
Ells	**O**-bren	Ells	**Han** o-**bert**	Ells	**O**-brin	Ells	**Ha**-gin o-**bert**
Imperfet		*Past Plusquamperfet*		*Imperfet past*		*Plusquamperfet past*	
Jo	O-**bri**-a	Jo	Ha-**vi**-a o-**bert**	Jo	O-**brís**	Jo	Ha-**gués** o-**bert**
Tu	O-**bri**-es	Tu	Ha-**vi**-es o-**bert**	Tu	O-**brís**-sis	Tu	Ha-**gués**-sis o-**bert**
Ell	O-**bri**-a	Ell	Ha-**vi**-a o-**bert**	Ell	O-**brís**	Ell	Ha-**gués** o-**bert**
No.	O-**brí**-em	Nos.	Ha-**ví**-em o-**bert**	Nos	O-**brís**-sim	Nos.	Ha-**gués**-sim o-**bert**
Vos.	O-**brí**-eu	Vos.	Ha-**ví**-eu o-**bert**	Vos.	O-**brís**-siu	Vos.	Ha-**gués**-siu o-**bert**
Ells	O-**bri**-en	Ells	Ha-**vi**-en o-**bert**	Ells	O-**bris**-sin	Ells	Ha-**gués**-sin o-**bert**

Past Simple		*Past Perifrastic*		*Past Anterior perifrastic*
Jo	O-**brí**	Jo	Vaig o-brir	Vaig ha-**ver** o-**bert**
Tu	O-**bri**-res	Tu	Vas o-brir	Vas ha-**ver** o-**bert**
Ell	O-**brí**	Ell	Va o-brir	Va ha-**ver** o-**bert**
Nos	O-**brí**-rem	Nos.	Vam o-brir	Vam ha-**ver** o-**bert**
Vos.	O-**brí**-reu	Vos.	Vau o-brir	Vau ha-**ver** o-**bert**
Ells	O-**bri**-ren	Ells	Van o-brir	Van ha-**ver** o-**bert**

Future Simple		*Future Compound*	
Jo	O-bri-**ré**	Jo	Hau-**ré** o-**bert**
Tu	O-bri-**ràs**	Tu	Hau-**ràs** o-**bert**
Ell	O-bri-**rà**	Ell	Hau-**rà** o-**bert**
Nos.	O-bri-**rem**	Nos.	Hau-**rem** o-**bert**
Vos.	O-bri-**reu**	Vos.	Hau-**reu** o-**bert**
Ells	O-bri-**ran**	Ells	Hau-**ran** o-**bert**

Conditional Simple		*Conditional Compound*		**IMPERATIVE**	
Jo	O-bri-**ri**-a	Jo	Hau-**ri**-a o-**bert**		
Tu	O-bri-**ri**-es	Tu	Hau-**ri**-es o-**bert**	**O**-bre	*(Tu)*
Ell	O-bri-**ri**-a	Ell	Hau-**ri**-a o-**bert**	**O**-bri	*(Ell)*
Nos	O-bri-**rí**-em	Nos.	Hau-**rí**-em o-**bert**	**O**-**brim**	*(Nos.)*
Vos.	O-bri-**rí**-eu	Vos.	Hau-**rí**-eu o-**bert**	**O**-**briu**	*(Vos.)*
Ells	O-bri-**ri**-en	Ells	Hau-**ri**-en o-**bert**	**O**-brin	*(Ells)*

IMPERSONAL		
	SIMPLE	**COMPOUND**
Infinitive	O-**brir**	Ha-**ver** o-**bert**
Participle	O-**bert**	-
Gerund	O-**brint**	Ha-**vent** o-**bert**

TO PLAY - JUGAR

PERSONAL				
INDICATIVE			**SUBJUNCTIVE**	
SIMPLE	**COMPOUND**		**SIMPLE**	**COMPOUND**
Present	*Past Indefinite*		*Present*	*Past Perfet*
Jo **Ju**-go	Jo **He** Ju-**gat**		Jo **Ju**-gui	Jo **Ha**-gi Ju-**gat**
Tu **Ju**-gues	Tu **Has** Ju-**gat**		Tu **Ju**-guis	Tu **Ha**-gis Ju-**gat**
Ell **Ju**-ga	Ell **Ha** Ju-**gat**		Ell **Ju**-gui	Ell **Ha**-gi Ju-**gat**
No. Ju-**guem**	Nos. **Hem** Ju-**gat**		Nos. Ju-**guem**	Nos. **Hà**-gim Ju-**gat**
Vos. Ju-**gueu**	Vos. **Heu** Ju-**gat**		Vos. Ju-**gueu**	Vos. **Hà**-giu Ju-**gat**
Ells **Ju**-guen	Ells **Han** Ju-**gat**		Ells **Ju**-guin	Ells **Ha**-gin Ju-**gat**
Imperfet	*Past Plusquamperfet*		*Imperfet past*	*Plusquamperfet past*
Jo Ju-**ga**-va	Jo Ha-**vi**-a Ju-**gat**		Jo Ju-**gués**	Jo Ha-**gués** Ju-**gat**
Tu Ju-**ga**-ves	Tu Ha-**vi**-es Ju-**gat**		Tu Ju-**gues**-sis	Tu Ha-**gues**-sis Ju-**gat**
Ell Ju-**ga**-va	Ell Ha-**vi**-a Ju-**gat**		Ell Ju-**gués**	Ell Ha-**gués** Ju-**gat**
No. Ju-**gà**-vem	Nos. Ha-**ví**-em Ju-**gat**		Nos Ju-**gués**-sim	Nos. Ha-**gués**-sim Ju-**gat**
Vos. Ju-**gà**-veu	Vos. Ha-**ví**-eu Ju-**gat**		Vos. Ju-**gués**-siu	Vos. Ha-**gués**-siu Ju-**gat**
Ells Ju-**ga**-ven	Ells Ha-**vi**-en Ju-**gat**		Ells Ju-**gués**-sin	Ells Ha-**gués**-sin Ju-**gat**

Past Simple	*Past Perifrastic*	*Past Anterior perifrastic*
Jo Ju-**guí**	Jo **Vaig** Ju-**gar**	**Vaig** ha-**ver** Ju-**gat**
Tu Ju-**ga**-res	Tu **Vas** Ju-**gar**	**Vas** ha-**ver** Ju-**gat**
Ell Ju-**gà**	Ell **Va** Ju-**gar**	**Va** ha-**ver** Ju-**gat**
Nos Ju-**gà**-rem	Nos. **Vam** Ju-**gar**	**Vam** ha-**ver** Ju-**gat**
Vos Ju-**gà**-reu	Vos. **Vau** Ju-**gar**	**Vau** ha-**ver** Ju-**gat**
Ells Ju-**ga**-ren	Ells **Van** Ju-**gar**	**Van** ha-**ver** Ju-**gat**

Future Simple	*Future Compound*
Jo Ju-ga-**ré**	Jo Hau-**ré** Ju-**gat**
Tu Ju-ga-**ràs**	Tu Hau-**ràs** Ju-**gat**
Ell Ju-ga-**rà**	Ell Hau-**rà** Ju-**gat**
Nos. Ju-ga-**rem**	Nos. Hau-**rem** Ju-**gat**
Vos. Ju-ga-**reu**	Vos. Hau-**reu** Ju-**gat**
Ells Ju-ga-**ran**	Ells Hau-**ran** Ju-**gat**

Conditional Simple	*Conditional Compound*	**IMPERATIVE**	
Jo Ju-ga-**ri**-a	Jo Hau-**ri**-a Ju-**gat**		
Tu Ju-ga-**ri**-es	Tu Hau-**ri**-es Ju-**gat**	**Ju**-ga	*(Tu)*
Ell Ju-ga-**ri**-a	Ell Hau-**ri**-a Ju-**gat**	**Ju**-gui	*(Ell)*
Nos Ju-ga-**rí**-em	Nos. Hau-**rí**-em Ju-**gat**	Ju-**guem**	*(Nos.)*
Vos. Ju-ga-**rí**-eu	Vos. Hau-**rí**-eu Ju-**gat**	Ju-**gueu**	*(Vos.)*
Ells Ju-ga-**ri**-en	Ells Hau-**ri**-en Ju-**gat**	**Ju**-guin	*(Ells)*

IMPERSONAL		
	SIMPLE	**COMPOUND**
Infinitive	Ju-**gar**	Ha-**ver** Ju-**gat**
Participle	Ju-**gat**	-
Gerund	Ju-**gant**	Ha-**vent** Ju-**gat**

TO PUT - POSAR

PERSONAL				
INDICATIVE			**SUBJUNCTIVE**	
SIMPLE	**COMPOUND**		**SIMPLE**	**COMPOUND**

INDICATIVE / SUBJUNCTIVE

Present		*Past Indefinite*		*Present*		*Past Perfet*	
Jo	**Po**-so	Jo	**He** po-sat	Jo	**Po**-si	Jo	**Ha**-gi po-**sat**
Tu	**Po**-ses	Tu	**Has** po-sat	Tu	**Po**-sis	Tu	**Ha**-gis po-**sat**
Ell	**Po**-sa	Ell	**Ha** po-sat	Ell	**Po**-si	Ell	**Ha**-gi po-**sat**
No.	Po-**sem**	Nos.	**Hem** po-sat	Nos.	Po-**sem**	Nos.	**Hà**-gim po-**sat**
Vos.	Po-**seu**	Vos.	**Heu** po-sat	Vos.	Po-**seu**	Vos.	**Hà**-giu po-**sat**
Ells	**Po**-sen	Ells	**Han** po-sat	Ells	**Po**-sin	Ells	**Ha**-gin po-**sat**

Imperfet		*Past Plusquamperfet*		*Imperfet past*		*Plusquamperfet past*	
Jo	Po-**sa**-va	Jo	Ha-**vi**-a po-**sat**	Jo	Po-**sés**	Jo	Ha-**gués** po-**sat**
Tu	Po-**sa**-ves	Tu	Ha-**vi**-es po-**sat**	Tu	Po-**ses**-sis	Tu	Ha-**gues**-sis po-**sat**
Ell	Po-**sa**-va	Ell	Ha-**vi**-a po-**sat**	Ell	Po-**sés**	Ell	Ha-**gués** po-**sat**
No.	Po-**sà**-vem	Nos.	Ha-**ví**-em po-**sat**	Nos	Po-**sés**-sim	Nos.	Ha-**gués**-sim po-**sat**
Vos.	Po-**sà**-veu	Vos.	Ha-**ví**-eu po-**sat**	Vos.	Po-**sés**-siu	Vos.	Ha-**gués**-siu po-**sat**
Ells	Po-**sa**-ven	Ells	Ha-**vi**-en po-**sat**	Ells	Po-**ses**-sin	Ells	Ha-**gues**-sin po-**sat**

Past Simple		*Past Perifrastic*		*Past Anterior perifrastic*
Jo	Po-**sí**	Jo	**Vaig** po-sar	**Vaig** ha-**ver** po-sat
Tu	Po-**sa**-res	Tu	**Vas** po-sar	**Vas** ha-**ver** po-sat
Ell	Po-**sà**	Ell	**Va** po-sar	**Va** ha-**ver** po-sat
Nos	Po-**sà**-rem	Nos.	**Vam** po-sar	**Vam** ha-**ver** po-sat
Vos.	Po-**sà**-reu	Vos.	**Vau** po-sar	**Vau** ha-**ver** po-sat
Ells	Po-**sa**-ren	Ells	**Van** po-sar	**Van** ha-**ver** po-sat

Future Simple		*Future Compound*	
Jo	Po-sa-**ré**	Jo	Hau-**ré** po-**sat**
Tu	Po-sa-**ràs**	Tu	Hau-**ràs** po-**sat**
Ell	Po-sa-**rà**	Ell	Hau-**rà** po-**sat**
Nos.	Po-sa-**rem**	Nos.	Hau-**rem** po-**sat**
Vos.	Po-sa-**reu**	Vos.	Hau-**reu** po-**sat**
Ells	Po-sa-**ran**	Ells	Hau-**ran** po-**sat**

Conditional Simple		*Conditional Compound*		**IMPERATIVE**	
Jo	Po-sa-**ri**-a	Jo	Hau-**ri**-a po-**sat**		
Tu	Po-sa-**ri**-es	Tu	Hau-**ri**-es po-**sat**	**Po**-sa	*(Tu)*
Ell	Po-sa-**ri**-a	Ell	Hau-**ri**-a po-**sat**	**Po**-si	*(Ell)*
Nos	Po-sa-**rí**-em	Nos.	Hau-**rí**-em po-**sat**	Po-**sem**	*(Nos.)*
Vos.	Po-sa-**rí**-eu	Vos.	Hau-**rí**-eu po-**sat**	Po-**seu**	*(Vos.)*
Ells	Po-sa-**ri**-en	Ells	Hau-**ri**-en po-**sat**	**Po**-sin	*(Ells)*

IMPERSONAL		
	SIMPLE	**COMPOUND**
Infinitive	Po-**sar**	Ha-**ver** po-**sat**
Participle	Po-**sat**	-
Gerund	Po-**sant**	Ha-**vent** po-**sat**

TO READ - LLEGIR

PERSONAL				
INDICATIVE			**SUBJUNCTIVE**	
SIMPLE	**COMPOUND**		**SIMPLE**	**COMPOUND**

INDICATIVE / SUBJUNCTIVE

Present		*Past Indefinite*		*Present*		*Past Perfet*	
Jo	Lle-**gei**-xo	Jo	**He** lle-**git**	Jo	Lle-**gei**-xi	Jo	**Ha**-gi lle-**git**
Tu	Lle-**gei**-xes	Tu	**Has** lle-**git**	Tu	Lle-**gei**-xis	Tu	**Ha**-gis lle-**git**
Ell	Lle-**geix**	Ell	**Ha** lle-**git**	Ell	Lle-**gei**-xi	Ell	**Ha**-gi lle-**git**
No.	Lle-**gim**	Nos	**Hem** lle-**git**	Nos	Lle-**gim**	Nos	**Hà**-gim lle-**git**
Vos.	Lle-**giu**	Vos.	**Heu** lle-**git**	Vos.	Lle-**giu**	Vos.	**Hà**-giu lle-**git**
Ells	Lle-**gei**-xen	Ells	**Han** lle-**git**	Ells	Lle-**gei**-xin	Ells	**Ha**-gin lle-**git**

Imperfet		*Past Plusquamperfet*		*Imperfet past*		*Plusquamperfet past*	
Jo	Lle-gi-a	Jo	Ha-**vi**-a lle-**git**	Jo	Lle-**gís**	Jo	Ha-**gués** lle-**git**
Tu	Lle-gi-es	Tu	Ha-**vi**-es lle-**git**	Tu	Lle-**gis**-sis	Tu	Ha-**gues**-sis lle-**git**
Ell	Lle-gi-a	Ell	Ha-**vi**-a lle-**git**	Ell	Lle-**gís**	Ell	Ha-**gués** lle-**git**
No.	Lle-**gí**-em	Nos	Ha-**ví**-em lle-**git**	Nos	Lle-**gís**-sim	Nos	Ha-**gués**-sim lle-**git**
Vos.	Lle-**gí**-eu	Vos.	Ha-**ví**-eu lle-**git**	Vos.	Lle-**gís**-siu	Vos.	Ha-**gués**-siu lle-**git**
Ells	Lle-gi-en	Ells	Ha-**vi**-en lle-**git**	Ells	Lle-**gis**-sin	Ells	Ha-**gues**-sin lle-**git**

Past Simple		*Past Perifrastic*		*Past Anterior perifrastic*
Jo	Lle-**gí**	Jo	**Vaig** lle-**gir**	**Vaig** ha-**ver** lle-**git**
Tu	Lle-gi-res	Tu	**Vas** lle-**gir**	**Vas** ha-**ver** lle-**git**
Ell	Lle-**gí**	Ell	**Va** lle-**gir**	**Va** ha-**ver** lle-**git**
Nos	Lle-**gí**-rem	Nos.	**Vam** lle-**gir**	**Vam** ha-**ver** lle-**git**
Vos.	Lle-**gí**-reu	Vos.	**Vau** lle-**gir**	**Vau** ha-**ver** lle-**git**
Ells	Lle-gi-ren	Ells	**Van** lle-**gir**	**Van** ha-**ver** lle-**git**

Future Simple		*Future Compound*	
Jo	Lle-gi-**ré**	Jo	Hau-**ré** lle-**git**
Tu	Lle-gi-**ràs**	Tu	Hau-**ràs** lle-**git**
Ell	Lle-gi-**rà**	Ell	Hau-**rà** lle-**git**
Nos.	Lle-gi-**rem**	Nos.	Hau-**rem** lle-**git**
Vos.	Lle-gi-**reu**	Vos.	Hau-**reu** lle-**git**
Ells	Lle-gi-**ran**	Ells	Hau-**ran** lle-**git**

Conditional Simple		*Conditional Compound*		**IMPERATIVE**	
Jo	Lle-gi-**ri**-a	Jo	Hau-**ri**-a lle-**git**		
Tu	Lle-gi-**ri**-es	Tu	Hau-**ri**-es lle-**git**	Lle-**geix**	(Tu)
Ell	Lle-gi-**ri**-a	Ell	Hau-**ri**-a lle-**git**	Lle-**gei**-xi	(Ell)
Nos	Lle-gi-**rí**-em	Nos.	Hau-**rí**-em lle-**git**	Lle-**gim**	(Nos.)
Vos.	Lle-gi-**rí**-eu	Vos.	Hau-**rí**-eu lle-**git**	Lle-**giu**	(Vos.)
Ells	Lle-gi-**ri**-en	Ells	Hau-**ri**-en lle-**git**	Lle-**gei**-xin	(Ells)

IMPERSONAL		
	SIMPLE	**COMPOUND**
Infinitive	Lle-**gir**	Ha-**ver** lle-**git**
Participle	Lle-**git**	-
Gerund	Lle-**gint**	Ha-**vent** lle-**git**

TO RECEIVE - REBRE

PERSONAL							
INDICATIVE				**SUBJUNCTIVE**			
SIMPLE		**COMPOUND**		**SIMPLE**		**COMPOUND**	
Present		*Past Indefinite*		*Present*		*Past Perfet*	
Jo	**Re**-bo	Jo	**He** re-**but**	Jo	**Re**-bi	Jo	**Ha**-gi re-**but**
Tu	**Reps**	Tu	**Has** re-**but**	Tu	**Re**-bis	Tu	**Ha**-gis re-**but**
Ell	**Rep**	Ell	**Ha** re-**but**	Ell	**Re**-bi	Ell	**Ha**-gi re-**but**
No.	**Re-bem**	Nos.	**Hem** re-**but**	Nos.	**Re-bem**	Nos.	**Hà**-gim re-**but**
Vos.	**Re-beu**	Vos.	**Heu** re-**but**	Vos.	**Re-beu**	Vos.	**Hà**-giu re-**but**
Ells	**Re**-ben	Ells	**Han** re-**but**	Ells	**Re**-bin	Ells	**Ha**-gin re-**but**
Imperfet		*Past Plusquamperfet*		*Imperfet past*		*Plusquamperfet past*	
Jo	Re-**bi**-a	Jo	Ha-**vi**-a re-**but**	Jo	Re-**bés**	Jo	Ha-**gués** re-**but**
Tu	Re-**bi**-es	Tu	Ha-**vi**-es re-**but**	Tu	Re-**bes**-sis	Tu	Ha-**gues**-sis re-**but**
Ell	Re-**bi**-a	Ell	Ha-**vi**-a re-**but**	Ell	Re-**bés**	Ell	Ha-**gués** re-**but**
No.	Re-**bí**-em	Nos.	Ha-**ví**-em re-**but**	Nos	Re-**bés**-sim	Nos.	Ha-**gués**-sim re-**but**
Vos.	Re-**bí**-eu	Vos.	Ha-**ví**-eu re-**but**	Vos.	Re-**bés**-siu	Vos.	Ha-**gués**-siu re-**but**
Ells	Re-**bi**-en	Ells	Ha-**vi**-en re-**but**	Ells	Re-**bes**-sin	Ells	Ha-**gues**-sin re-**but**

Past Simple		*Past Perifrastic*		*Past Anterior perifrastic*
Jo	Re-**bí**	Jo	**Vaig** re-**bre**	**Vaig** ha-**ver** re-**but**
Tu	Re-**be**-res	Tu	**Vas** re-**bre**	**Vas** ha-**ver** re-**but**
Ell	Re-**bé**	Ell	**Va** re-**bre**	**Va** ha-**ver** re-**but**
Nos	Re-**bé**-rem	Nos.	**Vam** re-**bre**	**Vam** ha-**ver** re-**but**
Vos.	Re-**bé**-reu	Vos.	**Vau** re-**bre**	**Vau** ha-**ver** re-**but**
Ells	Re-**be**-ren	Ells	**Van** re-**bre**	**Van** ha-**ver** re-**but**

Future Simple		*Future Compound*	
Jo	Re-**bré**	Jo	Hau-**ré** re-**but**
Tu	Re-**bràs**	Tu	Hau-**ràs** re-**but**
Ell	Re-**brà**	Ell	Hau-**rà** re-**but**
Nos.	Re-**brem**	Nos.	Hau-**rem** re-**but**
Vos.	Re-**breu**	Vos.	Hau-**reu** re-**but**
Ells	Re-**bran**	Ells	Hau-**ran** re-**but**

Conditional Simple		*Conditional Compound*		**IMPERATIVE**	
Jo	Re-**bri**-a	Jo	Hau-ri-a re-**but**		
Tu	Re-**bri**-es	Tu	Hau-**ri**-es re-**but**	**Rep**	(Tu)
Ell	Re-**bri**-a	Ell	Hau-**ri**-a re-**but**	**Re**-bi	(Ell)
Nos	Re-**brí**-em	Nos.	Hau-**rí**-em re-**but**	**Re-bem**	(Nos.)
Vos.	Re-**brí**-eu	Vos.	Hau-**rí**-eu re-**but**	**Re-beu**	(Vos.)
Ells	Re-**bri**-en	Ells	Hau-**ri**-en re-**but**	**Re**-bin	(Ells)

IMPERSONAL		
	SIMPLE	**COMPOUND**
Infinitive	Re-**bre**	Ha-**ver** re-**but**
Participle	Re-**but**	-
Gerund	Re-**bent**	Ha-**vent** re-**but**

TO REMEMBER - RECORDAR

PERSONAL							
INDICATIVE				SUBJUNCTIVE			
SIMPLE		COMPOUND		SIMPLE		COMPOUND	
Present		*Past Indefinite*		*Present*		*Past Perfet*	
Jo	Re-**cor**-do	Jo	**He** re-cor-**dat**	Jo	Re-**cor**-di	Jo	**Ha**-gi re-cor-**dat**
Tu	Re-**cor**-des	Tu	**Has** re-cor-**dat**	Tu	Re-**cor**-dis	Tu	**Ha**-gis re-cor-**dat**
Ell	Re-**cor**-da	Ell	**Ha** re-cor-**dat**	Ell	Re-**cor**-di	Ell	**Ha**-gi re-cor-**dat**
No.	Re-cor-**dem**	Nos.	**Hem** re-cor-**dat**	Nos.	Re-cor-**dem**	Nos.	**Hà**-gim re-cor-**dat**
Vos.	Re-cor-**deu**	Vos.	**Heu** re-cor-**dat**	Vos.	Re-cor-**deu**	Vos.	**Hà**-giu re-cor-**dat**
Ells	Re-**cor**-den	Ells	**Han** re-cor-**dat**	Ells	Re-**cor**-din	Ells	**Ha**-gin re-cor-**dat**
Imperfet		*Past Plusquamperfet*		*Imperfet past*		*Plusquamperfet past*	
Jo	Re-cor-**da**-va	Jo	Ha-**vi**-a re-cor-**dat**	Jo	Re-cor-**dés**	Jo	Ha-**gués** re-cor-**dat**
Tu	Re-cor-**da**-ves	Tu	Ha-**vi**-es re-cor-**dat**	Tu	Re-cor-**des**-sis	Tu	Ha-**gues**-sis re-cor-**dat**
Ell	Re-cor-**da**-va	Ell	Ha-**vi**-a re-cor-**dat**	Ell	Re-cor-**dés**	Ell	Ha-**gués** re-cor-**dat**
No.	Re-cor-**dà**-vem	Nos.	Ha-**ví**-em re-cor-**dat**	Nos	Re-cor-**dés**-sim	Nos.	Ha-**gués**-sim re-cor-**dat**
Vos.	Re-cor-**dà**-veu	Vos.	Ha-**ví**-eu re-cor-**dat**	Vos.	Re-cor-**dés**-siu	Vos.	Ha-**gués**-siu re-cor-**dat**
Ells	Re-cor-**da**-ven	Ells	Ha-**vi**-en re-cor-**dat**	Ells	Re-cor-**des**-sin	Ells	Ha-**gues**-sin re-cor-**dat**

Past Simple		*Past Perifrastic*		*Past Anterior perifrastic*
Jo	Re-cor-**dí**	Jo	**Vaig** re-cor-**dar**	**Vaig** ha-**ver** re-cor-**dat**
Tu	Re-cor-**da**-res	Tu	**Vas** re-cor-**dar**	**Vas** ha-**ver** re-cor-**dat**
Ell	Re-cor-**dà**	Ell	**Va** re-cor-**dar**	**Va** ha-**ver** re-cor-**dat**
Nos	Re-cor-**dà**-rem	Nos.	**Vam** re-cor-**dar**	**Vam** ha-**ver** re-cor-**dat**
Vos.	Re-cor-**dà**-reu	Vos.	**Vau** re-cor-**dar**	**Vau** ha-**ver** re-cor-**dat**
Ells	Re-cor-**da**-ren	Ells	**Van** re-cor-**dar**	**Van** ha-**ver** re-cor-**dat**

Future Simple		*Future Compound*	
Jo	Re-cor-da-**ré**	Jo	Hau-**ré** re-cor-**dat**
Tu	Re-cor-da-**ràs**	Tu	Hau-**ràs** re-cor-**dat**
Ell	Re-cor-da-**rà**	Ell	Hau-**rà** re-cor-**dat**
Nos.	Re-cor-da-**rem**	Nos.	Hau-**rem** re-cor-**dat**
Vos.	Re-cor-da-**reu**	Vos.	Hau-**reu** re-cor-**dat**
Ells	Re-cor-da-**ran**	Ells	Hau-**ran** re-cor-**dat**

Conditional Simple		*Conditional Compound*		IMPERATIVE	
Jo	Re-cor-da-**ri**-a	Jo	Hau-**ri**-a re-cor-**dat**		
Tu	Re-cor-da-**ri**-es	Tu	Hau-**ri**-es re-cor-**dat**	Re-**cor**-da	(Tu)
Ell	Re-cor-da-**ri**-a	Ell	Hau-**ri**-a re-cor-**dat**	Re-**cor**-di	(Ell)
Nos	Re-cor-da-**rí**-em	Nos.	Hau-**rí**-em re-cor-**dat**	Re-cor-**dem**	(Nos.)
Vos.	Re-cor-da-**rí**-eu	Vos.	Hau-**rí**-eu re-cor-**dat**	Re-cor-**deu**	(Vos.)
Ells	Re-cor-da-**ri**-en	Ells	Hau-**ri**-en re-cor-**dat**	Re-**cor**-din	(Ells)

IMPERSONAL		
	SIMPLE	COMPOUND
Infinitive	Re-cor-**dar**	Ha-**ver** re-cor-**dat**
Participle	Re-cor-**dat**	-
Gerund	Re-cor-**dant**	Ha-**vent** re-cor-**dat**

TO REPEAT - REPETIR

PERSONAL							
INDICATIVE				**SUBJUNCTIVE**			
SIMPLE		**COMPOUND**		**SIMPLE**		**COMPOUND**	
Present		*Past Indefinite*		*Present*		*Past Perfet*	
Jo	Re-pe-**tei**-xo	Jo	**He** re-pe-**tit**	Jo	Re-pe-**tei**-xi	Jo	**Ha**-gi re-pe-**tit**
Tu	Re-pe-**tei**-xes	Tu	**Has** re-pe-**tit**	Tu	Re-pe-**tei**-xis	Tu	**Ha**-gis re-pe-**tit**
Ell	Re-pe-**teix**	Ell	**Ha** re-pe-**tit**	Ell	Re-pe-**tei**-xi	Ell	**Ha**-gi re-pe-**tit**
No.	Re-pe-**tim**	Nos	**Hem** re-pe-**tit**	Nos	Re-pe-**tim**	Nos	**Hà**-gim re-pe-**tit**
Vos.	Re-pe-**tiu**	Vos.	**Heu** re-pe-**tit**	Vos.	Re-pe-**tiu**	Vos.	**Hà**-giu re-pe-**tit**
Ells	Re-pe-**tei**-xen	Ells	**Han** re-pe-**tit**	Ells	Re-pe-**tei**-xin	Ells	**Ha**-gin re-pe-**tit**
Imperfet		*Past Plusquamperfet*		*Imperfet past*		*Plusquamperfet past*	
Jo	Re-pe-**ti**-a	Jo	Ha-**vi**-a re-pe-**tit**	Jo	Re-pe-**tís**	Jo	Ha-**gués** re-pe-**tit**
Tu	Re-pe-**ti**-es	Tu	Ha-**vi**-es re-pe-**tit**	Tu	Re-pe-**tis**-sis	Tu	Ha-**gues**-sis re-pe-**tit**
Ell	Re-pe-**ti**-a	Ell	Ha-**vi**-a re-pe-**tit**	Ell	Re-pe-**tís**	Ell	Ha-**gués** re-pe-**tit**
No.	Re-pe-**tí**-em	Nos	Ha-**ví**-em re-pe-**tit**	Nos	Re-pe-**tís**-sim	Nos	Ha-**gués**-sim re-pe-**tit**
Vos.	Re-pe-**tí**-eu	Vos.	Ha-**ví**-eu re-pe-**tit**	Vos.	Re-pe-**tís**-siu	Vos.	Ha-**gués**-siu re-pe-**tit**
Ells	Re-pe-**ti**-en	Ells	Ha-**vi**-en re-pe-**tit**	Ells	Re-pe-**tis**-sin	Ells	Ha-**gues**-sin re-pe-**tit**

Past Simple		*Past Perifrastic*		*Past Anterior perifrastic*
Jo	Re-pe-**tí**	Jo	**Vaig** re-pe-**tir**	**Vaig** ha-**ver** re-pe-**tit**
Tu	Re-pe-**ti**-res	Tu	**Vas** re-pe-**tir**	**Vas** ha-**ver** re-pe-**tit**
Ell	Re-pe-**tí**	Ell	**Va** re-pe-**tir**	**Va** ha-**ver** re-pe-**tit**
Nos	Re-pe-**tí**-rem	Nos.	**Vam** re-pe-**tir**	**Vam** ha-**ver** re-pe-**tit**
Vos.	Re-pe-**tí**-reu	Vos.	**Vau** re-pe-**tir**	**Vau** ha-**ver** re-pe-**tit**
Ells	Re-pe-**ti**-ren	Ells	**Van** re-pe-**tir**	**Van** ha-**ver** re-pe-**tit**

Future Simple		*Future Compound*	
Jo	Re-pe-ti-**ré**	Jo	Hau-**ré** re-pe-**tit**
Tu	Re-pe-ti-**ràs**	Tu	Hau-**ràs** re-pe-**tit**
Ell	Re-pe-ti-**rà**	Ell	Hau-**rà** re-pe-**tit**
Nos.	Re-pe-ti-**rem**	Nos.	Hau-**rem** re-pe-**tit**
Vos.	Re-pe-ti-**reu**	Vos.	Hau-**reu** re-pe-**tit**
Ells	Re-pe-ti-**ran**	Ells	Hau-**ran** re-pe-**tit**

Conditional Simple		*Conditional Compound*		**IMPERATIVE**	
Jo	Re-pe-ti-**ri**-a	Jo	Hau-**ri**-a re-pe-**tit**		
Tu	Re-pe-ti-**ri**-es	Tu	Hau-**ri**-es re-pe-**tit**	Re-pe-**teix**	*(Tu)*
Ell	Re-pe-ti-**ri**-a	Ell	Hau-**ri**-a re-pe-**tit**	Re-pe-**tei**-xi	*(Ell)*
Nos	Re-pe-ti-**rí**-em	Nos.	Hau-**rí**-em re-pe-**tit**	Re-pe-**tim**	*(Nos.)*
Vos.	Re-pe-ti-**rí**-eu	Vos.	Hau-**rí**-eu re-pe-**tit**	Re-pe-**tiu**	*(Vos.)*
Ells	Re-pe-ti-**ri**-en	Ells	Hau-**ri**-en re-pe-**tit**	Re-pe-**tei**-xin	*(Ells)*

IMPERSONAL		
	SIMPLE	**COMPOUND**
Infinitive	Re-pe-**tir**	Ha-**ver** re-pe-**tit**
Participle	Re-pe-**tit**	-
Gerund	Re-pe-**tint**	Ha-**vent** re-pe-**tit**

TO RETURN - RETORNAR

PERSONAL					
INDICATIVE			**SUBJUNCTIVE**		
SIMPLE		**COMPOUND**	**SIMPLE**		**COMPOUND**
Present		*Past Indefinite*	*Present*		*Past Perfet*
Jo	Re-**tor**-no	Jo	**He** re-tor-**nat**	Jo	Re-**tor**-ni	Jo	**Ha**-gi re-tor-**nat**
Tu	Re-**tor**-nes	Tu	**Has** re-tor-**nat**	Tu	Re-**tor**-nis	Tu	**Ha**-gis re-tor-**nat**
Ell	Re-**tor**-na	Ell	**Ha** re-tor-**nat**	Ell	Re-**tor**-ni	Ell	**Ha**-gi re-tor-**nat**
No.	Re-tor-**nem**	Nos.	**Hem** re-tor-**nat**	Nos.	Re-tor-**nem**	Nos.	**Hà**-gim re-tor-**nat**
Vos.	Re-tor-**neu**	Vos.	**Heu** re-tor-**nat**	Vos.	Re-tor-**neu**	Vos.	**Hà**-giu re-tor-**nat**
Ells	Re-**tor**-nen	Ells	**Han** re-tor-**nat**	Ells	Re-**tor**-nin	Ells	**Ha**-gin re-tor-**nat**
Imperfet		*Past Plusquamperfet*	*Imperfet past*		*Plusquamperfet past*
Jo	Re-tor-**na**-va	Jo	Ha-**vi**-a re-tor-**nat**	Jo	Re-tor-**nés**	Jo	Ha-**gués** re-tor-**nat**
Tu	Re-tor-**na**-ves	Tu	Ha-**vi**-es re-tor-**nat**	Tu	Re-tor-**nes**-sis	Tu	Ha-**gues**-sis re-tor-**nat**
Ell	Re-tor-**na**-va	Ell	Ha-**vi**-a re-tor-**nat**	Ell	Re-tor-**nés**	Ell	Ha-**gués** re-tor-**nat**
No.	Re-tor-**nà**-vem	Nos.	Ha-**ví**-em re-tor-**nat**	Nos	Re-tor-**nés**-sim	Nos.	Ha-**gués**-sim re-tor-**nat**
Vos.	Re-tor-**nà**-veu	Vos.	Ha-**ví**-eu re-tor-**nat**	Vos.	Re-tor-**nés**-siu	Vos.	Ha-**gués**-siu re-tor-**nat**
Ells	Re-tor-**na**-ven	Ells	Ha-**vi**-en re-tor-**nat**	Ells	Re-tor-**nes**-sin	Ells	Ha-**gues**-sin re-tor-**nat**

Past Simple		*Past Perifrastic*	*Past Anterior perifrastic*
Jo	Re-tor-**ní**	Jo	**Vaig** re-tor-**nar**	**Vaig** ha-**ver** re-tor-**nat**
Tu	Re-tor-**na**-res	Tu	**Vas** re-tor-**nar**	**Vas** ha-**ver** re-tor-**nat**
Ell	Re-tor-**nà**	Ell	**Va** re-tor-**nar**	**Va** ha-**ver** re-tor-**nat**
Nos	Re-tor-**nà**-rem	Nos.	**Vam** re-tor-**nar**	**Vam** ha-**ver** re-tor-**nat**
Vos.	Re-tor-**nà**-reu	Vos.	**Vau** re-tor-**nar**	**Vau** ha-**ver** re-tor-**nat**
Ells	Re-tor-**na**-ren	Ells	**Van** re-tor-**nar**	**Van** ha-**ver** re-tor-**nat**

Future Simple		*Future Compound*	
Jo	Re-tor-na-**ré**	Jo	Hau-**ré** re-tor-**nat**
Tu	Re-tor-na-**ràs**	Tu	Hau-**ràs** re-tor-**nat**
Ell	Re-tor-na-**rà**	Ell	Hau-**rà** re-tor-**nat**
Nos.	Re-tor-na-**rem**	Nos.	Hau-**rem** re-tor-**nat**
Vos.	Re-tor-na-**reu**	Vos.	Hau-**reu** re-tor-**nat**
Ells	Re-tor-na-**ran**	Ells	Hau-**ran** re-tor-**nat**

Conditional Simple		*Conditional Compound*		**IMPERATIVE**	
Jo	Re-tor-na-**ri**-a	Jo	Hau-**ri**-a re-tor-**nat**		
Tu	Re-tor-na-**ri**-es	Tu	Hau-**ri**-es re-tor-**nat**	Re-**tor**-na	*(Tu)*
Ell	Re-tor-na-**ri**-a	Ell	Hau-**ri**-a re-tor-**nat**	Re-**tor**-ni	*(Ell)*
Nos	Re-tor-na-**rí**-em	Nos.	Hau-**rí**-em re-tor-**nat**	Re-tor-**nem**	*(Nos.)*
Vos.	Re-tor-na-**rí**-eu	Vos.	Hau-**rí**-eu re-tor-**nat**	Re-tor-**neu**	*(Vos.)*
Ells	Re-tor-na-**ri**-en	Ells	Hau-**ri**-en re-tor-**nat**	Re-**tor**-nin	*(Ells)*

IMPERSONAL		
	SIMPLE	**COMPOUND**
Infinitive	Re-tor-**nar**	Ha-**ver** re-tor-**nat**
Participle	Re-tor-**nat**	-
Gerund	Re-tor-**nant**	Ha-**vent** re-tor-n**at**

TO RUN – CÓRRER

PERSONAL					
INDICATIVE			**SUBJUNCTIVE**		
SIMPLE	**COMPOUND**		**SIMPLE**	**COMPOUND**	
Present	*Past Indefinite*		*Present*	*Past Perfet*	
Jo **Cor**-ro	Jo	**He** cor-re-**gut**	Jo **Cor**-ri	Jo	**Ha**-gi cor-re-**gut**
Tu **Cor**-res	Tu	**Has** cor-re-**gut**	Tu **Cor**-ris	Tu	**Ha**-gis cor-re-**gut**
Ell **Cor**-re	Ell	**Ha** cor-re-**gut**	Ell **Cor**-ri	Ell	**Ha**-gi cor-re-**gut**
No. Cor-**rem**	Nos.	**Hem** cor-re-**gut**	Nos. Cor-**rem**	Nos.	**Hà**-gim cor-re-**gut**
Vos. Cor-**reu**	Vos.	**Heu** cor-re-**gut**	Vos. Cor-**reu**	Vos.	**Hà**-giu cor-re-**gut**
Ells **Cor**-ren	Ells	**Han** cor-re-**gut**	Ells **Cor**-rin	Ells	**Ha**-gin cor-re-**gut**
Imperfet	*Past Plusquamperfet*		*Imperfet past*	*Plusquamperfet past*	
Jo Cor-**ri**-a	Jo	**Ha-vi**-a cor-re-**gut**	Jo Cor-re-**gués**	Jo	**Ha-gués** cor-re-**gut**
Tu Cor-**ri**-es	Tu	**Ha-vi**-es cor-re-**gut**	Tu Cor-re-**gues**-sis	Tu	**Ha-gues**-sis cor-re-**gut**
Ell Cor-**ri**-a	Ell	**Ha-vi**-a cor-re-**gut**	Ell Cor-re-**gués**	Ell	**Ha-gués** cor-re-**gut**
No. Cor-**rí**-em	Nos.	**Ha-ví**-em cor-re-**gut**	Nos. Cor-re-**gués**-sim	Nos.	**Ha-gués**-sim cor-re-**gut**
Vos. Cor-**rí**-eu	Vos.	**Ha-ví**-eu cor-re-**gut**	Vos. Cor-re-**gués**-siu	Vos.	**Ha-gués**-siu cor-re-**gut**
Ells Cor-**ri**-en	Ells	**Ha-vi**-en cor-re-**gut**	Ells Cor-re-**gues**-sin	Ells	**Ha-gues**-sin cor-re-**gut**

Past Simple	*Past Perifrastic*	*Past Anterior perifrastic*
Jo Cor-re-**guí**	Jo **Vaig cór**-rer	**Vaig** ha-**ver** cor-re-**gut**
Tu Cor-re-**gue**-res	Tu **Vas cór**-rer	**Vas** ha-**ver** cor-re-**gut**
Ell Cor-re-**gué**	Ell **Va cór**-rer	**Va** ha-**ver** cor-re-**gut**
Nos. Cor-re-**gué**-rem	Nos. **Vam cór**-rer	**Vam** ha-**ver** cor-re-**gut**
Vos. Cor-re-**gué**-reu	Vos. **Vau cór**-rer	**Vau** ha-**ver** cor-re-**gut**
Ells Cor-re-**gue**-ren	Ells **Van cór**-rer	**Van** ha-**ver** cor-re-**gut**

Future Simple	*Future Compound*
Jo Cor-re-**ré**	Jo Hau-**ré** cor-re-**gut**
Tu Cor-re-**ràs**	Tu Hau-**ràs** cor-re-**gut**
Ell Cor-re-**rà**	Ell Hau-**rà** cor-re-**gut**
Nos. **Cór**-re-**rem**	Nos. Hau-**rem** cor-re-**gut**
Vos. **Cór**-re-**reu**	Vos. Hau-**reu** cor-re-**gut**
Ells Cor-re-**ran**	Ells Hau-**ran** cor-re-**gut**

Conditional Simple	*Conditional Compound*	**IMPERATIVE**	
Jo Cor-re-**ri**-a	Jo Hau-**ri**-a cor-re-**gut**		
Tu Cor-re-**ri**-es	Tu Hau-**ri**-es cor-re-**gut**	**Cor**-re	*(Tu)*
Ell Cor-re-**ri**-a	Ell Hau-**ri**-a cor-re-**gut**	**Cor**-ri	*(Ell)*
Nos. Cor-re-**rí**-em	Nos. Hau-**rí**-em cor-re-**gut**	Cor-re-**guem** / cor-**rem**	*(Nos.)*
Vos. Cor-re-**rí**-eu	Vos. Hau-**rí**-eu cor-re-**gut**	Cor-**reu**	*(Vos.)*
Ells Cor-re-**ri**-en	Ells Hau-**ri**-en cor-re-**gut**	**Cor**-rin	*(Ells)*

IMPERSONAL		
	SIMPLE	**COMPOUND**
Infinitive	**Cór**-rer	Ha-**ver** cor-re-**gut**
Participle	Cor-re-**gut**	-
Gerund	Cor-**rent**	Ha-**vent** cor-re-**gut**

TO SAY - DIR

PERSONAL							

INDICATIVE				SUBJUNCTIVE			
SIMPLE		COMPOUND		SIMPLE		COMPOUND	
Present		*Past Indefinite*		*Present*		*Past Perfet*	
Jo	**Dic**	Jo	**He dit**	Jo	**Di**-gui	Jo	**Ha**-gi **dit**
Tu	**Dius**	Tu	**Has dit**	Tu	**Di**-guis	Tu	**Ha**-gis **dit**
Ell	**Diu**	Ell	**Ha dit**	Ell	**Di**-gui	Ell	**Ha**-gi **dit**
No.	Di-**em**	Nos.	**Hem dit**	Nos.	Di-**guem**	Nos.	**Hà**-gim **dit**
Vos.	Di-**eu**	Vos.	**Heu dit**	Vos.	Di-**gueu**	Vos.	**Hà**-giu **dit**
Ells	**Di**-uen	Ells	**Han dit**	Ells	**Di**-guin	Ells	**Ha**-gin **dit**
Imperfet		*Past Plusquamperfet*		*Imperfet past*		*Plusquamperfet past*	
Jo	**De**-ia	Jo	Ha-**vi**-a **dit**	Jo	Di-**gués**	Jo	Ha-**gués dit**
Tu	**De**-ies	Tu	Ha-**vi**-es **dit**	Tu	Di-**gues**-sis	Tu	Ha-**gues**-sis **dit**
Ell	**De**-ia	Ell	Ha-**vi**-a **dit**	Ell	Di-**gués**	Ell	Ha-**gués dit**
No.	**Dè**-iem	Nos.	Ha-**ví**-em **dit**	Nos.	Di-**gués**-sim	Nos.	Ha-**gués**-sim **dit**
Vos.	**Dè**-ieu	Vos.	Ha-**ví**-eu **dit**	Vos.	Di-**gués**-siu	Vos.	Ha-**gués**-siu **dit**
Ells	**De**-ien	Ells	Ha-**vi**-en **dit**	Ells	Di-**gues**-sin	Ells	Ha-**gues**-sin **dit**

Past Simple		*Past Perifrastic*		*Past Anterior perifrastic*			
Jo	Di-**guí**	Jo	**Vaig dir**	**Vaig** ha-**ver dit**			
Tu	Di-**gue**-res	Tu	**Vas dir**	**Vas** ha-**ver dit**			
Ell	Di-**gué**	Ell	**Va dir**	**Va** ha-**ver dit**			
Nos.	Di-**gué**-rem	Nos.	**Vam dir**	**Vam** ha-**ver dit**			
Vos.	Di-**gué**-reu	Vos.	**Vau dir**	**Vau** ha-**ver dit**			
Ells	Di-**gue**-ren	Ells	**Van dir**	**Van** ha-**ver dit**			

Future Simple		*Future Compound*					
Jo	Di-**ré**	Jo	Hau-**ré dit**				
Tu	Di-**ràs**	Tu	Hau-**ràs dit**				
Ell	Di-**rà**	Ell	Hau-**rà dit**				
Nos.	Di-**rem**	Nos.	Hau-**rem dit**				
Vos.	Di-**reu**	Vos.	Hau-**reu dit**				
Ells	Di-**ran**	Ells	Hau-**ran dit**				

Conditional Simple		*Conditional Compound*		IMPERATIVE			
Jo	Di-**ri**-a	Jo	Hau-ri-a **dit**				
Tu	Di-**ri**-es	Tu	Hau-ri-es **dit**	**Di**-gues		(Tu)	
Ell	Di-**ri**-a	Ell	Hau-ri-a **dit**	**Di**-gui		(Ell)	
Nos.	Di-**rí**-em	Nos.	Hau-rí-em **dit**	Di-**guem**		(Nos.)	
Vos.	Di-**rí**-eu	Vos.	Hau-rí-eu **dit**	Di-**gueu**		(Vos.)	
Ells	Di-**ri**-en	Ells	Hau-ri-en **dit**	**Di**-guin		(Ells)	

IMPERSONAL		
	SIMPLE	COMPOUND
Infinitive	**Dir**	Ha-**ver** dit
Participle	Dit	-
Gerund	Di-**ent**	Ha-**vent** dit

TO SCREAM - CRIDAR

PERSONAL							
INDICATIVE				**SUBJUNCTIVE**			
SIMPLE		**COMPOUND**		**SIMPLE**		**COMPOUND**	
Present		*Past Indefinite*		*Present*		*Past Perfet*	
Jo	**Cri**-do	Jo	**He** cri-**dat**	Jo	**Cri**-di	Jo	**Ha**-gi cri-**dat**
Tu	**Cri**-des	Tu	**Has** cri-**dat**	Tu	**Cri**-dis	Tu	**Ha**-gis cri-**dat**
Ell	**Cri**-da	Ell	**Ha** cri-**dat**	Ell	**Cri**-di	Ell	**Ha**-gi cri-**dat**
No.	Cri-**dem**	Nos.	**Hem** cri-**dat**	Nos.	Cri-**dem**	Nos.	**Hà**-gim cri-**dat**
Vos.	Cri-**deu**	Vos.	**Heu** cri-**dat**	Vos.	Cri-**deu**	Vos.	**Hà**-giu cri-**dat**
Ells	**Cri**-den	Ells	**Han** cri-**dat**	Ells	**Cri**-din	Ells	**Ha**-gin cri-**dat**
Imperfet		*Past Plusquamperfet*		*Imperfet past*		*Plusquamperfet past*	
Jo	Cri-**da**-va	Jo	Ha-**vi**-a cri-**dat**	Jo	Cri-**dés**	Jo	Ha-**gués** cri-**dat**
Tu	Cri-**da**-ves	Tu	Ha-**vi**-es cri-**dat**	Tu	Cri-**des**-sis	Tu	Ha-**gues**-sis cri-**dat**
Ell	Cri-**da**-va	Ell	Ha-**vi**-a cri-**dat**	Ell	Cri-**dés**	Ell	Ha-**gués** cri-**dat**
No.	Cri-**dà**-vem	Nos.	Ha-**ví**-em cri-**dat**	Nos	Cri-**dés**-sim	Nos.	Ha-**gués**-sim cri-**dat**
Vos.	Cri-**dà**-veu	Vos.	Ha-**ví**-eu cri-**dat**	Vos.	Cri-**dés**-siu	Vos.	Ha-**gués**-siu cri-**dat**
Ells	Cri-**da**-ven	Ells	Ha-**vi**-en cri-**dat**	Ells	Cri-**des**-sin	Ells	Ha-**gues**-sin cri-**dat**

Past Simple		*Past Perifrastic*		*Past Anterior perifrastic*
Jo	Cri-**dí**	Jo	**Vaig** cri-**dar**	**Vaig** ha-**ver** cri-**dat**
Tu	Cri-**da**-res	Tu	**Vas** cri-**dar**	**Vas** ha-**ver** cri-**dat**
Ell	Cri-**dà**	Ell	**Va** cri-**dar**	**Va** ha-**ver** cri-**dat**
Nos	Cri-**dà**-rem	Nos.	**Vam** cri-**dar**	**Vam** ha-**ver** cri-**dat**
Vos.	Cri-**dà**-reu	Vos.	**Vau** cri-**dar**	**Vau** ha-**ver** cri-**dat**
Ells	Cri-**da**-ren	Ells	**Van** cri-**dar**	**Van** ha-**ver** cri-**dat**

Future Simple		*Future Compound*	
Jo	Cri-da-**ré**	Jo	Hau-**ré** cri-**dat**
Tu	Cri-da-**ràs**	Tu	Hau-**ràs** cri-**dat**
Ell	Cri-da-**rà**	Ell	Hau-**rà** cri-**dat**
Nos.	Cri-da-**rem**	Nos.	Hau-**rem** cri-**dat**
Vos.	Cri-da-**reu**	Vos.	Hau-**reu** cri-**dat**
Ells	Cri-da-**ran**	Ells	Hau-**ran** cri-**dat**

Conditional Simple		*Conditional Compound*		**IMPERATIVE**	
Jo	Cri-da-**ri**-a	Jo	Hau-**ri**-a cri-**dat**		
Tu	Cri-da-**ri**-es	Tu	Hau-**ri**-es cri-**dat**	**Cri**-da	*(Tu)*
Ell	Cri-da-**ri**-a	Ell	Hau-**ri**-a cri-**dat**	**Cri**-di	*(Ell)*
Nos	Cri-da-**rí**-em	Nos.	Hau-**rí**-em cri-**dat**	Cri-**dem**	*(Nos.)*
Vos.	Cri-da-**rí**-eu	Vos.	Hau-**rí**-eu cri-**dat**	Cri-**deu**	*(Vos.)*
Ells	Cri-da-**rí**-en	Ells	Hau-**rí**-en cri-**dat**	**Cri**-din	*(Ells)*

IMPERSONAL		
	SIMPLE	**COMPOUND**
Infinitive	Cri-**dar**	Ha-**ver** cri-**dat**
Participle	Cri-**dat**	-
Gerund	Cri-**dant**	Ha-**vent** cri-**dat**

TO SEE - VEURE

PERSONAL			
INDICATIVE		**SUBJUNCTIVE**	
SIMPLE	COMPOUND	SIMPLE	COMPOUND

Present		*Past Indefinite*		*Present*		*Past Perfet*	
Jo	**Veig**	Jo	**He vist**	Jo	**Ve**-gi	Jo	**Ha**-gi **vist**
Tu	**Veus**	Tu	**Has vist**	Tu	**Ve**-gis	Tu	**Ha**-gis **vist**
Ell	**Veu**	Ell	**Ha vist**	Ell	**Ve**-gi	Ell	**Ha**-gi **vist**
No.	Ve-**iem**	Nos.	**Hem vist**	Nos.	Ve-**gem**	Nos.	**Hà**-gim **vist**
Vos.	Ve-**ieu**	Vos.	**Heu vist**	Vos.	Ve-**geu**	Vos.	**Hà**-giu **vist**
Ells	**Ve**-uen	Ells	**Han vist**	Ells	**Ve**-gin	Ells	**Ha**-gin **vist**

Imperfet		*Past Plusquamperfet*		*Imperfet past*		*Plusquamperfet past*	
Jo	**Ve**-ia	Jo	Ha-**vi**-a **vist**	Jo	Ve-**iés**	Jo	Ha-**gués vist**
Tu	**Ve**-ies	Tu	Ha-**vi**-es **vist**	Tu	Ve-**ies**-sis	Tu	Ha-**gues**-sis **vist**
Ell	**Ve**-ia	Ell	Ha-**vi**-a **vist**	Ell	Ve-**iés**	Ell	Ha-**gués vist**
No.	**Vè**-iem	Nos.	Ha-**ví**-em **vist**	Nos.	Ve-**iés**-sim	Nos.	Ha-**gués**-sim **vist**
Vos.	**Vè**-ieu	Vos.	Ha-**ví**-eu **vist**	Vos.	Ve-**iés**-siu	Vos.	Ha-**gués**-siu **vist**
Ells	**Ve**-ien	Ells	Ha-**vi**-en **vist**	Ells	Ve-**ies**-sin	Ells	Ha-**gues**-sin **vist**

Past Simple		*Past Perifrastic*		*Past Anterior perifrastic*
Jo	**Viu**	Jo	**Vaig veu-re**	**Vaig** ha-**ver vist**
Tu	Ve-**ie**-res	Tu	**Vas veu-re**	**Vas** ha-**ver vist**
Ell	Ve-**ié**	Ell	**Va veu-re**	**Va** ha-**ver vist**
Nos.	Ve-**ié**-rem	Nos.	**Vam veu-re**	**Vam** ha-**ver vist**
Vos.	Ve-**ié**-reu	Vos.	**Vau veu-re**	**Vau** ha-**ver vist**
Ells	Ve-**ie**-ren	Ells	**Van veu-re**	**Van** ha-**ver vist**

Future Simple		*Future Compound*	
Jo	Veu-**ré**	Jo	Hau-**ré vist**
Tu	Veu-**ràs**	Tu	Hau-**ràs vist**
Ell	Veu-**rà**	Ell	Hau-**rà vist**
Nos.	Veu-**rem**	Nos.	Hau-**rem vist**
Vos.	Veu-**reu**	Vos.	Hau-**reu vist**
Ells	Veu-**ran**	Ells	Hau-**ran vist**

Conditional Simple		*Conditional Compound*		**IMPERATIVE**	
Jo	Veu-**ri**-a	Jo	Hau-**ri**-a **vist**		
Tu	Veu-**ri**-es	Tu	Hau-**ri**-es **vist**	**Ve**-ges	*(Tu)*
Ell	Veu-**ri**-a	Ell	Hau-**ri**-a **vist**	**Ve**-gi	*(Ell)*
Nos.	Veu-**rí**-em	Nos.	Hau-**rí**-em **vist**	Ve-**gem**	*(Nos.)*
Vos.	Veu-**rí**-eu	Vos.	Hau-**rí**-eu **vist**	Ve-**geu** / Ve-**ieu**	*(Vos.)*
Ells	Veu-**ri**-en	Ells	Hau-**ri**-en **vist**	Ve-**gin**	*(Ells)*

IMPERSONAL		
	SIMPLE	COMPOUND
Infinitive	**Veu-re**	Ha-**ver vist**
Participle	Vist	-
Gerund	Ve-**ient**	Ha-**vent vist**

TO SEEM - SEMBLAR

PERSONAL							
INDICATIVE				SUBJUNCTIVE			
SIMPLE		COMPOUND			SIMPLE		COMPOUND
Present		*Past Indefinite*			*Present*		*Past Perfet*
Jo	**Sem**-blo	Jo	**He** sem-**blat**		Jo	**Sem**-bli	Jo	**Ha**-gi sem-**blat**
Tu	**Sem**-bles	Tu	**Has** sem-**blat**		Tu	**Sem**-blis	Tu	**Ha**-gis sem-**blat**
Ell	**Sem**-bla	Ell	**Ha** sem-**blat**		Ell	**Sem**-bli	Ell	**Ha**-gi sem-**blat**
No.	Sem-**blem**	Nos.	**Hem** sem-**blat**		Nos.	Sem-**blem**	Nos.	**Hà**-gim sem-**blat**
Vos.	Sem-**bleu**	Vos.	**Heu** sem-**blat**		Vos.	Sem-**bleu**	Vos.	**Hà**-giu sem-**blat**
Ells	**Sem**-blen	Ells	**Han** sem-**blat**		Ells	**Sem**-blin	Ells	**Ha**-gin sem-**blat**
Imperfet		*Past Plusquamperfet*			*Imperfet past*		*Plusquamperfet past*
Jo	Sem-**bla**-va	Jo	Ha-**vi**-a sem-**blat**		Jo	Sem-**blés**	Jo	Ha-**gués** sem-**blat**
Tu	Sem-**bla**-ves	Tu	Ha-**vi**-es sem-**blat**		Tu	Sem-**bles**-sis	Tu	Ha-**gues**-sis sem-**blat**
Ell	Sem-**bla**-va	Ell	Ha-**vi**-a sem-**blat**		Ell	Sem-**blés**	Ell	Ha-**gués** sem-**blat**
No.	Sem-**blà**-vem	Nos.	Ha-**ví**-em sem-**blat**		Nos	Sem-**blés**-sim	Nos.	Ha-**gués**-sim sem-**blat**
Vos.	Sem-**blà**-veu	Vos.	Ha-**ví**-eu sem-**blat**		Vos.	Sem-**blés**-siu	Vos.	Ha-**gués**-siu sem-**blat**
Ells	Sem-**bla**-ven	Ells	Ha-**vi**-en sem-**blat**		Ells	Sem-**bles**-sin	Ells	Ha-**gues**-sin sem-**blat**

Past Simple		*Past Perifrastic*		*Past Anterior perifrastic*
Jo	Sem-**blí**	Jo	**Vaig** sem-**blar**	**Vaig** ha-**ver** sem-**blat**
Tu	Sem-**bla**-res	Tu	**Vas** sem-**blar**	**Vas** ha-**ver** sem-**blat**
Ell	Sem-**blà**	Ell	**Va** sem-**blar**	**Va** ha-**ver** sem-**blat**
Nos	Sem-**blà**-rem	Nos.	**Vam** sem-**blar**	**Vam** ha-**ver** sem-**blat**
Vos.	Sem-**blà**-reu	Vos.	**Vau** sem-**blar**	**Vau** ha-**ver** sem-**blat**
Ells	Sem-**bla**-ren	Ells	**Van** sem-**blar**	**Van** ha-**ver** sem-**blat**

Future Simple		*Future Compound*	
Jo	Sem-bla-**ré**	Jo	Hau-**ré** sem-**blat**
Tu	Sem-bla-**ràs**	Tu	Hau-**ràs** sem-**blat**
Ell	Sem-bla-**rà**	Ell	Hau-**rà** sem-**blat**
Nos.	Sem-bla-**rem**	Nos.	Hau-**rem** sem-**blat**
Vos.	Sem-bla-**reu**	Vos.	Hau-**reu** sem-**blat**
Ells	Sem-bla-**ran**	Ells	Hau-**ran** sem-**blat**

Conditional Simple		*Conditional Compound*		IMPERATIVE		
Jo	Sem-bla-**ri**-a	Jo	Hau-**ri**-a sem-**blat**			
Tu	Sem-bla-**ri**-es	Tu	Hau-**ri**-es sem-**blat**	**Sem**-bla		*(Tu)*
Ell	Sem-bla-**ri**-a	Ell	Hau-**ri**-a sem-**blat**	**Sem**-bli		*(Ell)*
Nos	Sem-bla-**rí**-em	Nos.	Hau-**rí**-em sem-**blat**	Sem-**blem**		*(Nos.)*
Vos.	Sem-bla-**rí**-eu	Vos.	Hau-**rí**-eu sem-**blat**	Sem-**bleu**		*(Vos.)*
Ells	Sem-bla-**ri**-en	Ells	Hau-**ri**-en sem-**blat**	**Sem**-blin		*(Ells)*

IMPERSONAL		
	SIMPLE	COMPOUND
Infinitive	Sem-**blar**	Ha-**ver** sem-**blat**
Participle	Sem-**blat**	-
Gerund	Sem-**blant**	Ha-**vent** sem-**blat**

TO SELL - VENDRE

PERSONAL				
INDICATIVE			**SUBJUNCTIVE**	
SIMPLE	**COMPOUND**		**SIMPLE**	**COMPOUND**
Present	*Past Indefinite*		*Present*	*Past Perfet*
Jo **Venc**	Jo **He** ve-**nut**		Jo **Ven**-gui	Jo **Ha**-gi ve-**nut**
Tu **Vens**	Tu **Has** ve-**nut**		Tu **Ven**-guis	Tu **Ha**-gis ve-**nut**
Ell **Ven**	Ell **Ha** ve-**nut**		Ell **Ven**-gui	Ell **Ha**-gi ve-**nut**
No. Ve-**nem**	Nos. **Hem** ve-**nut**		Nos. **Ven**-guem	Nos. **Hà**-gim ve-**nut**
Vos. Ve-**neu**	Vos. **Heu** ve-**nut**		Vos. **Ven**-gueu	Vos. **Hà**-giu ve-**nut**
Ells **Ve**-nen	Ells **Han** ve-**nut**		Ells **Ven**-guin	Ells **Ha**-gin ve-**nut**
Imperfet	*Past Plusquamperfet*		*Imperfet past*	*Plusquamperfet past*
Jo Ve-**ni**-a	Jo Ha-**vi**-a ve-**nut**		Jo Ven-**gués**	Jo Ha-**gués** ve-**nut**
Tu Ve-**ni**-es	Tu Ha-**vi**-es ve-**nut**		Tu Ven-**gues**-sis	Tu Ha-**gues**-sis ve-**nut**
Ell Ve-**ni**-a	Ell Ha-**vi**-a ve-**nut**		Ell Ven-**gués**	Ell Ha-**gués** ve-**nut**
No. Ve-**ní**-em	Nos. Ha-**ví**-em ve-**nut**		Nos. Ven-**gués**-sim	Nos. Ha-**gués**-sim ve-**nut**
Vos. Ve-**ní**-eu	Vos. Ha-**ví**-eu ve-**nut**		Vos. Ven-**gués**-siu	Vos. Ha-**gués**-siu ve-**nut**
Ells Ve-**ni**-en	Ells Ha-**vi**-en ve-**nut**		Ells Ven-**gues**-sin	Ells Ha-**gues**-sin ve-**nut**

Past Simple	*Past Perifrastic*	*Past Anterior perifrastic*
Jo Ven-**guí**	Jo **Vaig ven**-dre	**Vaig** ha-**ver** ve-**nut**
Tu Ven-**gue**-res	Tu **Vas ven**-dre	**Vas** ha-**ver** ve-**nut**
Ell Ven-**gué**	Ell **Va ven**-dre	**Va** ha-**ver** ve-**nut**
Nos. Ven-**gué**-rem	Nos. **Vam ven**-dre	**Vam** ha-**ver** ve-**nut**
Vos. Ven-**gué**-reu	Vos. **Vau ven**-dre	**Vau** ha-**ver** ve-**nut**
Ells Ven-**gue**-ren	Ells **Van ven**-dre	**Van** ha-**ver** ve-**nut**

Future Simple	*Future Compound*
Jo Ven-**dré**	Jo Hau-**ré** ve-**nut**
Tu Ven-**dràs**	Tu Hau-**ràs** ve-**nut**
Ell Ven-**drà**	Ell Hau-**rà** ve-**nut**
Nos. Ven-**drem**	Nos. Hau-**rem** ve-**nut**
Vos. Ven-**dreu**	Vos. Hau-**reu** ve-**nut**
Ells Ven-**dran**	Ells Hau-**ran** ve-**nut**

Conditional Simple	*Conditional Compound*	**IMPERATIVE**	
Jo Ven-**dri**-a	Jo Hau-**ri**-a ve-**nut**		
Tu Ven-**dri**-es	Tu Hau-**ri**-es ve-**nut**	**Ven**	*(Tu)*
Ell Ven-**dri**-a	Ell Hau-**ri**-a ve-**nut**	**Ven**-gui	*(Ell)*
Nos. Ven-**drí**-em	Nos. Hau-**rí**-em ve-**nut**	**Ven**-guem	*(Nos.)*
Vos. Ven-**drí**-eu	Vos. Hau-**rí**-eu ve-**nut**	Ve-**neu**	*(Vos.)*
Ells Ven-**dri**-en	Ells Hau-**ri**-en ve-**nut**	**Ven**-guin	*(Ells)*

IMPERSONAL		
	SIMPLE	**COMPOUND**
Infinitive	**Ven**-dre	Ha-**ver** ve-**nut**
Participle	Ve-**nut**	-
Gerund	Ve-**nent**	Ha-**vent** ve-**nut**

TO SEND - ENVIAR

PERSONAL							
INDICATIVE				**SUBJUNCTIVE**			
SIMPLE		**COMPOUND**		**SIMPLE**		**COMPOUND**	
Present		*Past Indefinite*		*Present*		*Past Perfet*	
Jo	En-**vi**-o	Jo	**He** en-vi-**at**	Jo	En-**vi**-ï	Jo	**Ha**-gi en-vi-**at**
Tu	En-**vi**-es	Tu	**Has** en-vi-**at**	Tu	En-**vi**-ïs	Tu	**Ha**-gis en-vi-**at**
Ell	En-**vi**-a	Ell	**Ha** en-vi-**at**	Ell	En-**vi**-ï	Ell	**Ha**-gi en-vi-**at**
No.	En-vi-**em**	Nos.	**Hem** en-vi-**at**	Nos.	En-vi-**em**	Nos.	**Hà**-gim en-vi-**at**
Vos.	En-vi-**eu**	Vos.	**Heu** en-vi-**at**	Vos.	En-vi-**eu**	Vos.	**Hà**-giu en-vi-**at**
Ells	En-**vi**-en	Ells	**Han** en-vi-**at**	Ells	En-**vi**-in	Ells	**Ha**-gin en-vi-**at**
Imperfet		*Past Plusquamperfet*		*Imperfet past*		*Plusquamperfet past*	
Jo	En-vi-**a**-va	Jo	**Ha**-**vi**-a en-vi-**at**	Jo	En-vi-**és**	Jo	**Ha**-**gués** en-vi-**at**
Tu	En-vi-**a**-ves	Tu	**Ha**-**vi**-es en-vi-**at**	Tu	En-vi-**es**-sis	Tu	**Ha**-**gues**-sis en-vi-**at**
Ell	En-vi-**a**-va	Ell	**Ha**-**vi**-a en-vi-**at**	Ell	En-vi-**és**	Ell	**Ha**-**gués** en-vi-**at**
No.	En-vi-**à**-vem	Nos.	**Ha**-**ví**-em en-vi-**at**	Nos	En-vi-**és**-sim	Nos.	**Ha**-**gués**-sim en-vi-**at**
Vos.	En-vi-**à**-veu	Vos.	**Ha**-**ví**-eu en-vi-**at**	Vos.	En-vi-**és**-siu	Vos.	**Ha**-**gués**-siu en-vi-**at**
Ells	En-vi-**a**-ven	Ells	**Ha**-**vi**-en en-vi-**at**	Ells	En-vi-**es**-sin	Ells	**Ha**-**gues**-sin en-vi-**at**

Past Simple		*Past Perifrastic*		*Past Anterior perifrastic*
Jo	En-vi-**í**	Jo	**Vaig** en-vi-**ar**	**Vaig** ha-**ver** en-vi-**at**
Tu	En-vi-**a**-res	Tu	**Vas** en-vi-**ar**	**Vas** ha-**ver** en-vi-**at**
Ell	En-vi-**à**	Ell	**Va** en-vi-**ar**	**Va** ha-**ver** en-vi-**at**
Nos	En-vi-**à**-rem	Nos.	**Vam** en-vi-**ar**	**Vam** ha-**ver** en-vi-**at**
Vos.	En-vi-**à**-reu	Vos.	**Vau** en-vi-**ar**	**Vau** ha-**ver** en-vi-**at**
Ells	En-vi-**a**-ren	Ells	**Van** en-vi-**ar**	**Van** ha-**ver** en-vi-**at**

Future Simple		*Future Compound*	
Jo	En-vi-a-**ré**	Jo	Hau-**ré** en-vi-**at**
Tu	En-vi-a-**ràs**	Tu	Hau-**ràs** en-vi-**at**
Ell	En-vi-a-**rà**	Ell	Hau-**rà** en-vi-**at**
Nos.	En-vi-a-**rem**	Nos.	Hau-**rem** en-vi-**at**
Vos.	En-vi-a-**reu**	Vos.	Hau-**reu** en-vi-**at**
Ells	En-vi-a-**ran**	Ells	Hau-**ran** en-vi-**at**

Conditional Simple		*Conditional Compound*		**IMPERATIVE**	
Jo	En-vi-a-**ri**-a	Jo	Hau-**ri**-a en-vi-**at**		
Tu	En-vi-a-**ri**-es	Tu	Hau-**ri**-es en-vi-**at**	En-**vi**-a	(Tu)
Ell	En-vi-a-**ri**-a	Ell	Hau-**ri**-a en-vi-**at**	En-**vi**-ï	(Ell)
Nos	En-vi-a-**rí**-em	Nos.	Hau-**rí**-em en-vi-**at**	En-vi-**em**	(Nos.)
Vos.	En-vi-a-**rí**-eu	Vos.	Hau-**rí**-eu en-vi-**at**	En-vi-**eu**	(Vos.)
Ells	En-vi-a-**ri**-en	Ells	Hau-**ri**-en en-vi-**at**	En-**vi**-in	(Ells)

IMPERSONAL		
	SIMPLE	**COMPOUND**
Infinitive	En-vi-**ar**	Ha-**ver** en-vi-**at**
Participle	En-vi-**at**	-
Gerund	En-vi-**ant**	Ha-**vent** en-vi-**at**

TO SHOW - MOSTRAR

PERSONAL						
INDICATIVE				**SUBJUNCTIVE**		
SIMPLE		**COMPOUND**		**SIMPLE**		**COMPOUND**

INDICATIVE

SIMPLE		COMPOUND		SIMPLE		COMPOUND	
Present		*Past Indefinite*		*Present*		*Past Perfet*	
Jo	**Mos**-tro	Jo	**He** mos-**trat**	Jo	**Mos**-tri	Jo	**Ha**-gi mos-**trat**
Tu	**Mos**-tres	Tu	**Has** mos-**trat**	Tu	**Mos**-tris	Tu	**Ha**-gis mos-**trat**
Ell	**Mos**-tra	Ell	**Ha** mos-**trat**	Ell	**Mos**-tri	Ell	**Ha**-gi mos-**trat**
No.	Mos-**trem**	Nos.	**Hem** mos-**trat**	Nos.	Mos-**trem**	Nos.	**Hà**-gim mos-**trat**
Vos.	Mos-**treu**	Vos.	**Heu** mos-**trat**	Vos.	Mos-**treu**	Vos.	**Hà**-giu mos-**trat**
Ells	**Mos**-tren	Ells	**Han** mos-**trat**	Ells	**Mos**-trin	Ells	**Ha**-gin mos-**trat**
Imperfet		*Past Plusquamperfet*		*Imperfet past*		*Plusquamperfet past*	
Jo	Mos-**tra**-va	Jo	Ha-**vi**-a mos-**trat**	Jo	Mos-**trés**	Jo	Ha-**gués** mos-**trat**
Tu	Mos-**tra**-ves	Tu	Ha-**vi**-es mos-**trat**	Tu	Mos-**tres**-sis	Tu	Ha-**gues**-sis mos-**trat**
Ell	Mos-**tra**-va	Ell	Ha-**vi**-a mos-**trat**	Ell	Mos-**trés**	Ell	Ha-**gués** mos-**trat**
No.	Mos-**trà**-vem	Nos.	Ha-**ví**-em mos-**trat**	Nos	Mos-**trés**-sim	Nos.	Ha-**gués**-sim mos-**trat**
Vos.	Mos-**trà**-veu	Vos.	Ha-**ví**-eu mos-**trat**	Vos.	Mos-**trés**-siu	Vos.	Ha-**gués**-siu mos-**trat**
Ells	Mos-**tra**-ven	Ells	Ha-**vi**-en mos-**trat**	Ells	Mos-**tres**-sin	Ells	Ha-**gues**-sin mos-**trat**

Past Simple		*Past Perifrastic*		*Past Anterior perifrastic*
Jo	Mos-**trí**	Jo	**Vaig** mos-**trar**	**Vaig** ha-**ver** mos-**trat**
Tu	Mos-**tra**-res	Tu	**Vas** mos-**trar**	**Vas** ha-**ver** mos-**trat**
Ell	Mos-**trà**	Ell	**Va** mos-**trar**	**Va** ha-**ver** mos-**trat**
Nos	Mos-**trà**-rem	Nos.	**Vam** mos-**trar**	**Vam** ha-**ver** mos-**trat**
Vos.	Mos-**trà**-reu	Vos.	**Vau** mos-**trar**	**Vau** ha-**ver** mos-**trat**
Ells	Mos-**tra**-ren	Ells	**Van** mos-**trar**	**Van** ha-**ver** mos-**trat**

Future Simple		*Future Compound*	
Jo	Mos-tra-**ré**	Jo	Hau-**ré** mos-**trat**
Tu	Mos-tra-**ràs**	Tu	Hau-**ràs** mos-**trat**
Ell	Mos-tra-**rà**	Ell	Hau-**rà** mos-**trat**
Nos.	Mos-tra-**rem**	Nos.	Hau-**rem** mos-**trat**
Vos.	Mos-tra-**reu**	Vos.	Hau-**reu** mos-**trat**
Ells	Mos-tra-**ran**	Ells	Hau-**ran** mos-**trat**

Conditional Simple		*Conditional Compound*		IMPERATIVE	
Jo	Mos-tra-**ri**-a	Jo	Hau-**ri**-a mos-**trat**		
Tu	Mos-tra-**ri**-es	Tu	Hau-**ri**-es mos-**trat**	**Mos**-tra	(Tu)
Ell	Mos-tra-**ri**-a	Ell	Hau-**ri**-a mos-**trat**	**Mos**-tri	(Ell)
Nos	Mos-tra-**rí**-em	Nos.	Hau-**rí**-em mos-**trat**	Mos-**trem**	(Nos.)
Vos.	Mos-tra-**rí**-eu	Vos.	Hau-**rí**-eu mos-**trat**	Mos-**treu**	(Vos.)
Ells	Mos-tra-**ri**-en	Ells	Hau-**ri**-en mos-**trat**	**Mos**-trin	(Ells)

IMPERSONAL		
	SIMPLE	COMPOUND
Infinitive	Mos-**trar**	Ha-**ver** mos-**trat**
Participle	Mos-**trat**	-
Gerund	Mos-**trant**	Ha-**vent** mos-**trat**

TO SING - CANTAR

PERSONAL					
INDICATIVE			**SUBJUNCTIVE**		
SIMPLE	**COMPOUND**		**SIMPLE**	**COMPOUND**	
Present	*Past Indefinite*		*Present*	*Past Perfet*	
Jo **Can**-to	Jo **He** can-**tat**		Jo **Can**-ti	Jo **Ha**-gi can-**tat**	
Tu **Can**-tes	Tu **Has** can-**tat**		Tu **Can**-tis	Tu **Ha**-gis can-**tat**	
Ell **Can**-ta	Ell **Ha** can-**tat**		Ell **Can**-ti	Ell **Ha**-gi can-**tat**	
No. Can-**tem**	Nos. **Hem** can-**tat**		Nos. Can-**tem**	Nos. **Hà**-gim can-**tat**	
Vos. Can-**teu**	Vos. **Heu** can-**tat**		Vos. Can-**teu**	Vos. **Hà**-giu can-**tat**	
Ells **Can**-ten	Ells **Han** can-**tat**		Ells **Can**-tin	Ells **Ha**-gin can-**tat**	
Imperfet	*Past Plusquamperfet*		*Imperfet past*	*Plusquamperfet past*	
Jo Can-**ta**-va	Jo Ha-**vi**-a can-**tat**		Jo Can-**tés**	Jo Ha-**gués** can-**tat**	
Tu Can-**ta**-ves	Tu Ha-**vi**-es can-**tat**		Tu Can-**tes**-sis	Tu Ha-**gues**-sis can-**tat**	
Ell Can-**ta**-va	Ell Ha-**vi**-a can-**tat**		Ell Can-**tés**	Ell Ha-**gués** can-**tat**	
No. Can-**tà**-vem	Nos. Ha-**ví**-em can-**tat**		Nos Can-**tés**-sim	Nos. Ha-**gués**-sim can-**tat**	
Vos. Can-**tà**-veu	Vos. Ha-**ví**-eu can-**tat**		Vos. Can-**tés**-siu	Vos. Ha-**gués**-siu can-**tat**	
Ells Can-**ta**-ven	Ells Ha-**vi**-en can-**tat**		Ells Can-**tes**-sin	Ells Ha-**gues**-sin can-**tat**	

Past Simple	*Past Perifrastic*	*Past Anterior perifrastic*
Jo Can-**tí**	Jo **Vaig** can-**tar**	**Vaig** ha-**ver** can-**tat**
Tu Can-**ta**-res	Tu **Vas** can-**tar**	**Vas** ha-**ver** can-**tat**
Ell Can-**tà**	Ell **Va** can-**tar**	**Va** ha-**ver** can-**tat**
Nos Can-**tà**-rem	Nos. **Vam** can-**tar**	**Vam** ha-**ver** can-**tat**
Vos. Can-**tà**-reu	Vos. **Vau** can-**tar**	**Vau** ha-**ver** can-**tat**
Ells Can-**ta**-ren	Ells **Van** can-**tar**	**Van** ha-**ver** can-**tat**

Future Simple	*Future Compound*
Jo Can-ta-**ré**	Jo Hau-**ré** can-**tat**
Tu Can-ta-**ràs**	Tu Hau-**ràs** can-**tat**
Ell Can-ta-**rà**	Ell Hau-**rà** can-**tat**
Nos. Can-ta-**rem**	Nos. Hau-**rem** can-**tat**
Vos. Can-ta-**reu**	Vos. Hau-**reu** can-**tat**
Ells Can-ta-**ran**	Ells Hau-**ran** can-**tat**

Conditional Simple	*Conditional Compound*	**IMPERATIVE**	
Jo Can-ta-**ri**-a	Jo Hau-**ri**-a can-**tat**		
Tu Can-ta-**ri**-es	Tu Hau-**ri**-es can-**tat**	**Can**-ta	*(Tu)*
Ell Can-ta-**ri**-a	Ell Hau-**ri**-a can-**tat**	**Can**-ti	*(Ell)*
Nos Can-ta-**rí**-em	Nos. Hau-**rí**-em can-**tat**	Can-**tem**	*(Nos.)*
Vos. Can-ta-**rí**-eu	Vos. Hau-**rí**-eu can-**tat**	Can-**teu**	*(Vos.)*
Ells Can-ta-**ri**-en	Ells Hau-**ri**-en can-**tat**	**Can**-tin	*(Ells)*

IMPERSONAL		
	SIMPLE	**COMPOUND**
Infinitive	Can-**tar**	Ha-**ver** can-**tat**
Participle	Can-**tat**	-
Gerund	Can-**tant**	Ha-**vent** can-**tat**

TO SIT DOWN - SEURE

PERSONAL							
INDICATIVE				**SUBJUNCTIVE**			
SIMPLE		**COMPOUND**		**SIMPLE**		**COMPOUND**	
Present		*Past Indefinite*		*Present*		*Past Perfet*	
Jo	**Sec**	Jo	**He** se-**gut**	Jo	**Se**-gui	Jo	**Ha**-gi se-**gut**
Tu	**Seus**	Tu	**Has** se-**gut**	Tu	**Se**-guis	Tu	**Ha**-gis se-**gut**
Ell	**Seu**	Ell	**Ha** se-**gut**	Ell	**Se**-gui	Ell	**Ha**-gi se-**gut**
No.	Se-**iem**	Nos.	**Hem** se-**gut**	Nos.	Se-**guem**	Nos.	**Hà**-gim se-**gut**
Vos.	Se-**ieu**	Vos.	**Heu** se-**gut**	Vos.	Se-**gueu**	Vos.	**Hà**-giu se-**gut**
Ells	Se-**uen**	Ells	**Han** se-**gut**	Ells	Se-**guin**	Ells	**Ha**-gin se-**gut**
Imperfet		*Past Plusquamperfet*		*Imperfet past*		*Plusquamperfet past*	
Jo	**Se**-ia	Jo	Ha-**vi**-a se-**gut**	Jo	Se-**gués**	Jo	Ha-**gués** se-**gut**
Tu	**Se**-ies	Tu	Ha-**vi**-es se-**gut**	Tu	Se-**gues**-sis	Tu	Ha-**gues**-sis se-**gut**
Ell	**Se**-ia	Ell	Ha-**vi**-a se-**gut**	Ell	Se-**gués**	Ell	Ha-**gués** se-**gut**
No.	**Sè**-iem	Nos.	Ha-**ví**-em se-**gut**	Nos.	Se-**gués**-sim	Nos.	Ha-**gués**-sim se-**gut**
Vos.	**Sè**-ieu	Vos.	Ha-**ví**-eu se-**gut**	Vos.	Se-**gués**-siu	Vos.	Ha-**gués**-siu se-**gut**
Ells	**Se**-ien	Ells	Ha-**vi**-en se-**gut**	Ells	Se-**gues**-sin	Ells	Ha-**gues**-sin se-**gut**

Past Simple		*Past Perifrastic*		*Past Anterior perifrastic*
Jo	Se-**guí**	Jo	**Vaig** seu-re	**Vaig** ha-**ver** se-**gut**
Tu	Se-**gue**-res	Tu	**Vas** seu-re	**Vas** ha-**ver** se-**gut**
Ell	Se-**gué**	Ell	**Va** seu-re	**Va** ha-**ver** se-**gut**
Nos.	Se-**gué**-rem	Nos.	**Vam** seu-re	**Vam** ha-**ver** se-**gut**
Vos.	Se-**gué**-reu	Vos.	**Vau** seu-re	**Vau** ha-**ver** se-**gut**
Ells	Se-**gue**-ren	Ells	**Van** seu-re	**Van** ha-**ver** se-**gut**

Future Simple		*Future Compound*	
Jo	Seu-**ré**	Jo	Hau-**ré** se-**gut**
Tu	Seu-**ràs**	Tu	Hau-**ràs** se-**gut**
Ell	Seu-**rà**	Ell	Hau-**rà** se-**gut**
Nos.	Seu-**rem**	Nos.	Hau-**rem** se-**gut**
Vos.	Seu-**reu**	Vos.	Hau-**reu** se-**gut**
Ells	Seu-**ran**	Ells	Hau-**ran** se-**gut**

Conditional Simple		*Conditional Compound*		**IMPERATIVE**	
Jo	Seu-**ri**-a	Jo	Hau-**ri**-a se-**gut**		
Tu	Seu-**ri**-es	Tu	Hau-**ri**-es se-**gut**	**Seu**	*(Tu)*
Ell	Seu-**ri**-a	Ell	Hau-**ri**-a se-**gut**	**Se**-gui	*(Ell)*
Nos.	Seu-**rí**-em	Nos.	Hau-**rí**-em se-**gut**	Se-**guem**	*(Nos.)*
Vos.	Seu-**rí**-eu	Vos.	Hau-**rí**-eu se-**gut**	Se-**veu**	*(Vos.)*
Ells	Seu-**ri**-en	Ells	Hau-**ri**-en se-**gut**	**Se**-guin	*(Ells)*

IMPERSONAL		
	SIMPLE	**COMPOUND**
Infinitive	**Seu**-re	Ha-**ver** se-**gut**
Participle	Se-**gut**	-
Gerund	Se-**ient**	Ha-**vent** se-**gut**

TO SLEEP - DORMIR

PERSONAL							
INDICATIVE				SUBJUNCTIVE			
SIMPLE		COMPOUND		SIMPLE		COMPOUND	
Present		Past Indefinite		Predor-me		Past Perfet	
Jo	**Dor**-mo	Jo	**He** dor-**mit**	Jo	**Dor**-mi	Jo	**Ha**-gi dor-**mit**
Tu	**Dorms**	Tu	**Has** dor-**mit**	Tu	**Dor**-mis	Tu	**Ha**-gis dor-**mit**
Ell	**Dorm**	Ell	**Ha** dor-**mit**	Ell	**Dor**-mi	Ell	**Ha**-gi dor-**mit**
No.	Dor-**mim**	Nos.	**Hem** dor-**mit**	Nos.	Dor-**mim**	Nos.	**Hà**-gim dor-**mit**
Vos.	Dor-**miu**	Vos.	**Heu** dor-**mit**	Vos.	Dor-**miu**	Vos.	**Hà**-giu dor-**mit**
Ells	**Dor**-men	Ells	**Han** dor-**mit**	Ells	**Dor**-min	Ells	**Ha**-gin dor-**mit**
Imperfet		Past Plusquamperfet		Imperfet past		Plusquamperfet past	
Jo	Dor-**mi**-a	Jo	Ha-**vi**-a dor-**mit**	Jo	Dor-**mís**	Jo	Ha-**gués** dor-**mit**
Tu	Dor-**mi**-es	Tu	Ha-**vi**-es dor-**mit**	Tu	Dor-**mis**-sis	Tu	Ha-**gues**-sis dor-**mit**
Ell	Dor-**mi**-a	Ell	Ha-**vi**-a dor-**mit**	Ell	Dor-**mís**	Ell	Ha-**gués** dor-**mit**
No.	Dor-**mí**-em	Nos.	Ha-**ví**-em dor-**mit**	Nos	Dor-**mís**-sim	Nos.	Ha-**gués**-sim dor-**mit**
Vos.	Dor-**mí**-eu	Vos.	Ha-**ví**-eu dor-**mit**	Vos.	Dor-**mís**-siu	Vos.	Ha-**gués**-siu dor-**mit**
Ells	Dor-**mi**-en	Ells	Ha-**vi**-en dor-**mit**	Ells	Dor-**mis**-sin	Ells	Ha-**gues**-sin dor-**mit**

Past Simple		Past Perifrastic		Past Anterior perifrastic
Jo	Dor-**mí**	Jo	**Vaig** dor-**mir**	**Vaig** ha-**ver** dor-**mit**
Tu	Dor-**mi**-res	Tu	**Vas** dor-**mir**	**Vas** ha-**ver** dor-**mit**
Ell	Dor-**mí**	Ell	**Va** dor-**mir**	**Va** ha-**ver** dor-**mit**
Nos	Dor-**mí**-rem	Nos.	**Vam** dor-**mir**	**Vam** ha-**ver** dor-**mit**
Vos.	Dor-**mí**-reu	Vos.	**Vau** dor-**mir**	**Vau** ha-**ver** dor-**mit**
Ells	Dor-**mi**-ren	Ells	**Van** dor-**mir**	**Van** ha-**ver** dor-**mit**

Future Simple		Future Compound		
Jo	Dor-mi-**ré**	Jo	Hau-**ré** dor-**mit**	
Tu	Dor-mi-**ràs**	Tu	Hau-**ràs** dor-**mit**	
Ell	Dor-mi-**rà**	Ell	Hau-**rà** dor-**mit**	
Nos.	Dor-mi-**rem**	Nos.	Hau-**rem** dor-**mit**	
Vos.	Dor-mi-**reu**	Vos.	Hau-**reu** dor-**mit**	
Ells	Dor-mi-**ran**	Ells	Hau-**ran** dor-**mit**	

Conditional Simple		Conditional Compound		IMPERATIVE	
Jo	Dor-mi-**ri**-a	Jo	Hau-**ri**-a dor-**mit**		
Tu	Dor-mi-**ri**-es	Tu	Hau-**ri**-es dor-**mit**	**Dorm**	(Tu)
Ell	Dor-mi-**ri**-a	Ell	Hau-**ri**-a dor-**mit**	**Dor**-mi	(Ell)
Nos	Dor-mi-**rí**-em	Nos.	Hau-**rí**-em dor-**mit**	**Dor**-mim	(Nos.)
Vos.	Dor-mi-**rí**-eu	Vos.	Hau-**rí**-eu dor-**mit**	**Dor**-miu	(Vos.)
Ells	Dor-mi-**ri**-en	Ells	Hau-**ri**-en dor-**mit**	**Dor**-min	(Ells)

IMPERSONAL		
	SIMPLE	COMPOUND
Infinitive	Dor-**mir**	Ha-**ver** dor-**mit**
Participle	Dor-**mit**	-
Gerund	Dor-**mint**	Ha-**vent** dor-**mit**

TO SMILE - SOMRIURE

PERSONAL							
INDICATIVE				**SUBJUNCTIVE**			
SIMPLE		**COMPOUND**		**SIMPLE**		**COMPOUND**	
Present		*Past Indefinite*		*Present*		*Past Perfet*	
Jo	Som-**ric**	Jo	**He** som-ri-**gut**	Jo	Som-**ri**-gui	Jo	**Ha**-gi som-ri-**gut**
Tu	Som-**rius**	Tu	**Has** som-ri-**gut**	Tu	Som-**ri**-guis	Tu	**Ha**-gis som-ri-**gut**
Ell	Som-**riu**	Ell	**Ha** som-ri-**gut**	Ell	Som-**ri**-gui	Ell	**Ha**-gi som-ri-**gut**
No.	Som-ri-**em**	Nos.	**Hem** som-ri-**gut**	Nos.	Som-ri-**guem**	Nos.	**Hà**-gim som-ri-**gut**
Vos.	Som-ri-**eu**	Vos.	**Heu** som-ri-**gut**	Vos.	Som-ri-**gueu**	Vos.	**Hà**-giu som-ri-**gut**
Ells	Som-**ri**-uen	Ells	**Han** som-ri-**gut**	Ells	Som-**ri**-guin	Ells	**Ha**-gin som-ri-**gut**
Imperfet		*Past Plusquamperfet*		*Imperfet past*		*Plusquamperfet past*	
Jo	Som-**re**-ia	Jo	Ha-**vi**-a som-ri-**gut**	Jo	Som-ri-**gués**	Jo	Ha-**gués** som-ri-**gut**
Tu	Som-**re**-ies	Tu	Ha-**vi**-es som-ri-**gut**	Tu	Som-ri-**gues**-sis	Tu	Ha-**gues**-sis som-ri-**gut**
Ell	Som-**re**-ia	Ell	Ha-**vi**-a som-ri-**gut**	Ell	Som-ri-**gués**	Ell	Ha-**gués** som-ri-**gut**
No.	Som-**rè**-iem	Nos.	Ha-**ví**-em som-ri-**gut**	Nos	Som-ri-**gués**-sim	Nos.	Ha-**gués**-sim som-ri-**gut**
Vos.	Som-**rè**-ieu	Vos.	Ha-**ví**-eu som-ri-**gut**	Vos.	Som-ri-**gués**-siu	Vos.	Ha-**gués**-siu som-ri-**gut**
Ells	Som-**re**-ien	Ells	Ha-**vi**-en som-ri-**gut**	Ells	Som-ri-**gues**-sin	Ells	Ha-**gues**-sin som-ri-**gut**

Past Simple		*Past Perifrastic*		*Past Anterior perifrastic*
Jo	Som-ri-**guí**	Jo	**Vaig** som-**riu**-re	**Vaig** ha-**ver** som-ri-**gut**
Tu	Som-ri-**gue**-res	Tu	**Vas** som-**riu**-re	**Vas** ha-**ver** som-ri-**gut**
Ell	Som-ri-**gué**	Ell	**Va** som-**riu**-re	**Va** ha-**ver** som-ri-**gut**
Nos	Som-ri-**gué**-rem	Nos.	**Vam** som-**riu**-re	**Vam** ha-**ver** som-ri-**gut**
Vos.	Som-ri-**gué**-reu	Vos.	**Vau** som-**riu**-re	**Vau** ha-**ver** som-ri-**gut**
Ells	Som-ri-**gue**-ren	Ells	**Van** som-**riu**-re	**Van** ha-**ver** som-ri-**gut**

Future Simple		*Future Compound*	
Jo	Som-riu-**ré**	Jo	Hau-**ré** som-ri-**gut**
Tu	Som-riu-**ràs**	Tu	Hau-**ràs** som-ri-**gut**
Ell	Som-riu-**rà**	Ell	Hau-**rà** som-ri-**gut**
Nos.	Som-riu-**rem**	Nos.	Hau-**rem** som-ri-**gut**
Vos.	Som-riu-**reu**	Vos.	Hau-**reu** som-ri-**gut**
Ells	Som-riu-**ran**	Ells	Hau-**ran** som-ri-**gut**

Conditional Simple		*Conditional Compound*		**IMPERATIVE**	
Jo	Som-riu-**ri**-a	Jo	Hau-**ri**-a som-ri-**gut**		
Tu	Som-riu-**ri**-es	Tu	Hau-**ri**-es som-ri-**gut**	Som-**riu**	(Tu)
Ell	Som-riu-**ri**-a	Ell	Hau-**ri**-a som-ri-**gut**	Som-**ri**-gui	(Ell)
Nos	Som-riu-**rí**-em	Nos.	Hau-**rí**-em som-ri-**gut**	Som-ri-**guem**	(Nos.)
Vos.	Som-riu-**rí**-eu	Vos.	Hau-**rí**-eu som-ri-**gut**	Som-ri-**eu**	(Vos.)
Ells	Som-riu-**ri**-en	Ells	Hau-**ri**-en som-ri-**gut**	Som-ri-**guin**	(Ells)

IMPERSONAL		
	SIMPLE	**COMPOUND**
Infinitive	Som-**riu**-re	Ha-**ver** som-ri-**gut**
Participle	Som-ri-**gut**	-
Gerund	Som-ri-**ent**	Ha-**vent** som-ri-**gut**

TO SPEAK - PARLAR

PERSONAL						
INDICATIVE				**SUBJUNCTIVE**		
SIMPLE		**COMPOUND**		**SIMPLE**		**COMPOUND**
Present		*Past Indefinite*		*Present*		*Past Perfet*
Jo	**Par**-lo	Jo	**He** par-**lat**	Jo	**Par**-li	Jo	**Ha**-gi par-**lat**
Tu	**Par**-les	Tu	**Has** par-**lat**	Tu	**Par**-lis	Tu	**Ha**-gis par-**lat**
Ell	**Par**-la	Ell	**Ha** par-**lat**	Ell	**Par**-li	Ell	**Ha**-gi par-**lat**
No.	Par-**lem**	Nos.	**Hem** par-**lat**	Nos.	Par-**lem**	Nos.	**Hà**-gim par-**lat**
Vos.	Par-**leu**	Vos.	**Heu** par-**lat**	Vos.	Par-**leu**	Vos.	**Hà**-giu par-**lat**
Ells	**Par**-len	Ells	**Han** par-**lat**	Ells	**Par**-lin	Ells	**Ha**-gin par-**lat**
Imperfet		*Past Plusquamperfet*		*Imperfet past*		*Plusquamperfet past*
Jo	Par-**la**-va	Jo	Ha-**vi**-a par-**lat**	Jo	Par-**lés**	Jo	Ha-**gués** par-**lat**
Tu	Par-**la**-ves	Tu	Ha-**vi**-es par-**lat**	Tu	Par-**les**-sis	Tu	Ha-**gues**-sis par-**lat**
Ell	Par-**la**-va	Ell	Ha-**vi**-a par-**lat**	Ell	Par-**lés**	Ell	Ha-**gués** par-**lat**
No.	Par-**là**-vem	Nos.	Ha-**ví**-em par-**lat**	Nos	Par-**lés**-sim	Nos.	Ha-**gués**-sim par-**lat**
Vos.	Par-**là**-veu	Vos.	Ha-**ví**-eu par-**lat**	Vos.	Par-**lés**-siu	Vos.	Ha-**gués**-siu par-**lat**
Ells	Par-**la**-ven	Ells	Ha-**vi**-en par-**lat**	Ells	Par-**les**-sin	Ells	Ha-**gues**-sin par-**lat**

Past Simple		*Past Perifrastic*		*Past Anterior perifrastic*
Jo	Par-**lí**	Jo	**Vaig** par-**lar**	**Vaig** ha-**ver** par-**lat**
Tu	Par-**la**-res	Tu	**Vas** par-**lar**	**Vas** ha-**ver** par-**lat**
Ell	Par-**là**	Ell	**Va** par-**lar**	**Va** ha-**ver** par-**lat**
Nos	Par-**là**-rem	Nos.	**Vam** par-**lar**	**Vam** ha-**ver** par-**lat**
Vos.	Par-**là**-reu	Vos.	**Vau** par-**lar**	**Vau** ha-**ver** par-**lat**
Ells	Par-**la**-ren	Ells	**Van** par-**lar**	**Van** ha-**ver** par-**lat**

Future Simple		*Future Compound*	
Jo	Par-la-**ré**	Jo	Hau-**ré** par-**lat**
Tu	Par-la-**ràs**	Tu	Hau-**ràs** par-**lat**
Ell	Par-la-**rà**	Ell	Hau-**rà** par-**lat**
Nos.	Par-la-**rem**	Nos.	Hau-**rem** par-**lat**
Vos.	Par-la-**reu**	Vos.	Hau-**reu** par-**lat**
Ells	Par-la-**ran**	Ells	Hau-**ran** par-**lat**

Conditional Simple		*Conditional Compound*		**IMPERATIVE**	
Jo	Par-la-**ri**-a	Jo	Hau-**ri**-a par-**lat**		
Tu	Par-la-**ri**-es	Tu	Hau-**ri**-es par-**lat**	**Par**-la	*(Tu)*
Ell	Par-la-**ri**-a	Ell	Hau-**ri**-a par-**lat**	**Par**-li	*(Ell)*
Nos	Par-la-**rí**-em	Nos.	Hau-**rí**-em par-**lat**	Par-**lem**	*(Nos.)*
Vos.	Par-la-**rí**-eu	Vos.	Hau-**rí**-eu par-**lat**	Par-**leu**	*(Vos.)*
Ells	Par-la-**ri**-en	Ells	Hau-**ri**-en par-**lat**	**Par**-lin	*(Ells)*

IMPERSONAL		
	SIMPLE	**COMPOUND**
Infinitive	Par-**lar**	Ha-**ver** par-**lat**
Participle	Par-**lat**	-
Gerund	Par-**lant**	Ha-**vent** par-**lat**

TO STAND – AIXECAR-SE*

PERSONAL					
INDICATIVE			**SUBJUNCTIVE**		
SIMPLE		**COMPOUND**	**SIMPLE**		**COMPOUND**
Present		*Past Indefinite*	*Present*		*Past Perfet*
Jo	M'ai-**xe**-co	Jo	**M'he** ai-xe-cat	Jo	M'ai-**xe**-qui	Jo	**M'ha**-gi ai-xe-cat
Tu	T'ai-**xe**-ques	Tu	**T'has** ai-xe-cat	Tu	T'ai-**xe**-quis	Tu	**T'ha**-gis ai-xe-cat
Ell	S'ai-**xe**-ca	Ell	**S'ha** ai-xe-cat	Ell	S'ai-**xe**-qui	Ell	**S'ha**-gi ai-xe-cat
No.	Ens ai-xe-**quem**	Nos.	**Ens hem** ai-xe-cat	Nos.	Ens ai-xe-**quem**	Nos.	**Ens hà**-gim ai-xe-cat
Vos.	Us ai-xe-**queu**	Vos.	**Us heu** ai-xe-cat	Vos.	Us ai-xe-**queu**	Vos.	**Us hà**-giu ai-xe-cat
Ells	S'ai-**xe**-quen	Ells	**S'han** ai-xe-cat	Ells	S'ai-**xe**-quin	Ells	**S'ha**-gin ai-xe-cat

INDICATIVE — SIMPLE / COMPOUND · SUBJUNCTIVE — SIMPLE / COMPOUND

Present / **Past Indefinite** / **Present** / **Past Perfet**

	INDICATIVE SIMPLE		INDICATIVE COMPOUND		SUBJUNCTIVE SIMPLE		SUBJUNCTIVE COMPOUND
Jo	M'ai-**xe**-co	Jo	**M'he** ai-xe-cat	Jo	M'ai-**xe**-qui	Jo	**M'ha**-gi ai-xe-cat
Tu	T'ai-**xe**-ques	Tu	**T'has** ai-xe-cat	Tu	T'ai-**xe**-quis	Tu	**T'ha**-gis ai-xe-cat
Ell	S'ai-**xe**-ca	Ell	**S'ha** ai-xe-cat	Ell	S'ai-**xe**-qui	Ell	**S'ha**-gi ai-xe-cat
No.	Ens ai-xe-**quem**	Nos.	**Ens hem** ai-xe-cat	Nos.	Ens ai-xe-**quem**	Nos.	**Ens hà**-gim ai-xe-cat
Vos.	Us ai-xe-**queu**	Vos.	**Us heu** ai-xe-cat	Vos.	Us ai-xe-**queu**	Vos.	**Us hà**-giu ai-xe-cat
Ells	S'ai-**xe**-quen	Ells	**S'han** ai-xe-cat	Ells	S'ai-**xe**-quin	Ells	**S'ha**-gin ai-xe-cat

Imperfet / **Past Plusquamperfet** / **Imperfet past** / **Plusquamperfet past**

	INDICATIVE SIMPLE		INDICATIVE COMPOUND		SUBJUNCTIVE SIMPLE		SUBJUNCTIVE COMPOUND
Jo	M'ai-xe-**ca**-va	Jo	**M'ha**-**vi**-a ai-xe-cat	Jo	M'ai-xe-**qués**	Jo	M'ha-**gués** ai-xe-cat
Tu	T'ai-xe-**ca**-ves	Tu	**T'ha**-**vi**-es ai-xe-cat	Tu	T'ai-xe-**ques**-sis	Tu	T'ha-**gués**-sis ai-xe-cat
Ell	S'ai-xe-**ca**-va	Ell	**S'ha**-**vi**-a ai-xe-cat	Ell	S'ai-xe-**qués**	Ell	S'ha-**gués** ai-xe-cat
No.	Ens ai-xe-**cà**-vem	Nos.	**Ens ha**-**ví**-em ai-xe-cat	Nos	Ens ai-xe-**qués**-sim	Nos.	Ens ha-**gués**-sim ai-xe-cat
Vos.	Us ai-xe-**cà**-veu	Vos.	**Us ha**-**ví**-eu ai-xe-cat	Vos.	Us ai-xe-**qués**-siu	Vos.	Us ha-**gués**-siu ai-xe-cat
Ells	S'ai-xe-**ca**-ven	Ells	**S'ha**-**vi**-en ai-xe-cat	Ells	S'ai-xe-**ques**-sin	Ells	S'ha-**gués**-sin ai-xe-cat

Past Simple / **Past Perifrastic**** / **Past Anterior periphrastic****

	Past Simple		Past Perifrastic**	Past Anterior periphrastic**
Jo	M'ai-xe-**quí**	Jo	**Vaig** ai.xe.car-me	**Vaig** ha.**ver**-me ai.xe.cat
Tu	T'ai-xe-**ca**-res	Tu	**Vas** ai.xe.car-te	**Vas** ha.**ver**-te ai.xe.cat
Ell	S'ai-xe-**cà**	Ell	**Va** ai.xe.car-se	**Va** ha.**ver**-se ai.xe.cat
Nos	Ens ai-xe-**cà**-rem	Nos	**Vam** ai.xe.car-nos	**Vam** ha.**ver**-nos ai.xe.cat
Vos.	Us ai-xe-**cà**-reu	Vos.	**Vau** ai.xe.car-vos	**Vau** ha.**ver**-vos ai.xe.cat
Ells	S'ai-xe-**ca**-ren	Ells	**Van** ai.xe.car-se	**Van** ha.**ver**-se ai.xe.cat

Future Simple / **Future Compound**

	Future Simple		Future Compound
Jo	M'ai-xe-ca-**ré**	Jo	**M'hau**-**ré** ai-xe-cat
Tu	M'ai-xe-ca-**ràs**	Tu	**T'hau**-**ràs** ai-xe-cat
Ell	S'ai-xe-ca-**rà**	Ell	**S'hau**-**rà** ai-xe-cat
Nos.	Ens ai-xe-ca-**rem**	Nos.	**Ens hau**-**rem** ai-xe-cat
Vos.	Us ai-xe-ca-**reu**	Vos.	**Us hau**-**reu** ai-xe-cat
Ells	S'ai-xe-ca-**ran**	Ells	**S'hau**-**ran** ai-xe-cat

Conditional Simple / **Conditional Compound** / **IMPERATIVE****

	Conditional Simple		Conditional Compound	IMPERATIVE**	
Jo	M'ai-xe-ca-**ri**-a	Jo	**M'hau**-**ri**-a ai-xe-cat		
Tu	T'ai-xe-ca-**ri**-es	Tu	**T'hau**-**ri**-es ai-xe-cat	Ai-**xe**-ca't	(Tu)
Ell	S'ai-xe-ca-**ri**-a	Ell	**S'hau**-**ri**-a ai-xe-cat	S'ai-**xe**-qui	(Ell)
Nos	Ens ai-xe-ca-**rí**-em	Nos.	**Ens hau**-**rí**-em ai-xe-cat	Ai-xe-**quem**-nos	(Nos.)
Vos	Us ai-xe-ca-**rí**-eu	Vos.	**Us hau**-**rí**-eu ai-xe-cat	Ai-xe-**queu**-vos	(Vos.)
Ells	S'ai-xe-ca-**ri**-en	Ells	**S'hau**-**ri**-en ai-xe-cat	S'ai-**xe**-quin	(Ells)

IMPERSONAL		
	SIMPLE	**COMPOUND**
Infinitive	Ai.xe.**car**-se	Ha.**ver**-se ai.xe.**cat**
Participle	Ai.xe.**cat**	-
Gerund	Ai.xe.**cant**-se	Ha.**vent**-se ai.xe.**cat**

*Aixecar-se is a reflexive verb, which means that the action takes places on the subject. It is build with the weak pronouns, EM, ET, ES, ENS, US, ES and their variations depending on the place they are written.
** When the pronoun goes behind the word it is attached to it by a hyphen. In this case the syllables are separated with dots, to appreciate the difference.

111

TO START - COMENÇAR

PERSONAL							
INDICATIVE				**SUBJUNCTIVE**			
SIMPLE		**COMPOUND**		**SIMPLE**		**COMPOUND**	
Present		*Past Indefinite*		*Present*		*Past Perfet*	
Jo	Co-**men**-ço	Jo	**He** Co-men-**çat**	Jo	Co-**men**-ci	Jo	**Ha**-gi Co-men-**çat**
Tu	Co-**men**-ces	Tu	**Has** Co-men-**çat**	Tu	Co-**men**-cis	Tu	**Ha**-gis Co-men-**çat**
Ell	Co-**men**-ça	Ell	**Ha** Co-men-**çat**	Ell	Co-**men**-ci	Ell	**Ha**-gi Co-men-**çat**
No.	Co-men-**cem**	Nos.	**Hem** Co-men-**çat**	Nos.	Co-men-**cem**	Nos.	**Hà**-gim Co-men-**çat**
Vos.	Co-men-**ceu**	Vos.	**Heu** Co-men-**çat**	Vos.	Co-men-**ceu**	Vos.	**Hà**-giu Co-men-**çat**
Ells	Co-**men**-cen	Ells	**Han** Co-men-**çat**	Ells	Co-**men**-cin	Ells	**Ha**-gin Co-men-**çat**
Imperfet		*Past Plusquamperfet*		*Imperfet past*		*Plusquamperfet past*	
Jo	Co-men-**ça**-va	Jo	**Ha**-**vi**-a Co-men-**çat**	Jo	Co-men-**cés**	Jo	**Ha**-**gués** Co-men-**çat**
Tu	Co-men-**ça**-ves	Tu	**Ha**-**vi**-es Co-men-**çat**	Tu	Co-men-**ces**-sis	Tu	**Ha**-**gues**-sis Co-men-**çat**
Ell	Co-men-**ça**-va	Ell	**Ha**-**vi**-a Co-men-**çat**	Ell	Co-men-**cés**	Ell	**Ha**-**gués** Co-men-**çat**
No.	Co-men-**çà**-vem	Nos.	**Ha**-**ví**-em Co-men-**çat**	Nos	Co-men-**cés**-sim	Nos.	**Ha**-**gués**-sim Co-men-**çat**
Vos.	Co-men-**çà**-veu	Vos.	**Ha**-**ví**-eu Co-men-**çat**	Vos.	Co-men-**cés**-siu	Vos.	**Ha**-**gués**-siu Co-men-**çat**
Ells	Co-men-**ça**-ven	Ells	**Ha**-**vi**-en Co-men-**çat**	Ells	Co-men-**ces**-sin	Ells	**Ha**-**gues**-sin Co-men-**çat**

Past Simple		*Past Perifrastic*		*Past Anterior perifrastic*			
Jo	Co-men-**cí**	Jo	**Vaig** Co-men-**çar**	**Vaig** ha-**ver** Co-men-**çat**			
Tu	Co-men-**ça**-res	Tu	**Vas** Co-men-**çar**	**Vas** ha-**ver** Co-men-**çat**			
Ell	Co-men-**çà**	Ell	**Va** Co-men-**çar**	**Va** ha-**ver** Co-men-**çat**			
Nos	Co-men-**çà**-rem	Nos.	**Vam** Co-men-**çar**	**Vam** ha-**ver** Co-men-**çat**			
Vos.	Co-men-**çà**-reu	Vos.		**Vau** ha-**ver** Co-men-**çat**			
Ells	Co-men-**ça**-ren	Ells	**Vau** Co-men-**çar**	**Van** ha-**ver** Co-men-**çat**			
			Van Co-men-**çar**				

Future Simple		*Future Compound*					
Jo	Co-men-ça-**ré**	Jo	Hau-**ré** Co-men-**çat**				
Tu	Co-men-ça-**ràs**	Tu	Hau-**ràs** Co-men-**çat**				
Ell	Co-men-ça-**rà**	Ell	Hau-**rà** Co-men-**çat**				
Nos.	Co-men-ça-**rem**	Nos.	Hau-**rem** Co-men-**çat**				
Vos.	Co-men-ça-**reu**	Vos.	Hau-**reu** Co-men-**çat**				
Ells	Co-men-ça-**ran**	Ells	Hau-**ran** Co-men-**çat**				

Conditional Simple		*Conditional Compound*		**IMPERATIVE**			
Jo	Co-men-ça-**ri**-a	Jo	Hau-**ri**-a Co-men-**çat**				
Tu	Co-men-ça-**ri**-es	Tu	Hau-**ri**-es Co-men-**çat**	Co-**men**-ça		*(Tu)*	
Ell	Co-men-ça-**ri**-a	Ell	Hau-**ri**-a Co-men-**çat**	Co-**men**-ci		*(Ell)*	
Nos	Co-men-ça-**rí**-em	Nos.	Hau-**rí**-em Co-men-**çat**	Co-men-**cem**		*(Nos.)*	
Vos.	Co-men-ça-**rí**-eu	Vos.	Hau-**rí**-eu Co-men-**çat**	Co-men-**ceu**		*(Vos.)*	
Ells	Co-men-ça-**ri**-en	Ells	Hau-**ri**-en Co-men-**çat**	Co-**men**-cin		*(Ells)*	

IMPERSONAL		
	SIMPLE	**COMPOUND**
Infinitive	Co-men-**çar**	Ha-**ver** Co-men-**çat**
Participle	Co-men-**çat**	-
Gerund	Co-men-**çant**	Ha-**vent** Co-men-**çat**

TO STAY - ESTAR

PERSONAL				
INDICATIVE			**SUBJUNCTIVE**	
SIMPLE	**COMPOUND**		**SIMPLE**	**COMPOUND**

Present		*Past Indefinite*		*Present*		*Past Perfet*	
Jo	Es-**tic**	Jo	He es-**tat**	Jo	Es-**ti**-gui	Jo	**Ha**-gi es-**tat**
Tu	Es-**tàs**	Tu	**Has** es-**tat**	Tu	Es-**ti**-guis	Tu	**Ha**-gis es-**tat**
Ell	Es-**tà**	Ell	**Ha** es-**tat**	Ell	Es-**ti**-gui	Ell	**Ha**-gi es-**tat**
No.	Es-**tem**	Nos.	**Hem** es-**tat**	Nos.	Es-ti-**guem**	Nos.	**Hà**-gim es-**tat**
Vos.	Es-**teu**	Vos.	**Heu** es-**tat**	Vos.	Es-ti-**gueu**	Vos.	**Hà**-giu es-**tat**
Ells	Es-**tan**	Ells	**Han** es-**tat**	Ells	Es-**ti**-guin	Ells	**Ha**-gin es-**tat**

Imperfet		*Past Plusquamperfet*		*Imperfet past*		*Plusquamperfet past*	
Jo	Es-**ta**-va	Jo	Ha-**vi**-a es-**tat**	Jo	Es-ti-**gués**	Jo	Ha-**gués** es-**tat**
Tu	Es-**ta**-ves	Tu	Ha-**vi**-es es-**tat**	Tu	Es-ti-**gues**-sis	Tu	Ha-**gues**-sis es-**tat**
Ell	Es-**ta**-va	Ell	Ha-**vi**-a es-**tat**	Ell	Es-ti-**gués**	Ell	Ha-**gués** es-**tat**
No.	Es-**tà**-vem	Nos.	Ha-**ví**-em es-**tat**	Nos	Es-ti-**gués**-sim	Nos.	Ha-**gués**-sim es-**tat**
Vos.	Es-**tà**-veu	Vos.	Ha-**ví**-eu es-**tat**	Vos.	Es-ti-**gués**-siu	Vos.	Ha-**gués**-siu es-**tat**
Ells	Es-**ta**-ven	Ells	Ha-**vi**-en es-**tat**	Ells	Es-ti-**gues**-sin	Ells	Ha-**gues**-sin es-**tat**

Past Simple		*Past Perifrastic*		*Past Anterior perifrastic*
Jo	Es-ti-**guí**	Jo	**Vaig** es-**tar**	**Vaig** ha-**ver** es-**tat**
Tu	Es-ti-**gue**-res	Tu	**Vas** es-**tar**	**Vas** ha-**ver** es-**tat**
Ell	Es-ti-**gué**	Ell	**Va** es-**tar**	**Va** ha-**ver** es-**tat**
Nos	Es-ti-**gué**-rem	Nos.	**Vam** es-**tar**	**Vam** ha-**ver** es-**tat**
Vos.	Es-ti-**gué**-reu	Vos.	**Vau** es-**tar**	**Vau** ha-**ver** es-**tat**
Ells	Es-ti-**gue**-ren	Ells	**Van** es-**tar**	**Van** ha-**ver** es-**tat**

Future Simple		*Future Compound*	
Jo	Es-ta-**ré**	Jo	Hau-**ré** es-**tat**
Tu	Es-ta-**ràs**	Tu	Hau-**ràs** es-**tat**
Ell	Es-ta-**rà**	Ell	Hau-**rà** es-**tat**
Nos.	Es-ta-**rem**	Nos.	Hau-**rem** es-**tat**
Vos.	Es-ta-**reu**	Vos.	Hau-**reu** es-**tat**
Ells	Es-ta-**ran**	Ells	Hau-**ran** es-**tat**

Conditional Simple		*Conditional Compound*		**IMPERATIVE**	
Jo	Es-ta-**ri**-a	Jo	Hau-ri-a es-**tat**		
Tu	Es-ta-**ri**-es	Tu	Hau-**ri**-es es-**tat**	Es-**ti**-gues	*(Tu)*
Ell	Es-ta-**ri**-a	Ell	Hau-**ri**-a es-**tat**	Es-**ti**-gui	*(Ell)*
Nos	Es-ta-**rí**-em	Nos.	Hau-**rí**-em es-**tat**	Es-ti-**guem**	*(Nos.)*
Vos.	Es-ta-**rí**-eu	Vos.	Hau-**rí**-eu es-**tat**	Es-ti-**gueu**	*(Vos.)*
Ells	Es-ta-**ri**-en	Ells	Hau-**ri**-en es-**tat**	Es-**ti**-guin	*(Ells)*

IMPERSONAL		
	SIMPLE	**COMPOUND**
Infinitive	Es-**tar**	Ha-**ver** es-**tat**
Participle	Es-**tat**	-
Gerund	Es-**tant**	Ha-**vent** es-**tat**

TO TAKE - PRENDRE

PERSONAL							
INDICATIVE				SUBJUNCTIVE			
SIMPLE		COMPOUND		SIMPLE		COMPOUND	
Present		*Past Indefinite*		*Present*		*Past Perfet*	
Jo	**Prenc**	Jo	**He pres**	Jo	**Pren**-gui	Jo	**Ha**-gi **pres**
Tu	**Prens**	Tu	**Has pres**	Tu	**Pren**-guis	Tu	**Ha**-gis **pres**
Ell	**Pren**	Ell	**Ha pres**	Ell	**Pren**-gui	Ell	**Ha**-gi **pres**
No.	Pre-**nem**	Nos.	**Hem pres**	Nos.	Pren-**guem**	Nos	**Hà**-gim **pres**
Vos.	Pre-**neu**	Vos.	**Heu pres**	Vos.	Pren-**gueu**	Vos.	**Hà**-giu **pres**
Ells	**Pre**-nen	Ells	**Han pres**	Ells	**Pren**-guin	Ells	**Ha**-gin **pres**
Imperfet		*Past Plusquamperfet*		*Imperfet past*		*Plusquamperfet past*	
Jo	Pre-**ni**-a	Jo	Ha-**vi**-a **pres**	Jo	Pren-**gués**	Jo	Ha-**gués pres**
Tu	Pre-**ni**-es	Tu	Ha-**vi**-es **pres**	Tu	Pren-**gues**-sis	Tu	Ha-**gues**-sis **pres**
Ell	Pre-**ni**-a	Ell	Ha-**vi**-a **pres**	Ell	Pren-**gués**	Ell	Ha-**gués pres**
No.	Pre-**ní**-em	Nos.	Ha-**ví**-em **pres**	Nos.	Pren-**gués**-sim	Nos	Ha-**gués**-sim **pres**
Vos.	Pre-**ní**-eu	Vos.	Ha-**ví**-eu **pres**	Vos.	Pren-**gués**-siu	Vos.	Ha-**gués**-siu **pres**
Ells	Pre-**ni**-en	Ells	Ha-**vi**-en **pres**	Ells	Pren-**gues**-sin	Ells	Ha-**gues**-sin **pres**

Past Simple		*Past Perifrastic*		*Past Anterior perifrastic*
Jo	Pren-**guí**	Jo	**Vaig** pre-**ndre**	**Vaig** ha-**ver pres**
Tu	Pren-**gue**-res	Tu	**Vas** pre-**ndre**	**Vas** ha-**ver pres**
Ell	Pren-**gué**	Ell	**Va** pre-**ndre**	**Va** ha-**ver pres**
Nos.	Pren-**gué**-rem	Nos.	**Vam** pre-**ndre**	**Vam** ha-**ver pres**
Vos.	Pren-**gué**-reu	Vos.	**Vau** pre-**ndre**	**Vau** ha-**ver pres**
Ells	Pren-**gue**-ren	Ells	**Van** pre-**ndre**	**Van** ha-**ver pres**

Future Simple		*Future Compound*	
Jo	Pren-**dré**	Jo	Hau-**ré pres**
Tu	Pren-**dràs**	Tu	Hau-**ràs pres**
Ell	Pren-**drà**	Ell	Hau-**rà pres**
Nos.	Pren-**drem**	Nos.	Hau-**rem pres**
Vos.	Pren-**dreu**	Vos.	Hau-**reu pres**
Ells	Pren-**dran**	Ells	Hau-**ran pres**

Conditional Simple		*Conditional Compound*		IMPERATIVE	
Jo	Pren-**dri**-a	Jo	Hau-**ri**-a **pres**		
Tu	Pren-**dri**-es	Tu	Hau-**ri**-es **pres**	**Pren**	*(Tu)*
Ell	Pren-**dri**-a	Ell	Hau-**ri**-a **pres**	**Pren**-gui	*(Ell)*
Nos.	Pren-**drí**-em	Nos.	Hau-**rí**-em **pres**	Pren-**guem**	*(Nos.)*
Vos.	Pren-**drí**-eu	Vos.	Hau-**rí**-eu **pres**	Pre-**neu**	*(Vos.)*
Ells	Pren-**dri**-en	Ells	Hau-**ri**-en **pres**	**Pren**-guin	*(Ells)*

IMPERSONAL		
	SIMPLE	COMPOUND
Infinitive	Pren-**dre**	Ha-**ver pres**
Participle	**Pres**	-
Gerund	Pre-n**ent**	Ha-**vent pres**

114

TO TALK - PARLAR

PERSONAL						

INDICATIVE			SUBJUNCTIVE		
SIMPLE	COMPOUND		SIMPLE	COMPOUND	

Present / Past Indefinite / Present / Past Perfet

	SIMPLE		COMPOUND		SIMPLE		COMPOUND
Present		*Past Indefinite*		*Present*		*Past Perfet*	
Jo	**Par**-lo	Jo	**He** par-**lat**	Jo	**Par**-li	Jo	**Ha**-gi par-**lat**
Tu	**Par**-les	Tu	**Has** par-**lat**	Tu	**Par**-lis	Tu	**Ha**-gis par-**lat**
Ell	**Par**-la	Ell	**Ha** par-**lat**	Ell	**Par**-li	Ell	**Ha**-gi par-**lat**
No.	Par-**lem**	Nos.	**Hem** par-**lat**	Nos.	Par-**lem**	Nos.	**Hà**-gim par-**lat**
Vos.	Par-**leu**	Vos.	**Heu** par-**lat**	Vos.	Par-**leu**	Vos.	**Hà**-giu par-**lat**
Ells	**Par**-len	Ells	**Han** par-**lat**	Ells	**Par**-lin	Ells	**Ha**-gin par-**lat**
Imperfet		*Past Plusquamperfet*		*Imperfet past*		*Plusquamperfet past*	
Jo	Par-**la**-va	Jo	Ha-**vi**-a par-**lat**	Jo	Par-**lés**	Jo	Ha-**gués** par-**lat**
Tu	Par-**la**-ves	Tu	Ha-**vi**-es par-**lat**	Tu	Par-**les**-sis	Tu	Ha-**gues**-sis par-**lat**
Ell	Par-**la**-va	Ell	Ha-**vi**-a par-**lat**	Ell	Par-**lés**	Ell	Ha-**gués** par-**lat**
No.	Par-**là**-vem	Nos.	Ha-**ví**-em par-**lat**	Nos	Par-**lés**-sim	Nos.	Ha-**gués**-sim par-**lat**
Vos.	Par-**là**-veu	Vos.	Ha-**ví**-eu par-**lat**	Vos.	Par-**lés**-siu	Vos.	Ha-**gués**-siu par-**lat**
Ells	Par-**la**-ven	Ells	Ha-**vi**-en par-**lat**	Ells	Par-**les**-sin	Ells	Ha-**gues**-sin par-**lat**

Past Simple		*Past Perifrastic*		*Past Anterior perifrastic*
Jo	Par-**lí**	Jo	**Vaig** par-**lar**	**Vaig** ha-**ver** par-**lat**
Tu	Par-**la**-res	Tu	**Vas** par-**lar**	**Vas** ha-**ver** par-**lat**
Ell	Par-**là**	Ell	**Va** par-**lar**	**Va** ha-**ver** par-**lat**
Nos	Par-**là**-rem	Nos.	**Vam** par-**lar**	**Vam** ha-**ver** par-**lat**
Vos	Par-**là**-reu	Vos.	**Vau** par-**lar**	**Vau** ha-**ver** par-**lat**
Ells	Par-**la**-ren	Ells	**Van** par-**lar**	**Van** ha-**ver** par-**lat**

Future Simple		*Future Compound*	
Jo	Par-la-**ré**	Jo	Hau-**ré** par-**lat**
Tu	Par-la-**ràs**	Tu	Hau-**ràs** par-**lat**
Ell	Par-la-**rà**	Ell	Hau-**rà** par-**lat**
Nos.	Par-la-**rem**	Nos.	Hau-**rem** par-**lat**
Vos.	Par-la-**reu**	Vos.	Hau-**reu** par-**lat**
Ells	Par-la-**ran**	Ells	Hau-**ran** par-**lat**

Conditional Simple		*Conditional Compound*		IMPERATIVE	
Jo	Par-la-**ri**-a	Jo	Hau-**ri**-a par-**lat**		
Tu	Par-la-**ri**-es	Tu	Hau-**ri**-es par-**lat**	**Par**-la	*(Tu)*
Ell	Par-la-**ri**-a	Ell	Hau-**ri**-a par-**lat**	**Par**-li	*(Ell)*
Nos	Par-la-**rí**-em	Nos.	Hau-**rí**-em par-**lat**	Par-**lem**	*(Nos.)*
Vos	Par-la-**rí**-eu	Vos.	Hau-**rí**-eu par-**lat**	Par-**leu**	*(Vos.)*
Ells	Par-la-**ri**-en	Ells	Hau-**ri**-en par-**lat**	**Par**-lin	*(Ells)*

IMPERSONAL		
	SIMPLE	COMPOUND
Infinitive	Par-**lar**	Ha-**ver** par-**lat**
Participle	Par-**lat**	-
Gerund	Par-**lant**	Ha-**vent** par-**lat**

115

TO TEACH - ENSENYAR

PERSONAL							
INDICATIVE				**SUBJUNCTIVE**			
SIMPLE		**COMPOUND**		**SIMPLE**		**COMPOUND**	
Present		*Past Indefinite*		*Present*		*Past Perfet*	
Jo	En-**se**-nyo	Jo	**He** en-se-**nyat**	Jo	En-**se**-nyi	Jo	**Ha**-gi en-se-**nyat**
Tu	En-**se**-nyes	Tu	**Has** en-se-**nyat**	Tu	En-**se**-nyis	Tu	**Ha**-gis en-se-**nyat**
Ell	En-**se**-nya	Ell	**Ha** en-se-**nyat**	Ell	En-**se**-nyi	Ell	**Ha**-gi en-se-**nyat**
No.	En-se-**nyem**	Nos.	**Hem** en-se-**nyat**	Nos.	En-se-**nyem**	Nos.	**Hà**-gim en-se-**nyat**
Vos.	En-se-**nyeu**	Vos.	**Heu** en-se-**nyat**	Vos.	En-se-**nyeu**	Vos.	**Hà**-giu en-se-**nyat**
Ells	En-**se**-nyen	Ells	**Han** en-se-**nyat**	Ells	En-**se**-nyin	Ells	**Ha**-gin en-se-**nyat**
Imperfet		*Past Plusquamperfet*		*Imperfet past*		*Plusquamperfet past*	
Jo	En-se-**nya**-va	Jo	Ha-**vi**-a en-se-**nyat**	Jo	En-se-**nyés**	Jo	Ha-**gués** en-se-**nyat**
Tu	En-se-**nya**-ves	Tu	Ha-**vi**-es en-se-**nyat**	Tu	En-se-**nyes**-sis	Tu	Ha-**gues**-sis en-se-**nyat**
Ell	En-se-**nya**-va	Ell	Ha-**vi**-a en-se-**nyat**	Ell	En-se-**nyés**	Ell	Ha-**gués** en-se-**nyat**
No.	En-se-**nyà**-vem	Nos.	Ha-**ví**-em en-se-**nyat**	Nos	En-se-**nyés**-sim	Nos.	Ha-**gués**-sim en-se-**nyat**
Vos.	En-se-**nyà**-veu	Vos.	Ha-**ví**-eu en-se-**nyat**	Vos.	En-se-**nyés**-siu	Vos.	Ha-**gués**-siu en-se-**nyat**
Ells	En-se-**nya**-ven	Ells	Ha-**vi**-en en-se-**nyat**	Ells	En-se-**nyes**-sin	Ells	Ha-**gues**-sin en-se-**nyat**

Past Simple		*Past Perifrastic*		*Past Anterior perifrastic*
Jo	En-se-**nyí**	Jo	**Vaig** en-se-**nyar**	**Vaig** ha-**ver** en-se-**nyat**
Tu	En-se-**nya**-res	Tu	**Vas** en-se-**nyar**	**Vas** ha-**ver** en-se-**nyat**
Ell	En-se-**nyà**	Ell	**Va** en-se-**nyar**	**Va** ha-**ver** en-se-**nyat**
Nos	En-se-**nyà**-rem	Nos.	**Vam** en-se-**nyar**	**Vam** ha-**ver** en-se-**nyat**
Vos.	En-se-**nyà**-reu	Vos.	**Vau** en-se-**nyar**	**Vau** ha-**ver** en-se-**nyat**
Ells	En-se-**nya**-ren	Ells	**Van** en-se-**nyar**	**Van** ha-**ver** en-se-**nyat**

Future Simple		*Future Compound*	
Jo	En-se-nya-**ré**	Jo	Hau-**ré** en-se-**nyat**
Tu	En-se-nya-**ràs**	Tu	Hau-**ràs** en-se-**nyat**
Ell	En-se-nya-**rà**	Ell	Hau-**rà** en-se-**nyat**
Nos.	En-se-nya-**rem**	Nos.	Hau-**rem** en-se-**nyat**
Vos.	En-se-nya-**reu**	Vos.	Hau-**reu** en-se-**nyat**
Ells	En-se-nya-**ran**	Ells	Hau-**ran** en-se-**nyat**

Conditional Simple		*Conditional Compound*		**IMPERATIVE**	
Jo	En-se-nya-**ri**-a	Jo	Hau-**ri**-a en-se-**nyat**		
Tu	En-se-nya-**ri**-es	Tu	Hau-**ri**-es en-se-**nyat**	En-**se**-nya	*(Tu)*
Ell	En-se-nya-**ri**-a	Ell	Hau-**ri**-a en-se-**nyat**	En-**se**-nyi	*(Ell)*
Nos	En-se-nya-**rí**-em	Nos.	Hau-**rí**-em en-se-**nyat**	En-se-**nyem**	*(Nos.)*
Vos.	En-se-nya-**rí**-eu	Vos.	Hau-**rí**-eu en-se-**nyat**	En-se-**nyeu**	*(Vos.)*
Ells	En-se-nya-**ri**-en	Ells	Hau-**ri**-en en-se-**nyat**	En-**se**-nyin	*(Ells)*

IMPERSONAL		
	SIMPLE	**COMPOUND**
Infinitive	En-se-**nyar**	Ha-**ver** en-se-**nyat**
Participle	En-se-**nyat**	-
Gerund	En-se-**nyant**	Ha-**vent** en-se-**nyat**

TO THINK - PENSAR

PERSONAL					
INDICATIVE			**SUBJUNCTIVE**		
SIMPLE	**COMPOUND**		**SIMPLE**	**COMPOUND**	
Present	*Past Indefinite*		*Present*	*Past Perfet*	
Jo **Pen**-so	Jo **He** pen-**sat**		Jo **Pen**-si	Jo **Ha**-gi pen-**sat**	
Tu **Pen**-ses	Tu **Has** pen-**sat**		Tu **Pen**-sis	Tu **Ha**-gis pen-**sat**	
Ell **Pen**-sa	Ell **Ha** pen-**sat**		Ell **Pen**-si	Ell **Ha**-gi pen-**sat**	
No. Pen-**sem**	Nos. **Hem** pen-**sat**		Nos. Pen-**sem**	Nos. **Hà**-gim pen-**sat**	
Vos. Pen-**seu**	Vos. **Heu** pen-**sat**		Vos. Pen-**seu**	Vos. **Hà**-giu pen-**sat**	
Ells **Pen**-sen	Ells **Han** pen-**sat**		Ells **Pen**-sin	Ells **Ha**-gin pen-**sat**	
Imperfet	*Past Plusquamperfet*		*Imperfet past*	*Plusquamperfet past*	
Jo Pen-**sa**-va	Jo Ha-**vi**-a pen-**sat**		Jo Pen-**sés**	Jo Ha-**gués** pen-**sat**	
Tu Pen-**sa**-ves	Tu Ha-**vi**-es pen-**sat**		Tu Pen-ses-sis	Tu Ha-**gues**-sis pen-**sat**	
Ell Pen-**sa**-va	Ell Ha-**vi**-a pen-**sat**		Ell Pen-**sés**	Ell Ha-**gués** pen-**sat**	
No. Pen-**sà**-vem	Nos. Ha-**ví**-em pen-**sat**		Nos Pen-**sés**-sim	Nos. Ha-**gués**-sim pen-**sat**	
Vos. Pen-**sà**-veu	Vos. Ha-**ví**-eu pen-**sat**		Vos. Pen-**sés**-siu	Vos. Ha-**gués**-siu pen-**sat**	
Ells Pen-**sa**-ven	Ells Ha-**vi**-en pen-**sat**		Ells Pen-**ses**-sin	Ells Ha-**gues**-sin pen-**sat**	
Past Simple	*Past Perifrastic*	*Past Anterior perifrastic*			
Jo Pen-**sí**	Jo **Vaig** pen-**sar**	**Vaig** ha-**ver** pen-**sat**			
Tu Pen-**sa**-res	Tu **Vas** pen-**sar**	**Vas** ha-**ver** pen-**sat**			
Ell Pen-**sà**	Ell **Va** pen-**sar**	**Va** ha-**ver** pen-**sat**			
Nos Pen-**sà**-rem	Nos. **Vam** pen-**sar**	**Vam** ha-**ver** pen-**sat**			
Vos. Pen-**sà**-reu	Vos. **Vau** pen-**sar**	**Vau** ha-**ver** pen-**sat**			
Ells Pen-**sa**-ren	Ells **Van** pen-**sar**	**Van** ha-**ver** pen-**sat**			
Future Simple	*Future Compound*				
Jo Pen-sa-**ré**	Jo Hau-**ré** pen-**sat**				
Tu Pen-sa-**ràs**	Tu Hau-**ràs** pen-**sat**				
Ell Pen-sa-**rà**	Ell Hau-**rà** pen-**sat**				
Nos. Pen-sa-**rem**	Nos. Hau-**rem** pen-**sat**				
Vos. Pen-sa-**reu**	Vos. Hau-**reu** pen-**sat**				
Ells Pen-sa-**ran**	Ells Hau-**ran** pen-**sat**				
Conditional Simple	*Conditional Compound*		**IMPERATIVE**		
Jo Pen-sa-**ri**-a	Jo Hau-**ri**-a pen-**sat**		**Pen**-sa	(Tu)	
Tu Pen-sa-**ri**-es	Tu Hau-**ri**-es pen-**sat**		**Pen**-si	(Ell)	
Ell Pen-sa-**ri**-a	Ell Hau-**ri**-a pen-**sat**		Pen-**sem**	(Nos.)	
Nos Pen-sa-**rí**-em	Nos. Hau-**rí**-em pen-**sat**		Pen-**seu**	(Vos.)	
Vos. Pen-sa-**rí**-eu	Vos. Hau-**rí**-eu pen-**sat**		**Pen**-sin	(Ells)	
Ells Pen-sa-**ri**-en	Ells Hau-**ri**-en pen-**sat**				

IMPERSONAL		
	SIMPLE	**COMPOUND**
Infinitive	Pen-**sar**	Ha-**ver** pen-**sat**
Participle	Pen-**sat**	-
Gerund	Pen-**sant**	Ha-**vent** pen-**sat**

TO TOUCH - TOCAR

PERSONAL							
INDICATIVE				**SUBJUNCTIVE**			
SIMPLE		**COMPOUND**		**SIMPLE**		**COMPOUND**	
Present		*Past Indefinite*		*Present*		*Past Perfet*	
Jo	**To**-co	Jo	**He** To-**cat**	Jo	**To**-qui	Jo	**Ha**-gi To-**cat**
Tu	**To**-ques	Tu	**Has** To-**cat**	Tu	**To**-quis	Tu	**Ha**-gis To-**cat**
Ell	**To**-ca	Ell	**Ha** To-**cat**	Ell	**To**-qui	Ell	**Ha**-gi To-**cat**
No.	To-**quem**	Nos.	**Hem** To-**cat**	Nos.	To-**quem**	Nos.	**Hà**-gim To-**cat**
Vos.	To-**queu**	Vos.	**Heu** To-**cat**	Vos.	To-**queu**	Vos.	**Hà**-giu To-**cat**
Ells	**To**-quen	Ells	**Han** To-**cat**	Ells	**To**-quin	Ells	**Ha**-gin To-**cat**
Imperfet		*Past Plusquamperfet*		*Imperfet past*		*Plusquamperfet past*	
Jo	To-**ca**-va	Jo	Ha-**vi**-a To-**cat**	Jo	To-**qués**	Jo	Ha-**gués** To-**cat**
Tu	To-**ca**-ves	Tu	Ha-**vi**-es To-**cat**	Tu	To-**ques**-sis	Tu	Ha-**gues**-sis To-**cat**
Ell	To-**ca**-va	Ell	Ha-**vi**-a To-**cat**	Ell	To-**qués**	Ell	Ha-**gués** To-**cat**
No.	To-**cà**-vem	Nos.	Ha-**ví**-em To-**cat**	Nos	To-**qués**-sim	Nos.	Ha-**gués**-sim To-**cat**
Vos.	To-**cà**-veu	Vos.	Ha-**ví**-eu To-**cat**	Vos.	To-**qués**-siu	Vos.	Ha-**gués**-siu To-**cat**
Ells	To-**ca**-ven	Ells	Ha-**vi**-en To-**cat**	Ells	To-**ques**-sin	Ells	Ha-**gues**-sin To-**cat**

Past Simple		*Past Perifrastic*		*Past Anterior perifrastic*
Jo	To-**quí**	Jo	**Vaig** To-**car**	**Vaig** ha-**ver** To-**cat**
Tu	To-**ca**-res	Tu	**Vas** To-**car**	**Vas** ha-**ver** To-**cat**
Ell	To-**cà**	Ell	**Va** To-**car**	**Va** ha-**ver** To-**cat**
Nos	To-**cà**-rem	Nos.	**Vam** To-**car**	**Vam** ha-**ver** To-**cat**
Vos.	To-**cà**-reu	Vos.	**Vau** To-**car**	**Vau** ha-**ver** To-**cat**
Ells	To-**ca**-ren	Ells	**Van** To-**car**	**Van** ha-**ver** To-**cat**

Future Simple		*Future Compound*	
Jo	To-ca-**ré**	Jo	Hau-**ré** To-**cat**
Tu	To-ca-**ràs**	Tu	Hau-**ràs** To-**cat**
Ell	To-ca-**rà**	Ell	Hau-**rà** To-**cat**
Nos.	To-ca-**rem**	Nos.	Hau-**rem** To-**cat**
Vos.	To-ca-**reu**	Vos.	Hau-**reu** To-**cat**
Ells	To-ca-**ran**	Ells	Hau-**ran** To-**cat**

Conditional Simple		*Conditional Compound*		**IMPERATIVE**	
Jo	To-ca-**ri**-a	Jo	Hau-ri-a To-**cat**		
Tu	To-ca-**ri**-es	Tu	Hau-**ri**-es To-**cat**	**To**-ca	*(Tu)*
Ell	To-ca-**ri**-a	Ell	Hau-**ri**-a To-**cat**	**To**-qui	*(Ell)*
Nos	To-ca-**rí**-em	Nos.	Hau-**rí**-em To-**cat**	To-**quem**	*(Nos.)*
Vos.	To-ca-**rí**-eu	Vos.	Hau-**rí**-eu To-**cat**	To-**queu**	*(Vos.)*
Ells	To-ca-**ri**-en	Ells	Hau-**ri**-en To-**cat**	**To**-quin	*(Ells)*

IMPERSONAL		
	SIMPLE	**COMPOUND**
Infinitive	To-**car**	Ha-**ver** To-**cat**
Participle	To-**cat**	-
Gerund	To-**cant**	Ha-**vent** To-**cat**

TO TRAVEL - VIATJAR

PERSONAL							
INDICATIVE				**SUBJUNCTIVE**			
SIMPLE		**COMPOUND**		**SIMPLE**		**COMPOUND**	
Present		*Past Indefinite*		*Present*		*Past Perfet*	
Jo	Vi-**at**-jo	Jo	**He** Vi-at-**jat**	Jo	Vi-**at**-gi	Jo	**Ha**-gi Vi-at-**jat**
Tu	Vi-**at**-ges	Tu	**Has** Vi-at-**jat**	Tu	Vi-**at**-gis	Tu	**Ha**-gis Vi-at-**jat**
Ell	Vi-**at**-ja	Ell	**Ha** Vi-at-**jat**	Ell	Vi-**at**-gi	Ell	**Ha**-gi Vi-at-**jat**
No.	Vi-at-**gem**	Nos.	**Hem** Vi-at-**jat**	Nos.	Vi-at-**gem**	Nos.	**Hà**-gim Vi-at-**jat**
Vos.	Vi-at-**geu**	Vos.	**Heu** Vi-at-**jat**	Vos.	Vi-at-**geu**	Vos.	**Hà**-giu Vi-at-**jat**
Ells	Vi-at-**gen**	Ells	**Han** Vi-at-**jat**	Ells	Vi-**at**-gin	Ells	**Ha**-gin Vi-at-**jat**
Imperfet		*Past Plusquamperfet*		*Imperfet past*		*Plusquamperfet past*	
Jo	Vi-at-**ja**-va	Jo	**Ha**-**vi**-a Vi-at-**jat**	Jo	Vi-at-**gés**	Jo	**Ha**-**gués** Vi-at-**jat**
Tu	Vi-at-**ja**-ves	Tu	**Ha**-**vi**-es Vi-at-**jat**	Tu	Vi-at-**ges**-sis	Tu	**Ha**-**gues**-sis Vi-at-**jat**
Ell	Vi-at-**ja**-va	Ell	**Ha**-**vi**-a Vi-at-**jat**	Ell	Vi-at-**gés**	Ell	**Ha**-**gués** Vi-at-**jat**
No.	Vi-at-**jà**-vem	Nos.	**Ha**-**ví**-em Vi-at-**jat**	Nos	Vi-at-**gés**-sim	Nos.	**Ha**-**gués**-sim Vi-at-**jat**
Vos.	Vi-at-**jà**-veu	Vos.	**Ha**-**ví**-eu Vi-at-**jat**	Vos.	Vi-at-**gés**-siu	Vos.	**Ha**-**gués**-siu Vi-at-**jat**
Ells	Vi-at-**ja**-ven	Ells	**Ha**-**vi**-en Vi-at-**jat**	Ells	Vi-at-**ges**-sin	Ells	**Ha**-**gues**-sin Vi-at-**jat**

Past Simple		*Past Perifrastic*		*Past Anterior perifrastic*
Jo	Vi-at-**gí**	Jo	**Vaig** Vi-at-**jar**	**Vaig** ha-**ver** Vi-at-**jat**
Tu	Vi-at-**ja**-res	Tu	**Vas** Vi-at-**jar**	**Vas** ha-**ver** Vi-at-**jat**
Ell	Vi-at-**jà**	Ell	**Va** Vi-at-**jar**	**Va** ha-**ver** Vi-at-**jat**
Nos	Vi-at-**jà**-rem	Nos.	**Vam** Vi-at-**jar**	**Vam** ha-**ver** Vi-at-**jat**
Vos.	Vi-at-**jà**-reu	Vos.	**Vau** Vi-at-**jar**	**Vau** ha-**ver** Vi-at-**jat**
Ells	Vi-at-**ja**-ren	Ells	**Van** Vi-at-**jar**	**Van** ha-**ver** Vi-at-**jat**

Future Simple		*Future Compound*	
Jo	Vi-at-ja-**ré**	Jo	Hau-**ré** Vi-at-**jat**
Tu	Vi-at-ja-**ràs**	Tu	Hau-**ràs** Vi-at-**jat**
Ell	Vi-at-ja-**rà**	Ell	Hau-**rà** Vi-at-**jat**
Nos.	Vi-at-ja-**rem**	Nos.	Hau-**rem** Vi-at-**jat**
Vos.	Vi-at-ja-**reu**	Vos.	Hau-**reu** Vi-at-**jat**
Ells	Vi-at-ja-**ran**	Ells	Hau-**ran** Vi-at-**jat**

Conditional Simple		*Conditional Compound*		**IMPERATIVE**	
Jo	Vi-at-ja-**ri**-a	Jo	Hau-**ri**-a Vi-at-**jat**		
Tu	Vi-at-ja-**ri**-es	Tu	Hau-**ri**-es Vi-at-**jat**	Vi-**at**-ja	*(Tu)*
Ell	Vi-at-ja-**ri**-a	Ell	Hau-**ri**-a Vi-at-**jat**	Vi-**at**-gi	*(Ell)*
Nos	Vi-at-ja-**rí**-em	Nos.	Hau-**rí**-em Vi-at-**jat**	Vi-at-**gem**	*(Nos.)*
Vos.	Vi-at-ja-**rí**-eu	Vos.	Hau-**rí**-eu Vi-at-**jat**	Vi-at-**geu**	*(Vos.)*
Ells	Vi-at-ja-**ri**-en	Ells	Hau-**ri**-en Vi-at-**jat**	Vi-**at**-gin	*(Ells)*

IMPERSONAL		
	SIMPLE	**COMPOUND**
Infinitive	Vi-at-**jar**	Ha-**ver** Vi-at-**jat**
Participle	Vi-at-**jat**	-
Gerund	Vi-at-**jant**	Ha-**vent** Vi-at-**jat**

TO UNDERSTAND - ENTENDRE

PERSONAL							
INDICATIVE				**SUBJUNCTIVE**			
SIMPLE		**COMPOUND**		**SIMPLE**		**COMPOUND**	
En-tèsent		*Past Indefinite*		*En-tèsent*		*Past Perfet*	
Jo	En-**tenc**	Jo	**He** en-**tès**	Jo	En-**ten**-gui	Jo	**Ha**-gi en-**tès**
Tu	En-**tens**	Tu	**Has** en-**tès**	Tu	En-**ten**-guis	Tu	**Ha**-gis en-**tès**
Ell	En-**tén**	Ell	**Ha** en-**tès**	Ell	En-**ten**-gui	Ell	**Ha**-gi en-**tès**
No.	En-te-**nem**	Nos.	**Hem** en-**tès**	Nos.	En-ten-**guem**	Nos	**Hà**-gim en-**tès**
Vos.	En-te-**neu**	Vos.	**Heu** en-**tès**	Vos.	En-ten-**gueu**	Vos.	**Hà**-giu en-**tès**
Ells	En-**te**-nen	Ells	**Han** en-**tès**	Ells	En-**ten**-guin	Ells	**Ha**-gin en-**tès**
Imperfet		*Past Plusquamperfet*		*Imperfet past*		*Plusquamperfet past*	
Jo	En-te-**ni**-a	Jo	**Ha**-**vi**-a en-**tès**	Jo	En-ten-**gués**	Jo	**Ha**-**gués** en-**tès**
Tu	En-te-**ni**-es	Tu	**Ha**-**vi**-es en-**tès**	Tu	En-ten-**gues**-sis	Tu	**Ha**-**gues**-sis en-**tès**
Ell	En-te-**ni**-a	Ell	**Ha**-**vi**-a en-**tès**	Ell	En-ten-**gués**	Ell	**Ha**-**gués** en-**tès**
No.	En-te-**ní**-em	Nos.	**Ha**-**ví**-em en-**tès**	Nos.	En-ten-**gués**-sim	Nos	**Ha**-**gués**-sim en-**tès**
Vos.	En-te-**ní**-eu	Vos.	**Ha**-**ví**-eu en-**tès**	Vos.	En-ten-**gués**-siu	Vos.	**Ha**-**gués**-siu en-**tès**
Ells	En-te-**ni**-en	Ells	**Ha**-**vi**-en en-**tès**	Ells	En-ten-**gues**-sin	Ells	**Ha**-**gues**-sin en-**tès**

Past Simple		*Past Perifrastic*		*Past Anterior perifrastic*
Jo	En-ten-**guí**	Jo	**Vaig** en-**ten**-dre	**Vaig** ha-**ver** en-**tès**
Tu	En-ten-**gue**-res	Tu	**Vas** en-**ten**-dre	**Vas** ha-**ver** en-**tès**
Ell	En-ten-**gué**	Ell	**Va** en-**ten**-dre	**Va** ha-**ver** en-**tès**
Nos.	En-ten-**gué**-rem	Nos.	**Vam** en-**ten**-dre	**Vam** ha-**ver** en-**tès**
Vos.	En-ten-**gué**-reu	Vos.	**Vau** en-**ten**-dre	**Vau** ha-**ver** en-**tès**
Ells	En-ten-**gue**-ren	Ells	**Van** en-**ten**-dre	**Van** ha-**ver** en-**tès**

Future Simple		*Future Compound*	
Jo	En-ten-**dré**	Jo	Hau-**ré** en-**tès**
Tu	En-ten-**dràs**	Tu	Hau-**ràs** en-**tès**
Ell	En-ten-**drà**	Ell	Hau-**rà** en-**tès**
Nos.	En-ten-**drem**	Nos.	Hau-**rem** en-**tès**
Vos.	En-ten-**dreu**	Vos.	Hau-**reu** en-**tès**
Ells	En-ten-**dran**	Ells	Hau-**ran** en-**tès**

Conditional Simple		*Conditional Compound*		**IMPERATIVE**	
Jo	En-ten-**dri**-a	Jo	Hau-**ri**-a en-**tès**		
Tu	En-ten-**dri**-es	Tu	Hau-**ri**-es en-**tès**	En-**tén**	(Tu)
Ell	En-ten-**dri**-a	Ell	Hau-**ri**-a en-**tès**	En-**ten**-gui	(Ell)
Nos.	En-ten-**drí**-em	Nos.	Hau-**rí**-em en-**tès**	En-ten-**guem**	(Nos.)
Vos.	En-ten-**drí**-eu	Vos.	Hau-**rí**-eu en-**tès**	En-te-**neu**	(Vos.)
Ells	En-ten-**dri**-en	Ells	Hau-**ri**-en en-**tès**	En-**ten**-guin	(Ells)

IMPERSONAL		
	SIMPLE	**COMPOUND**
Infinitive	En-ten-**dre**	Ha-**ver** en-**tès**
Participle	En-**tès**	-
Gerund	En-te-**nent**	Ha-**vent** en-**tès**

120

TO USE - UTILITZAR

PERSONAL							
INDICATIVE				**SUBJUNCTIVE**			
SIMPLE		**COMPOUND**		**SIMPLE**		**COMPOUND**	
Present		*Past Indefinite*		*Present*		*Past Perfet*	
Jo	U-ti-**lit**-zo	Jo	**He** u-ti-lit-**zat**	Jo	U-ti-**lit**-zi	Jo	**Ha**-gi u-ti-lit-**zat**
Tu	U-ti-**lit**-zes	Tu	**Has** u-ti-lit-**zat**	Tu	U-ti-**lit**-zis	Tu	**Ha**-gis u-ti-lit-**zat**
Ell	U-ti-**lit**-za	Ell	**Ha** u-ti-lit-**zat**	Ell	U-ti-**lit**-zi	Ell	**Ha**-gi u-ti-lit-**zat**
No.	U-ti-lit-**zem**	Nos.	**Hem** u-ti-lit-**zat**	Nos.	U-ti-lit-**zem**	Nos.	**Hà**-gim u-ti-lit-**zat**
Vos.	U-ti-lit-**zeu**	Vos.	**Heu** u-ti-lit-**zat**	Vos.	U-ti-lit-**zeu**	Vos.	**Hà**-giu u-ti-lit-**zat**
Ells	U-ti-**lit**-zen	Ells	**Han** u-ti-lit-**zat**	Ells	U-ti-**lit**-zin	Ells	**Ha**-gin u-ti-lit-**zat**
Imperfet		*Past Plusquamperfet*		*Imperfet past*		*Plusquamperfet past*	
Jo	U-ti-lit-**za**-va	Jo	Ha-**vi**-a u-ti-lit-**zat**	Jo	U-ti-lit-**zés**	Jo	Ha-**gués** u-ti-lit-**zat**
Tu	U-ti-lit-**za**-ves	Tu	Ha-**vi**-es u-ti-lit-**zat**	Tu	U-ti-lit-**zes**-sis	Tu	Ha-**gues**-sis u-ti-lit-**zat**
Ell	U-ti-lit-**za**-va	Ell	Ha-**vi**-a u-ti-lit-**zat**	Ell	U-ti-lit-**zés**	Ell	Ha-**gués** u-ti-lit-**zat**
No.	U-ti-lit-**zà**-vem	Nos.	Ha-**ví**-em u-ti-lit-**zat**	Nos	U-ti-lit-**zés**-sim	Nos.	Ha-**gués**-sim u-ti-lit-**zat**
Vos.	U-ti-lit-**zà**-veu	Vos.	Ha-**ví**-eu u-ti-lit-**zat**	Vos.	U-ti-lit-**zés**-siu	Vos.	Ha-**gués**-siu u-ti-lit-**zat**
Ells	U-ti-lit-**za**-ven	Ells	Ha-**vi**-en u-ti-lit-**zat**	Ells	U-ti-lit-**zes**-sin	Ells	Ha-**gues**-sin u-ti-lit-**zat**

Past Simple		*Past Perifrastic*		*Past Anterior perifrastic*
Jo	U-ti-lit-**zí**	Jo	**Vaig** u-ti-lit-**zar**	**Vaig** ha-**ver** u-ti-lit-**zat**
Tu	U-ti-lit-**za**-res	Tu	**Vas** u-ti-lit-**zar**	**Vas** ha-**ver** u-ti-lit-**zat**
Ell	U-ti-lit-**zà**	Ell	**Va** u-ti-lit-**zar**	**Va** ha-**ver** u-ti-lit-**zat**
Nos	U-ti-lit-**zà**-rem	Nos.	**Vam** u-ti-lit-**zar**	**Vam** ha-**ver** u-ti-lit-**zat**
Vos.	U-ti-lit-**zà**-reu	Vos.	**Vau** u-ti-lit-**zar**	**Vau** ha-**ver** u-ti-lit-**zat**
Ells	U-ti-lit-**za**-ren	Ells	**Van** u-ti-lit-**zar**	**Van** ha-**ver** u-ti-lit-**zat**

Future Simple		*Future Compound*	
Jo	U-ti-lit-za-**ré**	Jo	Hau-**ré** u-ti-lit-**zat**
Tu	U-ti-lit-za-**ràs**	Tu	Hau-**ràs** u-ti-lit-**zat**
Ell	U-ti-lit-za-**rà**	Ell	Hau-**rà** u-ti-lit-**zat**
Nos.	U-ti-lit-za-**rem**	Nos.	Hau-**rem** u-ti-lit-**zat**
Vos.	U-ti-lit-za-**reu**	Vos.	Hau-**reu** u-ti-lit-**zat**
Ells	U-ti-lit-za-**ran**	Ells	Hau-**ran** u-ti-lit-**zat**

Conditional Simple		*Conditional Compound*		**IMPERATIVE**	
Jo	U-ti-lit-za-**ri**-a	Jo	Hau-ri-a u-ti-lit-**zat**		
Tu	U-ti-lit-za-**ri**-es	Tu	Hau-**ri**-es u-ti-lit-**zat**	U-ti-**lit**-za	*(Tu)*
Ell	U-ti-lit-za-**ri**-a	Ell	Hau-**ri**-a u-ti-lit-**zat**	U-ti-**lit**-zi	*(Ell)*
Nos	U-ti-lit-za-**rí**-em	Nos.	Hau-**rí**-em u-ti-lit-**zat**	U-ti-lit-**zem**	*(Nos.)*
Vos.	U-ti-lit-za-**rí**-eu	Vos.	Hau-**rí**-eu u-ti-lit-**zat**	U-ti-lit-**zeu**	*(Vos.)*
Ells	U-ti-lit-za-**ri**-en	Ells	Hau-**ri**-en u-ti-lit-**zat**	U-ti-**lit**-zin	*(Ells)*

IMPERSONAL		
	SIMPLE	**COMPOUND**
Infinitive	U-ti-lit-**zar**	Ha-**ver** u-ti-lit-**zat**
Participle	U-ti-lit-**zat**	-
Gerund	U-ti-lit-**zant**	Ha-**vent** u-ti-lit-**zat**

121

TO WAIT - ESPERAR

PERSONAL							
INDICATIVE				**SUBJUNCTIVE**			
SIMPLE		**COMPOUND**		**SIMPLE**		**COMPOUND**	
Present		*Past Indefinite*		*Present*		*Past Perfet*	
Jo	Es-**pe**-ro	Jo	**He** es-pe-**rat**	Jo	Es-**pe**-ri	Jo	**Ha**-gi es-pe-**rat**
Tu	Es-**pe**-res	Tu	**Has** es-pe-**rat**	Tu	Es-**pe**-ris	Tu	**Ha**-gis es-pe-**rat**
Ell	Es-**pe**-ra	Ell	**Ha** es-pe-**rat**	Ell	Es-**pe**-ri	Ell	**Ha**-gi es-pe-**rat**
No.	Es-pe-**rem**	Nos.	**Hem** es-pe-**rat**	Nos.	Es-pe-**rem**	Nos.	**Hà**-gim es-pe-**rat**
Vos.	Es-pe-**reu**	Vos.	**Heu** es-pe-**rat**	Vos.	Es-pe-**reu**	Vos.	**Hà**-giu es-pe-**rat**
Ells	Es-**pe**-ren	Ells	**Han** es-pe-**rat**	Ells	Es-**pe**-rin	Ells	**Ha**-gin es-pe-**rat**
Imperfet		*Past Plusquamperfet*		*Imperfet past*		*Plusquamperfet past*	
Jo	Es-pe-**ra**-va	Jo	Ha-**vi**-a es-pe-**rat**	Jo	Es-pe-**rés**	Jo	Ha-**gués** es-pe-**rat**
Tu	Es-pe-**ra**-ves	Tu	Ha-**vi**-es es-pe-**rat**	Tu	Es-pe-**res**-sis	Tu	Ha-**gues**-sis es-pe-**rat**
Ell	Es-pe-**ra**-va	Ell	Ha-**vi**-a es-pe-**rat**	Ell	Es-pe-**rés**	Ell	Ha-**gués** es-pe-**rat**
No.	Es-pe-**rà**-vem	Nos.	Ha-**ví**-em es-pe-**rat**	Nos	Es-pe-**rés**-sim	Nos.	Ha-**gués**-sim es-pe-**rat**
Vos.	Es-pe-**rà**-veu	Vos.	Ha-**ví**-eu es-pe-**rat**	Vos.	Es-pe-**rés**-siu	Vos.	Ha-**gués**-siu es-pe-**rat**
Ells	Es-pe-**ra**-ven	Ells	Ha-**vi**-en es-pe-**rat**	Ells	Es-pe-**res**-sin	Ells	Ha-**gues**-sin es-pe-**rat**

Past Simple		*Past Perifrastic*		*Past Anterior perifrastic*			
Jo	Es-pe-**rí**	Jo	**Vaig** es-pe-rar	**Vaig** ha-**ver** es-pe-**rat**			
Tu	Es-pe-**ra**-res	Tu	**Vas** es-pe-rar	**Vas** ha-**ver** es-pe-**rat**			
Ell	Es-pe-**rà**	Ell	**Va** es-pe-rar	**Va** ha-**ver** es-pe-**rat**			
Nos	Es-pe-**rà**-rem	Nos.	**Vam** es-pe-rar	**Vam** ha-**ver** es-pe-**rat**			
Vos.	Es-pe-**rà**-reu	Vos.	**Vau** es-pe-rar	**Vau** ha-**ver** es-pe-**rat**			
Ells	Es-pe-**ra**-ren	Ells	**Van** es-pe-rar	**Van** ha-**ver** es-pe-**rat**			

Future Simple		*Future Compound*					
Jo	Es-pe-ra-**ré**	Jo	Hau-**ré** es-pe-**rat**				
Tu	Es-pe-ra-**ràs**	Tu	Hau-**ràs** es-pe-**rat**				
Ell	Es-pe-ra-**rà**	Ell	Hau-**rà** es-pe-**rat**				
Nos.	Es-pe-ra-**rem**	Nos.	Hau-**rem** es-pe-**rat**				
Vos.	Es-pe-ra-**reu**	Vos.	Hau-**reu** es-pe-**rat**				
Ells	Es-pe-ra-**ran**	Ells	Hau-**ran** es-pe-**rat**				

Conditional Simple		*Conditional Compound*		**IMPERATIVE**			
Jo	Es-pe-ra-**ri**-a	Jo	Hau-**ri**-a es-pe-**rat**				
Tu	Es-pe-ra-**ri**-es	Tu	Hau-**ri**-es es-pe-**rat**	Es-**pe**-ra		*(Tu)*	
Ell	Es-pe-ra-**ri**-a	Ell	Hau-**ri**-a es-pe-**rat**	Es-**pe**-ri		*(Ell)*	
Nos	Es-pe-ra-**rí**-em	Nos.	Hau-**rí**-em es-pe-**rat**	Es-pe-**rem**		*(Nos.)*	
Vos.	Es-pe-ra-**rí**-eu	Vos.	Hau-**rí**-eu es-pe-**rat**	Es-pe-**reu**		*(Vos.)*	
Ells	Es-pe-ra-**ri**-en	Ells	Hau-**ri**-en es-pe-**rat**	Es-**pe**-rin		*(Ells)*	

IMPERSONAL		
	SIMPLE	**COMPOUND**
Infinitive	Es-pe-**rar**	Ha-**ver** es-pe-**rat**
Participle	Es-pe-**rat**	-
Gerund	Es-pe-**rant**	Ha-**vent** es-pe-**rat**

TO WALK - CAMINAR

PERSONAL				
INDICATIVE			**SUBJUNCTIVE**	
SIMPLE	**COMPOUND**		**SIMPLE**	**COMPOUND**

INDICATIVE / SUBJUNCTIVE

SIMPLE		COMPOUND		SIMPLE		COMPOUND	
Present		*Past Indefinite*		*Present*		*Past Perfet*	
Jo	Ca-**mi**-no	Jo	**He** ca-mi-**nat**	Jo	Ca-**mi**-ni	Jo	**Ha**-gi ca-mi-**nat**
Tu	Ca-**mi**-nes	Tu	**Has** ca-mi-**nat**	Tu	Ca-**mi**-nis	Tu	**Ha**-gis ca-mi-**nat**
Ell	Ca-**mi**-na	Ell	**Ha** ca-mi-**nat**	Ell	Ca-**mi**-ni	Ell	**Ha**-gi ca-mi-**nat**
No.	Ca-mi-**nem**	Nos.	**Hem** ca-mi-**nat**	Nos.	Ca-mi-**nem**	Nos.	**Hà**-gim ca-mi-**nat**
Vos.	Ca-mi-**neu**	Vos.	**Heu** ca-mi-**nat**	Vos.	Ca-mi-**neu**	Vos.	**Hà**-giu ca-mi-**nat**
Ells	Ca-**mi**-nen	Ells	**Han** ca-mi-**nat**	Ells	Ca-**mi**-nin	Ells	**Ha**-gin ca-mi-**nat**
Imperfet		*Past Plusquamperfet*		*Imperfet past*		*Plusquamperfet past*	
Jo	Ca-mi-**na**-va	Jo	Ha-**vi**-a ca-mi-**nat**	Jo	Ca-mi-**nés**	Jo	Ha-**gués** ca-mi-**nat**
Tu	Ca-mi-**na**-ves	Tu	Ha-**vi**-es ca-mi-**nat**	Tu	Ca-mi-**nes**-sis	Tu	Ha-**gues**-sis ca-mi-**nat**
Ell	Ca-mi-**na**-va	Ell	Ha-**vi**-a ca-mi-**nat**	Ell	Ca-mi-**nés**	Ell	Ha-**gués** ca-mi-**nat**
No.	Ca-mi-**nà**-vem	Nos.	Ha-**ví**-em ca-mi-**nat**	Nos	Ca-mi-**nés**-sim	Nos.	Ha-**gués**-sim ca-mi-**nat**
Vos.	Ca-mi-**nà**-veu	Vos.	Ha-**ví**-eu ca-mi-**nat**	Vos.	Ca-mi-**nés**-siu	Vos.	Ha-**gués**-siu ca-mi-**nat**
Ells	Ca-mi-**na**-ven	Ells	Ha-**vi**-en ca-mi-**nat**	Ells	Ca-mi-**nes**-sin	Ells	Ha-**gues**-sin ca-mi-**nat**

Past Simple		*Past Perifrastic*		*Past Anterior perifrastic*
Jo	Ca-mi-**ní**	Jo	**Vaig** ca-mi-nar	**Vaig** ha-**ver** ca-mi-**nat**
Tu	Ca-mi-**na**-res	Tu	**Vas** ca-mi-nar	**Vas** ha-**ver** ca-mi-**nat**
Ell	Ca-mi-**nà**	Ell	**Va** ca-mi-nar	**Va** ha-**ver** ca-mi-**nat**
Nos	Ca-mi-**nà**-rem	Nos.	**Vam** ca-mi-nar	**Vam** ha-**ver** ca-mi-**nat**
Vos.	Ca-mi-**nà**-reu	Vos.	**Vau** ca-mi-nar	**Vau** ha-**ver** ca-mi-**nat**
Ells	Ca-mi-**na**-ren	Ells	**Van** ca-mi-nar	**Van** ha-**ver** ca-mi-**nat**

Future Simple		*Future Compound*	
Jo	Ca-mi-na-**ré**	Jo	Hau-**ré** ca-mi-**nat**
Tu	Ca-mi-na-**ràs**	Tu	Hau-**ràs** ca-mi-**nat**
Ell	Ca-mi-na-**rà**	Ell	Hau-**rà** ca-mi-**nat**
Nos.	Ca-mi-na-**rem**	Nos.	Hau-**rem** ca-mi-**nat**
Vos.	Ca-mi-na-**reu**	Vos.	Hau-**reu** ca-mi-**nat**
Ells	Ca-mi-na-**ran**	Ells	Hau-**ran** ca-mi-**nat**

Conditional Simple		*Conditional Compound*		IMPERATIVE	
Jo	Ca-mi-na-**ri**-a	Jo	Hau-**ri**-a ca-mi-**nat**		
Tu	Ca-mi-na-**ri**-es	Tu	Hau-**ri**-es ca-mi-**nat**	Ca-**mi**-na	*(Tu)*
Ell	Ca-mi-na-**ri**-a	Ell	Hau-**ri**-a ca-mi-**nat**	Ca-**mi**-ni	*(Ell)*
Nos	Ca-mi-na-**rí**-em	Nos.	Hau-**rí**-em ca-mi-**nat**	Ca-mi-**nem**	*(Nos.)*
Vos.	Ca-mi-na-**rí**-eu	Vos.	Hau-**rí**-eu ca-mi-**nat**	Ca-mi-**neu**	*(Vos.)*
Ells	Ca-mi-na-**ri**-en	Ells	Hau-**ri**-en ca-mi-**nat**	Ca-**mi**-nin	*(Ells)*

IMPERSONAL		
	SIMPLE	**COMPOUND**
Infinitive	Ca-mi-**nar**	Ha-**ver** ca-mi-**nat**
Participle	Ca-mi-**nat**	-
Gerund	Ca-mi-**nant**	Ha-**vent** ca-mi-**nat**

TO WANT - VOLER

PERSONAL							
INDICATIVE				**SUBJUNCTIVE**			
SIMPLE		**COMPOUND**		**SIMPLE**		**COMPOUND**	
Present		*Past Indefinite*		*Present*		*Past Perfet*	
Jo	**Vull**	Jo	**He** vol-**gut**	Jo	**Vul**-gui	Jo	**Ha**-gi vol-**gut**
Tu	**Vols**	Tu	**Has** vol-**gut**	Tu	**Vul**-guis	Tu	**Ha**-gis vol-**gut**
Ell	**Vol**	Ell	**Ha** vol-**gut**	Ell	**Vul**-gui	Ell	**Ha**-gi vol-**gut**
No.	Vo-**lem**	Nos.	**Hem** vol-**gut**	Nos.	Vul-**guem**	Nos.	**Hà**-gim vol-**gut**
Vos.	Vo-**leu**	Vos.	**Heu** vol-**gut**	Vos.	Vul-**gueu**	Vos.	**Hà**-giu vol-**gut**
Ells	**Vo**-len	Ells	**Han** vol-**gut**	Ells	**Vul**-guin	Ells	**Ha**-gin vol-**gut**
Imperfet		*Past Plusquamperfet*		*Imperfet past*		*Plusquamperfet past*	
Jo	Vo-**li**-a	Jo	**Ha**-**vi**-a vol-**gut**	Jo	Vol-**gués**	Jo	**Ha**-**gués** vol-**gut**
Tu	Vo-**li**-es	Tu	**Ha**-**vi**-es vol-**gut**	Tu	Vol-**gues**-sis	Tu	**Ha**-**gues**-sis vol-**gut**
Ell	Vo-**li**-a	Ell	**Ha**-**vi**-a vol-**gut**	Ell	Vol-**gués**	Ell	**Ha**-**gués** vol-**gut**
No.	Vo-**lí**-em	Nos.	**Ha**-**ví**-em vol-**gut**	Nos.	Vol-**gués**-sim	Nos.	**Ha**-**gués**-sim vol-**gut**
Vos.	Vo-**lí**-eu	Vos.	**Ha**-**ví**-eu vol-**gut**	Vos.	Vol-**gués**-siu	Vos.	**Ha**-**gués**-siu vol-**gut**
Ells	Vo-**li**-en	Ells	**Ha**-**vi**-en vol-**gut**	Ells	Vol-**gues**-sin	Ells	**Ha**-**gues**-sin vol-**gut**

Past Simple		*Past Perifrastic*		*Past Anterior perifrastic*
Jo	Vol-**guí**	Jo	**Vaig** vo-**ler**	**Vaig** ha-**ver** vol-**gut**
Tu	Vol-**gue**-res	Tu	**Vas** **vo**-ler	**Vas** ha-**ver** vol-**gut**
Ell	Vol-**gué**	Ell	**Va** **vo**-ler	**Va** ha-**ver** vol-**gut**
Nos.	Vol-**gué**-rem	Nos.	**Vam** **vo**-ler	**Vam** ha-**ver** vol-**gut**
Vos.	Vol-**gué**-reu	Vos.	**Vau** **vo**-ler	**Vau** ha-**ver** vol-**gut**
Ells	Vol-**gue**-ren	Ells	**Van** **vo**-ler	**Van** ha-**ver** vol-**gut**

Future Simple		*Future Compound*	
Jo	Vol-**dré**	Jo	Hau-**ré** vol-**gut**
Tu	Vol-**dràs**	Tu	Hau-**ràs** vol-**gut**
Ell	Vol-**drà**	Ell	Hau-**rà** vol-**gut**
Nos.	Vol-**drem**	Nos.	Hau-**rem** vol-**gut**
Vos.	Vol-**dreu**	Vos.	Hau-**reu** vol-**gut**
Ells	Vol-**dran**	Ells	Hau-**ran** vol-**gut**

Conditional Simple		*Conditional Compound*		**IMPERATIVE**	
Jo	Vol-**dri**-a	Jo	Hau-**ri**-a vol-**gut**		
Tu	Vol-**dri**-es	Tu	Hau-**ri**-es vol-**gut**	**Vul**-gues	*(Tu)*
Ell	Vol-**dri**-a	Ell	Hau-**ri**-a vol-**gut**	**Vul**-gui	*(Ell)*
Nos.	Vol-**drí**-em	Nos.	Hau-**rí**-em vol-**gut**	Vul-**guem**	*(Nos.)*
Vos.	Vol-**drí**-eu	Vos.	Hau-**rí**-eu vol-**gut**	Vul-**gueu**	*(Vos.)*
Ells	Vol-**dri**-en	Ells	Hau-**ri**-en vol-**gut**	**Vul**-guin	*(Ells)*

IMPERSONAL		
	SIMPLE	**COMPOUND**
Infinitive	**Vo**-ler	Ha-**ver** vol-**gut**
Participle	Vol-**gut**	-
Gerund	Vo-**lent**	Ha-**vent** vol-**gut**

TO WATCH - MIRAR

PERSONAL						
INDICATIVE			**SUBJUNCTIVE**			
SIMPLE	**COMPOUND**		**SIMPLE**	**COMPOUND**		
Present	*Past Indefinite*		*Present*	*Past Perfet*		
Jo **Mi**-ro	Jo He mi-**rat**		Jo **Mi**-ri	Jo **Ha**-gi mi-**rat**		
Tu **Mi**-res	Tu **Has** mi-**rat**		Tu **Mi**-ris	Tu **Ha**-gis mi-**rat**		
Ell **Mi**-ra	Ell **Ha** mi-**rat**		Ell **Mi**-ri	Ell **Ha**-gi mi-**rat**		
No. Mi-**rem**	Nos. **Hem** mi-**rat**		Nos. Mi-**rem**	Nos. **Hà**-gim mi-**rat**		
Vos. **Mi-reu**	Vos. **Heu** mi-**rat**		Vos. **Mi-reu**	Vos. **Hà**-giu mi-**rat**		
Ells **Mi**-ren	Ells **Han** mi-**rat**		Ells **Mi**-rin	Ells **Ha**-gin mi-**rat**		
Imperfet	*Past Plusquamperfet*		*Imperfet past*	*Plusquamperfet past*		
Jo Mi-**ra**-va	Jo Ha-**vi**-a mi-**rat**		Jo Mi-**rés**	Jo Ha-**gués** mi-**rat**		
Tu Mi-**ra**-ves	Tu Ha-**vi**-es mi-**rat**		Tu Mi-**res**-sis	Tu Ha-**gues**-sis mi-**rat**		
Ell Mi-**ra**-va	Ell Ha-**vi**-a mi-**rat**		Ell Mi-**rés**	Ell Ha-**gués** mi-**rat**		
No. Mi-**rà**-vem	Nos. Ha-**ví**-em mi-**rat**		Nos Mi-**rés**-sim	Nos. Ha-**gués**-sim mi-**rat**		
Vos. Mi-**rà**-veu	Vos. Ha-**ví**-eu mi-**rat**		Vos. Mi-**rés**-siu	Vos. Ha-**gués**-siu mi-**rat**		
Ells Mi-**ra**-ven	Ells Ha-**vi**-en mi-**rat**		Ells Mi-**res**-sin	Ells Ha-**gues**-sin mi-**rat**		
Past Simple	*Past Perifrastic*	*Past Anterior perifrastic*				
Jo Mi-**rí**	Jo **Vaig** mi-**rar**	**Vaig** ha-**ver** mi-**rat**				
Tu Mi-**ra**-res	Tu **Vas** mi-**rar**	**Vas** ha-**ver** mi-**rat**				
Ell Mi-**rà**	Ell **Va** mi-**rar**	**Va** ha-**ver** mi-**rat**				
Nos Mi-**rà**-rem	Nos. **Vam** mi-**rar**	**Vam** ha-**ver** mi-**rat**				
Vos. Mi-**rà**-reu	Vos. **Vau** mi-**rar**	**Vau** ha-**ver** mi-**rat**				
Ells Mi-**ra**-ren	Ells **Van** mi-**rar**	**Van** ha-**ver** mi-**rat**				
Future Simple	*Future Compound*					
Jo Mi-ra-**ré**	Jo Hau-**ré** mi-**rat**					
Tu Mi-ra-**ràs**	Tu Hau-**ràs** mi-**rat**					
Ell Mi-ra-**rà**	Ell Hau-**rà** mi-**rat**					
Nos. Mi-ra-**rem**	Nos. Hau-**rem** mi-**rat**					
Vos. Mi-ra-**reu**	Vos. Hau-**reu** mi-**rat**					
Ells Mi-ra-**ran**	Ells Hau-**ran** mi-**rat**					
Conditional Simple	*Conditional Compound*		**IMPERATIVE**			
Jo Mi-ra-**ri**-a	Jo Hau-**ri**-a mi-**rat**					
Tu Mi-ra-**ri**-es	Tu Hau-**ri**-es mi-**rat**		**Mi**-ra	*(Tu)*		
Ell Mi-ra-**ri**-a	Ell Hau-**ri**-a mi-**rat**		**Mi**-ri	*(Ell)*		
Nos Mi-ra-**rí**-em	Nos. Hau-**rí**-em mi-**rat**		Mi-**rem**	*(Nos.)*		
Vos. Mi-ra-**rí**-eu	Vos. Hau-**rí**-eu mi-**rat**		Mi-**reu**	*(Vos.)*		
Ells Mi-ra-**ri**-en	Ells Hau-**ri**-en mi-**rat**		**Mi**-rin	*(Ells)*		

IMPERSONAL		
	SIMPLE	**COMPOUND**
Infinitive	Mi-**rar**	Ha-**ver** mi-**rat**
Participle	Mi-**rat**	-
Gerund	Mi-**rant**	Ha-**vent** mi-**rat**

TO WORK - TREBALLAR

PERSONAL							
INDICATIVE				**SUBJUNCTIVE**			
SIMPLE		**COMPOUND**		**SIMPLE**		**COMPOUND**	
Present		*Past Indefinite*		*Present*		*Past Perfet*	
Jo	Tre-**ba**-llo	Jo	**He** tre-ba-**llat**	Jo	Tre-**ba**-lli	Jo	**Ha**-gi tre-ba-**llat**
Tu	Tre-**ba**-lles	Tu	**Has** tre-ba-**llat**	Tu	Tre-**ba**-llis	Tu	**Ha**-gis tre-ba-**llat**
Ell	Tre-**ba**-lla	Ell	**Ha** tre-ba-**llat**	Ell	Tre-**ba**-lli	Ell	**Ha**-gi tre-ba-**llat**
No.	Tre-ba-**llem**	Nos.	**Hem** tre-ba-**llat**	Nos.	Tre-ba-**llem**	Nos.	**Hà**-gim tre-ba-**llat**
Vos.	Tre-ba-**lleu**	Vos.	**Heu** tre-ba-**llat**	Vos.	Tre-ba-**lleu**	Vos.	**Hà**-giu tre-ba-**llat**
Ells	Tre-**ba**-llen	Ells	**Han** tre-ba-**llat**	Ells	Tre-**ba**-llin	Ells	**Ha**-gin tre-ba-**llat**
Imperfet		*Past Plusquamperfet*		*Imperfet past*		*Plusquamperfet past*	
Jo	Tre-ba-**lla**-va	Jo	Ha-**vi**-a tre-ba-**llat**	Jo	Tre-ba-**llés**	Jo	Ha-**gués** tre-ba-**llat**
Tu	Tre-ba-**lla**-ves	Tu	Ha-**vi**-es tre-ba-**llat**	Tu	Tre-ba-**lles**-sis	Tu	Ha-**gues**-sis tre-ba-**llat**
Ell	Tre-ba-**lla**-va	Ell	Ha-**vi**-a tre-ba-**llat**	Ell	Tre-ba-**llés**	Ell	Ha-**gués** tre-ba-**llat**
No.	Tre-ba-**llà**-vem	Nos.	Ha-**ví**-em tre-ba-**llat**	Nos	Tre-ba-**llés**-sim	Nos.	Ha-**gués**-sim tre-ba-**llat**
Vos.	Tre-ba-**llà**-veu	Vos.	Ha-**ví**-eu tre-ba-**llat**	Vos.	Tre-ba-**llés**-siu	Vos.	Ha-**gués**-siu tre-ba-**llat**
Ells	Tre-ba-**lla**-ven	Ells	Ha-**vi**-en tre-ba-**llat**	Ells	Tre-ba-**lles**-sin	Ells	Ha-**gues**-sin tre-ba-**llat**

Past Simple		*Past Perifrastic*		*Past Anterior perifrastic*			
Jo	Tre-ba-**llí**	Jo	**Vaig** tre-ba-**llar**	**Vaig** ha-**ver** tre-ba-**llat**			
Tu	Tre-ba-**lla**-res	Tu	**Vas** tre-ba-**llar**	**Vas** ha-**ver** tre-ba-**llat**			
Ell	Tre-ba-**llà**	Ell	**Va** tre-ba-**llar**	**Va** ha-**ver** tre-ba-**llat**			
Nos	Tre-ba-**llà**-rem	Nos.	**Vam** tre-ba-**llar**	**Vam** ha-**ver** tre-ba-**llat**			
Vos.	Tre-ba-**llà**-reu	Vos.	**Vau** tre-ba-**llar**	**Vau** ha-**ver** tre-ba-**llat**			
Ells	Tre-ba-**lla**-ren	Ells	**Van** tre-ba-**llar**	**Van** ha-**ver** tre-ba-**llat**			

Future Simple		*Future Compound*					
Jo	Tre-ba-lla-**ré**	Jo	Hau-**ré** tre-ba-**llat**				
Tu	Tre-ba-lla-**ràs**	Tu	Hau-**ràs** tre-ba-**llat**				
Ell	Tre-ba-lla-**rà**	Ell	Hau-**rà** tre-ba-**llat**				
Nos.	Tre-ba-lla-**rem**	Nos.	Hau-**rem** tre-ba-**llat**				
Vos.	Tre-ba-lla-**reu**	Vos.	Hau-**reu** tre-ba-**llat**				
Ells	Tre-ba-lla-**ran**	Ells	Hau-**ran** tre-ba-**llat**				

Conditional Simple		*Conditional Compound*		**IMPERATIVE**			
Jo	Tre-ba-lla-**ri**-a	Jo	Hau-**ri**-a tre-ba-**llat**				
Tu	Tre-ba-lla-**ri**-es	Tu	Hau-**ri**-es tre-ba-**llat**	Tre-**ba**-lla		*(Tu)*	
Ell	Tre-ba-lla-**ri**-a	Ell	Hau-**ri**-a tre-ba-**llat**	Tre-**ba**-lli		*(Ell)*	
Nos	Tre-ba-lla-**rí**-em	Nos.	Hau-**rí**-em tre-ba-**llat**	Tre-ba-**llem**		*(Nos.)*	
Vos.	Tre-ba-lla-**rí**-eu	Vos.	Hau-**rí**-eu tre-ba-**llat**	Tre-ba-**lleu**		*(Vos.)*	
Ells	Tre-ba-lla-**ri**-en	Ells	Hau-**ri**-en tre-ba-**llat**	Tre-**ba**-llin		*(Ells)*	

IMPERSONAL		
	SIMPLE	**COMPOUND**
Infinitive	Tre-ba-**llar**	Ha-**ver** tre-ba-**llat**
Participle	Tre-ba-**llat**	-
Gerund	Tre-ba-**llant**	Ha-**vent** tre-ba-**llat**

TO WRITE - ESCRIURE

PERSONAL							
INDICATIVE				**SUBJUNCTIVE**			
SIMPLE		**COMPOUND**		**SIMPLE**		**COMPOUND**	
Present		*Past Indefinite*		*Present*		*Past Perfet*	
Jo	Es-**cric**	Jo	**He** es-**crit**	Jo	Es-**cri**-gui	Jo	**Ha**-gi es-**crit**
Tu	Es-**crius**	Tu	**Has** es-**crit**	Tu	Es-**cri**-guis	Tu	**Ha**-gis es-**crit**
Ell	Es-**criu**	Ell	**Ha** es-**crit**	Ell	Es-**cri**-gui	Ell	**Ha**-gi es-**crit**
No.	Es-cri-**vim**	Nos.	**Hem** es-**crit**	Nos.	Es-cri-**guem**	Nos.	**Hà**-gim es-**crit**
Vos.	Es-cri-**viu**	Vos.	**Heu** es-**crit**	Vos.	Es-cri-**gueu**	Vos.	**Hà**-giu es-**crit**
Ells	Es-**cri**-uen	Ells	**Han** es-**crit**	Ells	Es-**cri**-guin	Ells	**Ha**-gin es-**crit**
Imperfet		*Past Plusquamperfet*		*Imperfet past*		*Plusquamperfet past*	
Jo	Es-cri-**vi**-a	Jo	Ha-**vi**-a es-**crit**	Jo	Es-cri-**gués**	Jo	Ha-**gués** es-**crit**
Tu	Es-cri-**vi**-es	Tu	Ha-**vi**-es es-**crit**	Tu	Es-cri-**gues**-sis	Tu	Ha-**gues**-sis es-**crit**
Ell	Es-cri-**vi**-a	Ell	Ha-**vi**-a es-**crit**	Ell	Es-cri-**gués**	Ell	Ha-**gués** es-**crit**
No.	Es-cri-**ví**-em	Nos.	Ha-**ví**-em es-**crit**	Nos	Es-cri-**gués**-sim	Nos.	Ha-**gués**-sim es-**crit**
Vos.	Es-cri-**ví**-eu	Vos.	Ha-**ví**-eu es-**crit**	Vos.	Es-cri-**gués**-siu	Vos.	Ha-**gués**-siu es-**crit**
Ells	Es-cri-**vi**-en	Ells	Ha-**vi**-en es-**crit**	Ells	Es-cri-**gues**-sin	Ells	Ha-**gues**-sin es-**crit**

Past Simple		*Past Perifrastic*		*Past Anterior perifrastic*
Jo	Es-cri-**guí**	Jo	**Vaig** es-**criu**-re	**Vaig** ha-**ver** es-**crit**
Tu	Es-cri-**gue**-res	Tu	**Vas** es-**criu**-re	**Vas** ha-**ver** es-**crit**
Ell	Es-cri-**gué**	Ell	**Va** es-**criu**-re	**Va** ha-**ver** es-**crit**
Nos	Es-cri-**gué**-rem	Nos.	**Vam** es-**criu**-re	**Vam** ha-**ver** es-**crit**
Vos.	Es-cri-**gué**-reu	Vos.	**Vau** es-**criu**-re	**Vau** ha-**ver** es-**crit**
Ells	Es-cri-**gue**-ren	Ells	**Van** es-**criu**-re	**Van** ha-**ver** es-**crit**

Future Simple		*Future Compound*	
Jo	Es-criu-**ré**	Jo	Hau-**ré** es-**crit**
Tu	Es-criu-**ràs**	Tu	Hau-**ràs** es-**crit**
Ell	Es-criu-**rà**	Ell	Hau-**rà** es-**crit**
Nos.	Es-criu-rem	Nos.	Hau-**rem** es-**crit**
Vos.	Es-criu-reu	Vos.	Hau-**reu** es-**crit**
Ells	Es-criu-**ran**	Ells	Hau-**ran** es-**crit**

Conditional Simple		*Conditional Compound*		**IMPERATIVE**	
Jo	Es-criu-**ri**-a	Jo	Hau-**ri**-a es-**crit**		
Tu	Es-criu-**ri**-es	Tu	Hau-**ri**-es es-**crit**	Es-**criu**	(Tu)
Ell	Es-criu-**ri**-a	Ell	Hau-**ri**-a es-**crit**	Es-**cri**-gui	(Ell)
Nos	Es-criu-**rí**-em	Nos.	Hau-**rí**-em es-**crit**	Es-cri-**guem**	(Nos.)
Vos.	Es-criu-**rí**-eu	Vos.	Hau-**rí**-eu es-**crit**	Es-cri-**viu**	(Vos.)
Ells	Es-criu-**ri**-en	Ells	Hau-**ri**-en es-**crit**	Es-**cri**-guin	(Ells)

IMPERSONAL		
	SIMPLE	**COMPOUND**
Infinitive	Es-**criu**-re	Ha-**ver** es-**crit**
Participle	Es-**crit**	-
Gerund	Es-cri-**vint**	Ha-**vent** es-**crit**

Made in the USA
San Bernardino, CA
01 October 2015